To my fri... ...
...arian

MW01687046

Pipe Organs of British Columbia

Keep working hard!.

Christopher Dalton

A.W. de Jonge 2010.
See Page 151, 253, 236

Cover Photo: Holy Rosary Cathedral (R.C.), Vancouver

Pipe Organs of British Columbia

All rights reserved, including moral rights. No part of this publication may be reproduced or transmitted in any form or by any means electronic or mechanical including photocopying, recording or any information storage retrieval system without permission in writing from the author except by a reviewer or academic who may quote brief passages in a review or critical study.

Canadian Cataloguing in Publication Data

History
ISBN: 978-0-9865254-0-7

Pipe Organs of British Columbia / Christopher Dalton
1. Pipe Organs – History I. Title

© Christopher Dalton, 2010

First Edition 2010.

Cover Design and typesetting: Louise Beinhauer, L.B. Word Works

This book is dedicated with love and gratitude to my Mom and Dad.
They brought music into my life and soul.

Acknowledgements

This book would not have come to fruition if it wasn't for the vision, planning, support, and commitment of all those individuals who desired to have a pipe organ in their places of worship, theatres, concert halls, universities, or residences. Notably, those who came to British Columbia from England, the Netherlands and Germany, were the most influential in our course of attaining instruments of our own in this province.

From as early as 1970, I started recording stoplists and other pertinent information from pipe organs that I visited in this province. The first and most influential person who shared organ research with me and inspired me to complete this book was my dear friend Kathy Edge of Victoria. We met in 1980. She was doing a student employment project on pipe organs in the province and attending university there. She helped me a great deal, especially with Vancouver Island organs, and I reciprocated with what I knew about mainland organs. Kathy still has a passion for pipe organs and is organist at St. Andrew's (RC) Cathedral in Victoria. The next most important source in my quest for a complete record of extant organs here in B.C. was from the late Eugene M. Nye of Seattle, Washington. He visited British Columbia on a few occasions in the 1950s and compiled an extensive record of the instruments, including an inventory. Both Kathy Edge and I used this list in our respective projects.

A project like this involved a lot of field work and I was able to visit most of the organs listed in this book. I am very grateful to the organists, clergy, secretaries, caretakers, and other authorities who permitted me to compile information on their instruments. I have had the privilege of meeting most of the organ builders and technicians who were involved with these instruments professionally. Included in this group have been Casavant Frères representatives: J. Jean Girouard, Alex Bernhardt, John Darbyshire, and service affiliate Herb Huestis and his wife Marianne who still service organs in the region. Other organ builders include Stan Haddon, Ken Hodgson, Hugo Spilker, Adrian Koppejan, and still active builder, serviceman Grant Smalley. Finally those people who play the organ or simply dedicate themselves of their own accord to the appreciation and support of instruments in general and have gathered information on several examples, have been most helpful in assisting me in keeping my notes up to date and accurate. These individuals include the late D. Stuart Kennedy of Calgary, Alberta, the late Stuart Kolbinson of Victoria, Fr. Basil Foote of Westminster Abbey, Mission, and Douglas H. Adams & H. David Vuckson of Victoria.

In the tasks of compiling, transcribing, editing and moral and financial support I wish to thank the following people: my mother, Kay Dalton, sister, Louise Beinhauer, wife, Anne Dalton, and daughter Alison. Credit also goes to Dorothy Froese, President of the Victoria Chapter of the Royal Canadian College of Organists who contacted me in in 2007 and inspired me to resurrect and update the old unpublished 1983 manuscript of this book in order to make it available for the R.C.C.O.'s 2010 national convention to be held in Victoria.

Please accept my apologies if I have left anyone out who feels they should have their name mentioned. For all of you who have helped me complete this book, I express my sincere thanks.

CONTENTS

Preamble

Have you ever walked past a church, heard the sounds of an instrument being played from inside, but didn't know what it was or for some reason didn't go in and investigate? Chances are that it was a pipe organ. Have you ever been inside a building and noticed a neat row or several clusters of vertical pipes stacked together and wondered what they were? If you heard sounds emanating from them, that's probably another pipe organ. Ever been curious about an organ and wanted to know about it – where it came from, how large it is or when it was built? Well this book should satisfy that curiosity and give you insight into British Columbia's pipe organs. There are almost 200 of them scattered about the province. Most are in churches, but several are in private residences, recital halls and funeral homes. We even have one that is still in its original former movie theatre home. Some of these organs are over 100 years old and a few of them have been in their present locations all that time. Most of these organs were manufactured in eastern Canada, the United States, or Europe but in British Columbia there have been a few organ builders who designed and built organs within the province and one builder who was prominent enough to build instruments for Alberta and the United States as well. This book describes most of the extant ones and gives technical information on them as well. All you wanted to know about pipe organs in British Columbia but were afraid to ask. Well, ask no further, the answers are now in your hands.

This province's history of pipe organs takes its form in many ways and evolves with time. In the realm of musical instruments, the pipe organ is the largest and most steadfast of them, rendering faithful service in times of peace or war, natural or economic disasters, and times of economic prosperity and rapid growth. It has lived through it all and provided musical leadership for church music and singing as well as entertaining us at concerts. It once helped depict scenes at the movie theatres before there was sound with the film. These pipe organs are there for us. They are played to stir up and inspire us to greater soulful experiences. Through baptisms, christenings, weddings, funerals, it made its presence known – fixed sentinals of music waiting to have wind fill their lungs and to speak again from quiet whispers to thundering out in all their majesty.

The story of their history parallels and intermingles with the history of events in this province. Before there was a cross-Canada railway line, the organs in this province came from the United States or Europe, mainly by sailing ship via Cape Horn. The railway line gave the very fine eastern Canadian organ builders better opportunity to design and show B.C. residents their high quality craft. There are many interesting stories involving nobility and their influence on the organs that did arrive here. Sir James Douglas was involved in the acquisition of the oldest extant organ in the province. This instrument is a very important example of one the earliest organ builders in the United States and is one of very few remaining. This is part of our legacy. The largest organ to date, built by one of the finest builders in the world, was recently installed here. The legacy is evolving and there is a need to recognize, appreciate and preserve noteworthy examples of good organ building. It may seem to some that our instruments are modest in size and that our organ history is young, but here size doesn't matter as long as it fills the need and room adequately. There has never been a better time for building pipe organs than now. The knowledge, materials, and skills are available and within this province we have seen evidence of this especially over the last ten years. Here is the story about Pipe Organs in British Columbia.

Outline

Pipe Organs of British Columbia is a book about the history and development of extant organs in the province from the 1820s to 2009. Following this outline of the contents of the book is a brief summary describing how a pipe organ works and a simplified explanation of the different types of action used in its operation. The next topic covers the organ's history in this province summarizing its development and how circumstances have influenced what has been placed here from the early days of white settlement to the present.

The ensuing topics describe the stages of development of pipe organs by the country in which they were built. There is a chronological order of examples by date in three priorities: first, of the country, second, of its builders, and third of that builder's examples. Beginning with England, the country's builders, their locations, dates of manufacture, the Opus numbers where possible, and the present locations in this province of each of the examples is given. **Unless an asterisk appears after a particular example, the reader can find more detailed information on that example in Lists I and II at the back of the book**.

Organs from the United States, Canada, and mainland European countries of Germany, the Netherlands, and France follow the information on English-built organs and describe their respective contributions in a similar way. Following this is information on local installer-technicians, tracing from the first known organ servicemen to the present and outlining their individual experiences, traits, and more notable installations. There is a summary of how the organ has developed, what is evident now, and possibilities of the future for organ building technology in British Columbia. The final topic gives advice to parties interested in having an instrument installed, rebuilt, or merely serviced. The book contains illustrations of instruments with interesting case facades, consoles that are representative of the builders, and also some organ interior photographs.

Following this chapter, are three lists: a chronological order list, an alphabetical list of most of the organs in the province with further details, and a short dictionary of stop terminology and meanings.

List I, a chronological order chart, is an index of virtually every known extant pipe organ in the province. The age of the greatest number of pipes of the organ, not its arrival date in the province, is considered. After this date is the organ's present location, followed by the number of manuals, stops, ranks and finally its action type.

List II contains an alphabetical order of the location of each organ, be it in a church, institutation or a private owner's residence as of 2009. Each example has the number of stops and ranks the organ contains. There is a detailed account of each of these instruments giving the date it was built, its builder and/or installer, and the present location in the building of the case and console along with an appearance description. The type of action is mentioned as well as style of voicing if not otherwise obvious. Major changes or additions since the time of building are also mentioned along with location changes and, if the author has played the instrument, pertinent comments. Detailed specifications are also given.

List III is a short dictionary of stops, giving a definition of the different stop names relative to organs in British Columbia.

History Summary

Because of its geography, white settlement in B.C. didn't start developing until the mid 1800s and then with the gold rush, it came in droves making long-term planning and stability difficult to accomplish. Anglican, Catholic, and Methodist missionaries, in a drive to convert First Nations people to Christianity, were among the first settlers to arrive and did so by sailing ship. Many went up the coast in search of converts and brought their culture with them. Some carried portable reed pump organs to encourage the learning of hymns. There is even evidence to suggest that in some of the larger churches organized in these remote communities, there were pipe organs. However it was the reed organ that became more practical because of its portability and low maintenance. Even larger reed organs with two manuals and a pedal board were brought in. Eventually white settlers started gathering in the present day areas of Victoria and New Westminster. The first known records of pipe organs being brought into B.C. were by sailing vessel to Victoria from the east via Cape Horn at the southern tip of South America. The settlers in Victoria were predominately from England and were Anglicans. The city's two congregations of Christ Church and St. John the Divine developed rapidly. Christ Church's first instrument was a barrel organ that came from England in 1859. It was soon replaced in 1862 by a one manual pipe organ built by London's Bevington & Sons in 1856. Some of this organ still exists in a small portable instrument at the present Christ Church Cathedral. St. John the Divine's first organ was built in 1859 by J.W. Walker & Sons, London, and arrived at the church the following year. This organ is still pretty much intact today at St. John's Anglican Church in Duncan. Victoria's Reformed Episcopal Church of our Lord was formed as an offshoot congregation to Christ Church Cathedral. Joseph Cridge, who was a priest at the cathedral, protested some of the Anglican Church's ideas and moved with many followers, to form their own congregation in a church down the hill from the cathedral. This church's original organ was built in about 1827 by Thomas Appleton of Boston, Mass. In the 1860s this organ was destined for a church in Oregon, but the ship carrying it was wrecked enroute. The organ was somehow salvaged and brought to Victoria where it was repaired and installed in this church in 1876. It is still being used in services today and has the distinction of being one of only a few Appleton organs still in existence.

With the exception of the Appleton organ at Church of our Lord, the organs that arrived in the province up until 1880 were exclusively of English make. They were of good clear Victorian romantic voicing, had durable mechanical action, and good quality materials and workmanship for the most part. The only drawback was that they had underdeveloped Pedal divisions, a common problem with the style of voicing and a trait that would continue to occur until the arrival of neo-classical and neo-baroque voicing in 1956.

In 1889, with the completion of the trans-Canada railway line, Canadian-built organs arrived more easily from two Ontario firms: D.W. Karn of Woodstock and S.R. Warren & Son of Toronto. The Presbyterians were quick to bring in examples from Warren and two found their way to the congregations of St. Andrew's Presbyterian in Victoria and St. Andrew's in New Westminster. Among other places, Karn built a two-manual 20-stop tracker action organ installed in New Westminster's Holy Trinity Anglican Cathedral in 1889. With one exception, 1900 spelled the end to tracker action for a long time to come, but this year established a predominance of eastern Canadian-built organs for the province. In 1899, the corner-stone of Vancouver's Cathedral of the Holy Rosary was laid and the following year the first known (major size one at any rate) pipe organ in a Catholic church in B.C. was built by Karn-Warren. For the province, this example was of unprecedented size, voicing type, and action. A new replacement organ built by Casavant in 2000 has included several of the original organ's pipes.

In 1906, the first example of many organs to be installed in this province by the St. Hyacinthe, Québec firm of Casavant Frères Ltée. was built for and still functions at St. Paul's Anglican Church, Vancouver. Today an average of one out of every four pipe organs in B.C. is made by Casavant. The period of 1910-33 saw the development and end of tubular-pneumatic action in organs in British Columbia. This was also the start of unified style organs and the era of the theatre organ. At one time there were over 20 theatre organs in the Vancouver area alone. Many theatre organs still exist today in various forms and places. Also during this period, two organ technicians in the lower mainland started bringing in pipes and consoles from Aug Laukhuff of Weikersheim, Germany. The depression of the 1930s showed a marked drop in the number and quality of organ installations due to lack of money to invest and this encouraged the development in the unification type of organ until the late 1940s. This period, also spelled for awhile, the end to further projects for large downtown cathedral-type churches and placed emphasis on smaller more widespread suburban buildings.

Installations increased in the 1940s and 50s with Casavant being the sole Canadian builder of organs to challenge those using American and European components, as well as the growing interest in those making electronic substitutes for pipes. In 1956, the German builder Gebr. Späth of Ennetach-Mengen, built two organs for the province with neo-classical voicing, one of which was tracker action. The action didn't establish itself at that time, but the voicing style did, and during this period Hugo Spilker started up his shop in Victoria. Using pipes from Stinkens of Holland among other places, he used the classical voicing type and re-introduced the unification idea to several of his designs using a combined electric electro-pneumatic action to most instruments, all for the sake of economy and competitiveness. With his designs, organ location was usually in an optimum setting in the room and imaginative speaking pipe facades were reintroduced. Also during this period the English firms of Hill, Norman & Beard and Walker & Son gained a few new contracts but were unsuccessful in becoming established here. Seeing the writing on the wall, Casavant changed with the demand and in 1958 hired Lawrence Phelps as tonal director, who introduced a line of organs in neo-classic style voicing. From 1959-70, the company enjoyed its last boom period here in B.C. under Phelps' direction. In 1970, the first major size tracker-action organ of this period was built by Casavant for the University of British Columbia in Vancouver. From 1966-69, Ontario was actively represented again in B.C. by the Waterloo organ builder J.C. Hallman. Firmly establishing Stinkens as a major pipe supplier for the province, Hallman made a record 14 installations in three years, all of which were made with electric action and thirteen were unified. In 1975, Adrian Koppejan from the Netherlands set up his shop in Chilliwack to build tracker and electric slider action organs and was the first builder in the province to design mechanical action.

For those who are interested in statistics, of the 182 organs that will be mentioned in this book, the chronological order chart lists 177 of them and there are 145 stoplists in List II. Forty-nine of these are reasonably intact Casavant-built instruments from the period 1905-76 and decrease in proportion to others from 1969 onward. In the period from 1977-99 there was a void in their new installations for B.C. With three exceptions, all Casavant installations have electro-pneumatic action. Thirty-one organs are from various Ontario builders, 12 of which were built by Hallman and eight from Karn-Warren. Twenty organs come from builders in the United States, 11 are from England, three are from Germany, two are from the Netherlands, one is from France, one is from Switzerland, one is from Denmark and one from Ireland.

Of the custom designs that local installer-technicians have done, Hugo Spilker of Victoria continues to predominate with at least 30 major contracts to his name since the mid 1950s. In types of action, there are 34 tracker action examples, two of tubular-penumatic action, and two with an Austin-Universal style of action. The rest are electro-pneumatic, electric, electric slider, or a combination of these types. There are 62 organs that are extensively unified, many from the 1920s to '40s and then from the late 1960s to the present day. Besides the American theatre organ builders, the two Canadian firms of Hallman and G. Herald Keefer & Associates have installed many unified organs. On several occasions Hugo Spilker has installed this type and Casavant did it somewhat in the 1930s and '40s. Of the five still relatively intact instruments built for theatres, only one is in its original location which is at Vancouver's Orpheum Theatre, and it is also the only one in the country that has this distinction. There are 23 organs in the province that are not owned by churches. Of those that are, the United Church has 32, with their oldest example at Cumberland and the largest one is at Ryerson in Vancouver; the Anglican Church has 53, with their oldest intact one at St. John's Anglican Church in Duncan; the Roman Catholic Church has 17, with Victoria's St. Andrew's Cathedral being their oldest extant example; the Lutheran Church has 13; the Christian Reformed Church 11; various Baptist churches, seven; the Presbyterian Church which brought in some of the most significant early examples of Canadian builders now has only seven examples; the Canadian Reformed Church has four; and the Christian Scientist Church has two. No doubt there are other organs in various residences and a few churches in the province, but access to information and specific examples can sometimes be very difficult if not impossible to obtain. The largest extant organ in the province is the Hellmuth Wolff-built instrument with 61 stops controlling over 4,300 pipes at Victoria's Christ Church Cathedral.

Organs From England

The stately city of Victoria, with its many descendants from England, was to obtain several instruments from various builders of that country. Vancouver Island still has a unique collection of these tracker action Victorian romantically voiced instruments with an older one residing in the United Church at the central island ex-coal mining town of Cumberland. The organ was built in 1878 by A. Hunter of London and was moved to various locations in Victoria and Courtenay before coming to Cumberland. Although most of the six ranks of pipework are still intact in this one manual with pedal board instrument, the case has been altered somewhat.

Another organ to arrive on Vancouver Island is the 1856 Bevington & Sons, Soho, England instrument with records dating back to 1862, where it was presented as the second organ to Christ Church Cathedral in Victoria by Baroness Burdett-Coutts. The organ is at Christ Church now, but it has seen many changes since the original building was burned down in 1869, where parts of the instrument had to be replaced and then it was moved to several other places. At present, only about two ranks of the original organ's pipework remain intact.

The neighbouring Anglican parish of St. John the Divine was also to receive an organ through the kindness of Baroness Burdett-Coutts. A new J.W. Walker & Sons of London instrument built for the British Consulate in Nice, Italy, in 1859 was somehow re-routed to this church where it was used in 1860. In 1891 it was moved to St. Barnabas Anglican Church in Victoria where it stayed for two years. Finally it was moved to the congregation of St. John's Anglican Church in Duncan. The organ has since been moved to the new building of this congregation and it remains pretty much intact.

After Victoria's Christ Church Cathedral burned down in 1869, J.W. Walker was contracted to build an organ with two manuals, Pedal, and 17 ranks of pipes*. In 1872 it was completed and moved to the second building of Christ Church Cathedral. At that time it must have been one of the largest organs in the province. The instrument was later moved to the present third building of Christ Church Cathedral in 1929 where Chandos Dix of Vancouver enlarged it to three manuals and 31 speaking stops. Two later enlargement rebuilds in 1957 and 1980 changed the tonal design of the original Walker quite drastically, and the organ was removed in 2003-2004.

In 1962, J.W. Walker built an organ for Marpole United Church in Vancouver. This unified two manual 18-stop organ is the opposite to the 1859 organ at Duncan's St. John's Church in almost every sense. No other builder for the province has produced organs over a period longer than the 105 year span of the three examples that Walker has left us.

The oldest extant two-manual English built organ in B.C., arrived and was installed in St. Saviour's Anglican Church in Victoria in 1901 and has remained there virtually untouched ever since. The instrument was built in 1870 by A. Pease of Stoke, Newington County. The organ has 56-note manuals, a 30-note pedal board, 11 stops with an expressive Swell division, and a most elegant facade.

The largest pre-1900s organ in B.C. is the mechanical action 1890 Peter Conacher of Huddersfield instrument of three manuals, Pedal, and 24 stops, built for St. John the Divine Anglican Church in Victoria. It replaced the Walker organ installed in the then new building in 1860. This second organ was probably the first three manual organ in B.C., arriving in 1890, and remains as the province's oldest one of this keyboard size. The building that this organ was installed in, which was nick-named the "Iron Church", was made almost entirely of prefabricated riveted metal and became very noisy on windy days. It no doubt must have at times given the organ's forthright volume quite a challenge. In 1911, the property was sold to the Hudson's Bay Company and the building was torn down. The organ was sold to St. Paul's Naval and Garrison Church in nearby Esquimalt. The building it was housed in was much quieter in itself and had a near-the-water location at the naval base. However, cannon fire from a nearby battery created a great deal of noise and a serious vibration problem which caused concern as it was feared the building would soon fall apart. A decision was made to move the building with the organ to a quieter location up the hill, and this is where they both can be seen today.

One of the earliest residence organs to arrive in B.C. was the 1907 Spurdon Rutt of Leyton, London, tracker instrument of two manuals, Pedal and nine ranks for the studio of G. Jennings Burnett of Victoria*. This organ was sold to a Victoria theatre in 1912, was later moved up island and eventually was installed in Marpole United Church in Vancouver. In 1949, Stan Haddon of Vancouver converted the action to electro-pneumatic and in 1962 it was sold to Hugo Spilker of Victoria. He rebuilt, enlarged, and installed it in Oak Bay United Church, Victoria, but it has since been removed.

There are a few other examples of English origin instruments from about 1876 to 1900 but they are somewhat obscure and more or less drastically changed from the original builders' design ideas. The church of St. Michael & All Angels in Kelowna has a three manual 23 stop electro-pneumatic instrument containing parts of an English-made tracker organ dating from about 1876. The organ arrived in B.C. in 1901 and was installed in a Methodist church in Vancouver. The action has been changed twice and its chests rebuilt, but much of the original pipework apparently still remains.

The University of Victoria has a small tracker organ of one manual, no Pedal, and three stops in a practice room. Much of the pipework dates from about 1890 by an unknown English builder, but the rest of the organ was built by Hugo Spilker in 1962.

With the completion of the cross-Canada railway line in 1889, it became unnecessary to bring in pipe organs by sailing vessel and so fewer requests were made for instruments from England.

With one notable exception, the period of 1908 to 1957 was void of any English-built arrivals. 1938 saw the arrival of a most unusual organ for its period to Vancouver Island's Prince of Wales School in Cowichan. The organ was built in 1927 by Messrs. Harrison & Harrison, Durham, for the residence of W.N. Mitchell in Somerset. The Fairbridge Society obtained it and placed it in their school's chapel in Cowichan. Eventually it was sold to Christ Church Cathedral in Victoria, as a fill-in instrument while the main organ was moved and rebuilt in 1980. The Harrison & Harrison organ is not so unusual in its stoplist, but what is striking is that it has an integral case and mechanical action throughout, two traits that few other instruments of that period possess.

In 1957, with the advent of neo-classical voicing, the English firm of William Hill and Son and Norman & Beard, London, started building organs for the province with Harry Gore assisted by Stan Haddon of Vancouver as their district representatives. Their first contract was a major showpiece organ costing $41,000 for Christ Church Cathedral in Victoria*. The existing organ was rebuilt, revoiced and enlarged from 31 to 60 stops (48 ranks), and a new four manual console installed. That same year, St. Matthia's Anglican Church in Victoria contracted the firm to build a new two manual, ten stop organ. In 1960, they installed a new console and did some minor modifications to the organ at Canadian Memorial United Church in Vancouver.

Their last contract for the province was the installation of a two manual, 14 stop organ at St. Christopher's Anglican Church, West Vancouver in 1963. It remains as the sole Hill, Norman, & Beard organ left in the province, that has been virtually unchanged since installation. The St. Matthia's instrument was later enlarged by Hugo Spilker, and the Canadian Memorial organ was rebuilt and revoiced by Casavant in 1970. Its Hill, Norman, & Beard drawstop console lasted only ten years before action material faults became irreparable and the console replaced. Although the company gave B.C. some good examples in English neo-classical voicing sound, the quality in workmanship of the pipes and action was generally fairly poor. As mentioned earlier, the firm of J.W. Walker & Sons built an instrument for Marpole United Church, Vancouver, in 1962. This is their only example in the province, that was made in that century.

The last English-built organ installed in the province is the one manual tracker action instrument built in 1986 by Goetze & Gwynn for the St. Andrew's-Wesley United Church, Vancouver. The first organs that arrived were very solidly built and lasted well through the years. Most were built by smaller shops and much care was taken in the voicing. They possess a warm solid, tone with an open pure quality. The other examples that arrived during the 1950s and '60s were much different and were not particularly successful as there were Canadian builders that could offer instruments of comparable or superior quality.

Organs From The United States

When Rev. Joseph Cridge of Victoria's Christ Church Cathedral protested some of the Church of England's ideas, he broke away from the church and, with several members of the Cathedral, formed a new congregation following the American Reformed Episcopal Movement. Sir James Douglas gave them a piece of property just down hill from Christ Church and in 1876, they completed the new church building and named it Church of Our Lord. Douglas also gave them a pipe organ that he had acquired from a ship wreck off San Francisco. The instrument was built in about 1827 by the Boston, Mass. organ and cabinet builder Thomas Appleton. Appleton was one of the city's first and finest hand-made organ craftsmen and this example was built early in his career. It is believed that the organ was moved to two or three different locations before finally arriving in Victoria in about 1875. It was probably the first American-built organ to arrive in B.C. and is still used each Sunday by the congregation in their original building. The firms of S.S. Hamill, East Cambridge, Mass. and John Bergstrom of San Francisco did alterations to it in 1867and 1875, however, most of the original pipework and action still remains, making this instrument one of only three two manual Appleton organs known to exist and the oldest extant organ in the province.

Another small one manual tracker organ with origins in the United States is the 1878 example at the Kobald residence in Langley. Details of this organ are sketchy and it is unknown as to whether this organ, with stop names in French, was built in Quebec or the United States. The pipework is inscribed as the work of Samuel Pierce Organ Pipe Co. of Reading, Mass. Samuel Pierce was the foreman of a prominent American organ builder's pipe department before he formed his own business in 1847 and became one of the leading suppliers in the United States. It is not known at what time this organ arrived in British Columbia, but it was owned by a member of Rupert Foursquare Church, Vancouver, and set up there for several years. It gradually fell into disuse and was put up for sale. In 1979, it was sold to the organ builder Adrian Koppejan of Chilliwack. After carefully restoring the organ, he sold it to the Vanderpols later that year. The organ was acquired by daughter Norma and moved to her home.

The last American built pre-1900s tracker organ in B.C. is also the most recent arrival from that country. The organ, located in First Lutheran Church, Vancouver, was obtained through the auspices of the Organ Clearing House, Harrisville, New Hampshire, and is the first one in the province found through this organization. The Organ Clearing House issues lists of pre-owned organs in North America that are available for sale. The instrument was bought in 1981 through private sale and brought up from storage in Los Angeles, California. After rebuilding the action, reservoir, and stepping up some ranks one octave, it was installed the next year in the rear gallery of First Lutheran Church by Hugo Spilker and Grant Smalley of Victoria. The organ was built in about 1892 by Hinners & Albertsen of Pekin, Illinois. The company was established in Chicago, Illinois by John L. Hinners in 1879 and produced only reed organs until 1890. After moving to Pekin, Hinners formed a partnership with U.J. Albertsen and they started building pipe organs under the name of Hinners & Albertsen. Metal pipes were purchased from Anton Gottfried of Erie, Pennsylvania. Upon the retirement of Mr. Albertsen in 1902, the firm became the Hinners Organ Co. In 1910, the company rebuilt this organ. The firm continued to build tracker action organs until 1930. After producing more than 3,000 pipe organs, the company closed that line in 1936 and continued making reed organs until it went out of business in 1942. The organ at First Lutheran is the only example in B.C. from this builder

In the late 1800s, tubular-penumatic action was developed and gradually replaced trackers in new organ construction. The firm of W.W. Kimball & Company of Chicago was among many builders to use this type. The company started its operations by building reed organs in 1879 and embarked upon pipe organ building in 1891. Using designs and devices of Frederick W. Hedgeland, Kimball started building tubular-penumatic action organs in 1894 and expanded by building a huge new factory addition of five stories and 96,000 square feet the following year. They built two organs of tubular-penumatic action and straight unborrowed specifications that eventually reached this province. A 1905 example of their work, some of which still survives, is at the Willowby Christian Reformed Church in Langley. This organ spent several years in a Methodist church in Seattle, Washington. It came to this province in 1968 and eventually was sold to this church in 1975. Hugo Spilker of Victoria installed the organ after converting the action and supplying a new console and provided a facade from a 1913 Companie d'Orgues Canadiennes (Canadian Organ Company) instrument. Most of the existing pipework of the two manual, 11 stop organ is from Kimball's shop. The other early 1900s example of their work is the 1909 instrument at Duncan United Church, Duncan. Originally containing tubular-penumatic action, the two manual, eight stop organ was built for a private residence. The organ has since been altered including action change and new console but most of the pipework, case, and chests are original. A more recent example of Kimball's work can be seen at Sands Memorial Chapel of Chimes in Victoria. This organ was built in 1932, has electro-pneumatic action and is unified throughout. Another small unified organ is the 1937 example at the Christian Reformed Church in Terrace. Stan Haddon of Vancouver did some Kimball installations and the drawstop console at Coastal Church, Vancouver as well as some materials at Dunbar United Church, Vancouver came from Kimball.

The last period of major American involvement in this province was by the builders of theatre organs. Several theatres in the province purchased organs to entertain people with improvised music during the showing of silent movies. At one time in the 1920s, there were over 20 theatre organs in the Vancouver area alone and most of them were built by American firms especially Rudolf WurliTzer and Robert Morton. The theatre organ possessed several remarkable characteristics. Its pipe voicing along romantic lines, lacked upper-work and mixtures, but introduced several unique hybrid stops. What's more, these organs possessed percussive effects including toy counters (drums, cymbals, blocks, triangles etc.) and through pneumatic action, had control over other instruments added on, such as the marimba, xylophone, and piano. The organs were invariably located in single or double chambers behind screens and were mostly or entirely under expression. The consoles were always detached and somewhat portable; many were placed on hydraulic lifts that would rise up to stage level from the pit below. Tab stops were used exclusively and many were arranged in a horseshoe fashion above the manuals. The number of ranks these organs possessed was from about four to 15, and very high wind pressure and extensive unification were used to enable these rather small instruments to give full and diverse sound effects in rooms that in most cases were quite large and possessed poor acoustics. After sound was added to the motion pictures, the theatre organ lost its originally designated usefulness and most were removed from the theatres. 1927 was the last year this type of organ was installed in a theatre in the province and this era came to an end, but not without a lasting influence on future design ideas for ensuing organ installations. Many of the organs bought from theatres were converted and found their way to various churches and chapels and still can be seen today. Innovations in unification and early direct electric action that theatre organ builders devised are still being used, to some extent, on modern organ designs.

The firm of Robert Morton, Van Nuys, California, founded in the early 1900s, provided the oldest and greatest number of theatre-style organs for B.C. They now have only two examples here, starting with the Columbia-Bowell Funeral Chapel in New Westminster which was built in about 1914. Another small Morton organ that eventually found its way to a church is at North Lonsdale United Church in North Vancouver. It was originally built in the late 1920s but so little of it is now intact that it is virtually unrecognizable.

These two theatre organs were among several that were converted and installed in churches or funeral homes by Vancouver technician Stan Haddon. Like most other extant examples, these two organs had their percussive effects removed with the exception of the chimes. For the most part, the more intact theatre organs are to be found in private residences and are maintained by people who are more sympathetic to the original design idea. Although Robert Morton wasn't considered the largest or the most innovative of the theatre organ builders, such as the next firm that will be mentioned, it was believed by many that they built the highest quality theatre organs in action and voicing with the Tibia stop in particular, possessing a very fine sound.

The firm Rudolph WurliTzer of North Tonawanda, New York had, since the late 1800s, been a leading innovator of mechanical musical instruments and theatre organs. They built thousands of organs and, with the famous inventor Robert Hope-Jones, devised many unique action and voicing ideas. Unfortunately Hope-Jones fell into despair with the company, parted, and later committed suicide. Compared with Morton, WurliTzer's organs tended to be more heavily unified and used consoles of three and four manuals for the equivalent ranks that the former builder would use two manuals for. The province's two surviving examples have faired somewhat better than the Mortons mainly because they have been recognized for their importance and were left intact.

St Andrew's United Church* in Port Moody has an instrument of three ranks, installed in 1971 by Stan Haddon, with parts in it originating from WurliTzer. There is also a WurliTzer console at Paroisse Notre Dame de Lourdes in Maillardville. In the residence of Jim Tarling in Burnaby can be found a 1927, three manual, 77 stop organ that is very much intact and still used for playing music it was designed for. Perhaps the most significant WurliTzer which survives today is the last new theatre organ that arrived in the province in 1927. The directors of the Orpheum Theatre in Vancouver signed a contract for it which they later tried to cancel after hearing about sound being introduced to motion pictures. WurliTzer telegraphed them back with the reply that it was too late and the organ was already being shipped by rail and would soon be arriving. So the organ was installed but put to little use thereafter. Except for the occasional recital and the more classical side of it being used to back the Vancouver Symphony Orchestra, it is not used very much. It is, nevertheless, a famous, unique instrument in that it is the only extant original location theatre organ in Canada.

The Wicks Organ Company of Highland, Illinois was founded in 1906 and, specializing in direct electric action and unification designs, this versatile company has produced thousands of economically priced organs and continues as one of the largest American organ builders today. The only organ that Wicks built for this province was installed in Trinity Lutheran Church, Richmond, during 1975. The organ is again unified with electric action and two manuals, and has 21 stops controlling ten ranks of pipes voiced in the classical style, including a 32-foot Resultant in the Pedal division.

Another major sized American organ building firm was M.P. Möller of Hagarstown, Maryland. Founded in 1875, it ceased operation in 1992 after building over 11,000 instruments. There are four examples containing this firm's work. Highlands United Church in North Vancouver has a two manual, 18 stop organ originally built in 1920 by Möller. The largest and most intact Möller organ in B.C. is the three manual, 26 stop one built in 1924 and installed at Chown Memorial Chinese United Church, Vancouver, by Stan Haddon in 1955. Like with many theatre organs, Haddon was involved in acquiring, converting, and re-installing the Möller organs in various churches in the province. St. Helen's Anglican Church and Dunbar United Church in Vancouver both have organs that contain some pipework from Möller dating from 1951 to 1955.

Before joining with E.M. Skinner, the Aeolian Organ Company of the eastern United States built several organs. There is an Aeolian 16 rank player organ with keyboard at Butchart Gardens* on the Saanich Peninsula on Vancouver Island. It was built as Opus 1417 in 1920.

Henry Pilcher & Sons of Louisville, Kentucky, built an instrument in 1934 that is now located in St. Andrew's United Church in North Vancouver. This three manual, 47 stop organ was once played in recital by the late Virgil Fox. The company was founded in the 1830s by Henry Pilcher who had emigrated from England and opened a shop in Newark, New Jersey. Moving no less than six times before settling in Louisville in 1874, the firm built about 1,800 organs before being bought out by Möller in 1944.

To a very limited extent, the Seattle firm of Balcom & Vaughan has done some work on two lower mainland instruments. The organ at West Point Grey Baptist Church was originally built by the firm in 1954 but has since been rebuilt by Herald Keefer. In 1975, Balcom & Vaughan installed a new console and did tonal modifications to the Haddon-installed organ at First Christian Reformed Church in Abbotsford. The firm also supplied organ consoles and other components in some local custom installed organs. The firm no longer is in business.

The last two organs coming from the United States that will be mentioned were built by two different, reasonably small shops all based in the Washington — Oregon region. These builders specialized in mechanical action designs and construction and voicing ideas based on 16th and

17th century European thought which has been part of the neoclassical revival that predominated organ design from the 1950s until recently.

The first American builder to provide a classically voiced tracker organ for this province was John Brombaugh from Eugene, Oregon. He apprenticed with prominent eastern U.S. organ builders Fritz Noack and Charles Fisk before moving on as a journeyman for German organ builder Rudolph von Beckerath of Hamburg. In 1968 he started making his own instruments from an Ohio location before re-establishing operations in Eugene. His designs were always of mechanical action based on 16th and 17th century ideas with innovations of his own to complement them. Church of St. Barnabas (Anglican) of Victoria purchased one of his works, a seven rank, one manual and pedal board instrument in 1990. After building 66 instruments, John Brombaugh retired from the business in 2005.

The second U.S. builder of this tracker action revival style to provide B.C. a new instrument was Pasi Organ Builders, Inc. of Roy, Washington. Martin Pasi, a native of Austria, received four years of apprenticeship in that country at the Rieger Company. He moved to the U.S. in 1981 and worked with several builders before opening his own shop. Like Brombaugh, his instruments have been mechanical action and of baroque and classical period based ideas. In 1998, his firm installed the largest example of an American built tracker organ in the province, a two-manual, 31-stop instrument at West Vancouver United Church.

Organs Manufactured in Canada

Most Canadian-built organs to arrive in British Columbia came by train after the 1889 completion of the railway line connecting the Vancouver area with Ontario and points east. Two Ontario organ builders founded in the last half of the 1800s were the firms of D.W. Karn, Woodstock, and S.R. Warren & Son, Toronto. They were the first Canadian organ builders to send instruments to B.C.

D.W. Karn was one of Ontario's largest builders, producing reed organs and pianos as well as pipe organs. Some of their action ideas came as a result of a collaboration with the U.S. firm Austin Organs Inc. which was operating out of Detroit, Michigan at that time. Austin even provided many of the parts. Pipework was made by S.R. Warren but Karn had it voiced along Cavaille-Coll lines after he visited that famous builder in France. Above the solid foundation of eight foot tones found commonly in Victorian romantic voicing, Karn organs possessed a unique transparent brightness in the upper work and reeds were often voiced with a typical French style dry snarl to them.

An instrument believed to be originally built by Karn can be found at Holy Trinity Cathedral in New Westminster. It was built in c. 1889 with tracker action which has since been electrified and was enlarged and modified, thus making it difficult to imagine what it might have sounded like originally. Karn used an early example in non-tracker electric connections to the console devised by Austin and called Austin-Universal action, in many of its larger instruments built after

1890. With this type of action, pallets at the base of each of the pipes were activated by toggles connected to trackers. The trackers were moved by two or three primary and secondary pneumatic bellows which were given air by magnets controlled electrically from the console. This rather complicated design permitted the console to be detached from the case. With the speed of electricity through wires being faster than air passing through tubes, this action had a shorter time delay from key depression to pipe pallet opening than the tubular-penumatic type particularly in more remote console locations. However, the Austin-Universal design required a great deal of space to set up and in some cases was not as reliable (possibly due in part to the lack of knowledge by many technicians of this type) as were the alternatives at the time of tracker, tubular-penumatic, and the new electro-pneumatic types. Karn provided Austin-Universal action in the organ at St. Andrew's United Church (1893), Nanaimo.

S.R. Warren & Son of Toronto, was a close neighbour to Karn. Apart from making pipes for Karn, they also had the Austin Co. filing patents in their shop. It is believed that the firm might have had connections with the prominent inventor, Robert Hope-Jones. There were two organs built by S.R. Warren & Son for churches in British Columbia before the trans-continental railroad was completed. They were both destined for Vancouver Island churches. The first was a small, two manual, tracker action instrument installed in 1879 at Pandora Street Methodist Church, Victoria* and the second was a larger organ of similar design and 20 stops installed in 1881 at the former building of St. Andrew's Presbyterian Church, also in Victoria. The fate of the former organ is not known, but St. Andrew's organ was moved to the present building. The organ was re-built, altered and enlarged several times and a few of the original pipe ranks have survived to this time.

The only extant unmodified example of Warren's work in the province is the mechanical action organ at Emmanuel Pentecostal Church in New Westminster. The building is the organ's original home and was St. Andrew's Presbyterian Church at the time of its installation in 1891. As far as Canadian organ heritage is concerned in this province, this instrument is clearly the most significant remaining example of its type and deserves a closely scrutinized restoration. Upon examination of this organ, it is evident that Warren's high-quality caliber of work made him one of the finest builders in North America during his period. The remaining c. 1898 example of a Warren organ in B.C. is at St. John the Evangelist Anglican Church*, North Vancouver. It has not faired so well and has since had action and pipework changes.

In the early 1900s, it is believed that Karn was having financial difficulties, and when the wealthier S.R. Warren died, the two companies were merged and operated from Woodstock, Ontario, as Karn-Warren. In 1907, their last example of Austin-Universal action was in an organ that was later modified and is now at Paroisse Notre-Dames de Lourdes, Maillardville. After that, they built mostly straight un-unified electro-pneumatic organs as can be seen at Living Hope Christian Reformed Church (1910), Abbotsford.

At this time they also embarked on the manufacturing of theatre-style organs, adding on the usual percussive effects. Unlike the American theatre organ builders, they retained the classical appearance of the console using drawstops, kept the wind pressure down, and seldom made organs with extensive rank borrowing or unification. Unfortunately none of the Karn-Warren theatre organs in B.C. have survived, but other examples from this period can be seen at Church of the Good Shepherd (1910), Vancouver, and Ruth Morton Baptist Church (c. 1919), Vancouver. The 1917 organ at the Coastal Church in Vancouver is the largest extant Karn-Warren organ in the province. Containing three manuals and 35 stops, it is their only remaining example using some unification. Another church organ built by this firm is the 1915 organ at All Saints Anglican Church, Vernon.

Beset by financial difficulties, Karn-Warren closed down in 1921, however, the workers decided to buy out the company and carry on as a co-operative under the name of Woodstock Organ Company. In 1933, the largest Woodstock organ in the province, containing three manuals and 36 stops, was built at Vancouver's First Baptist Church*. The specifications were very similar to those of the Karn organ of nearby Holy Rosary Cathedral, but the console was built in theatre style with radiating tab stops. In 1977, an electronic substitute was purchased and all but the organ's chamber front facade were removed. Parts of this organ can now be found in the Hugo Spilker installations at Ladner Christian Reformed Church, Ladner, and the Canadian Reformed Church in Abbotsford as well as the Blok and Darbyshire-installed organ at the Christian Reformed Church in Smithers, among other places. On the pipework of many Woodstock organs can be found the name W. Robertson, one of the voicers of the company. Stan Haddon of Vancouver was involved in later Karn-Warren and Woodstock installations in the province. In 1950, Woodstock ceased operations and brought to a close Ontario's most prominent line of organ builders.

Another late 19th early 20th century organ builder from Ontario that has two instruments in B.C. is Edward Lye & Sons of Toronto. They built two, two-manual mechanical action instruments in about 1900 that eventually made their way to British Columbia. The organ at the Lakeside Presbyterian Church in Summerland has been there since 1929 and its 13 ranks of pipework and action are very much intact. The other instrument, at St. Paul's Lutheran Church in Nanaimo, is somewhat smaller and has had some pipe changes and action adjustment since it was built.

The next Canadian organ builder to send instruments into B.C. was the firm Casavant Frères Ltée. of St-Hyacinthe, Québec. The company was founded in 1879 by Samuel and Claver Casavant, two sons of Joseph Casavant who himself built organs in St-Hyacinthe from 1834 until his retirement in 1866. At this point, he turned his shop over to his apprentice, Eusêbe Brodeur, on the condition that his sons be trained in organ building. In 1878, Claver went to France for further studies with John Abbey of Versailles and soon after was joined by his brother. They returned to Canada the following year and instead of going back to work for Brodeur, founded their own company, Casavant Frères Ltée. Their first instruments were of mechanical action and in 1884, they started building some with tubular-penumatic action as well. In 1885, they were contracted to build their first major sized instrument, the four manual, 82 stop organ at Notre Dame Cathedral in Montreal. This organ was unique in that it partially incorporated their newly invented electro-pneumatic action. It was used extensively starting in 1892. Another invention of theirs was the Duval Patent adjustable combination action started in 1882 and now used by many other builders. Their last tracker organ during the romantic voicing period was built in 1902. Tubular pneumatic action organs continued to be built, especially in smaller organs, until about 1930. During the height of popularity of theatre-style organs in the 1910s and 20s, Casavant followed the trend and built several organs for theatres. During the depression and war years, Samuel Casavant's son Aristide and his brother-in-law F.N. Oliver, kept the company in business and expanded their operations into the church furniture line, still being done today. Also during this period, the company started building unified type organs. By 1947, about 90 percent of the organs used in Canada had been built by Casavant.

Casavant's last romantically voiced instruments were built in the 1950s and in 1958, Lawrence Phelps was hired as tonal director and started their transition over to neo-classic style voicing. In 1961, the company started building tracker action organs again. Lawrence Phelps resigned in about 1974 and was replaced by Gerhard Brunzema for a brief period until, like Phelps, he too formed his own organ building company. Hellmuth Wolff is another prominent Québec organ builder who also, at one time, worked with Casavant. In 1976, Casavant Frères was purchased by a New Brunswick furniture maker. By the firm's centennial year of 1979, more than 3,400 organs had been built. The company continues to prosper and is one of the largest and most widely respected of electro-pneumatic and tracker action organ builders in the world.

Although most of the pipe organs in Canada were built by Casavant and the company built more organs for British Columbia than any other firm, their proportion in the province is only about one out of every four. It is believed that the first contract they got, to design an organ destined for a B.C. location, was the 1906 Opus 264 instrument at St. Paul's Anglican Church in Vancouver. Still being played in its original location, this organ is their oldest extant example here. The only other extant Casavant organ in B.C. built during the period 1900 to 1909 is the Opus 293 instrument, the province's first twin case design, at St. Andrew's Catholic Cathedral in Victoria. It was their first contract on Vancouver Island and the organ had two manuals and 23 stops with tubular-penumatic action controlling 27 ranks of pipes. The organ now has a different action and a three-manual console.

From 1910 to 1919, Casavant had several contracts for new organs in the lower mainland and Vancouver Island. 1910 was a busy year starting with Opus 397 for Vancouver's Evangelistic Tabernacle building which was a former Methodist church. The organ has since been relocated to Westminster Abbey in Mission.

Later that year, they installed the second largest organ on Vancouver Island, Opus 400 with four manuals and 56 stops for Metropolitan Methodist Church, now Victoria Conservatory of Music in Victoria, and Opus 403 a short distance away at Centennial United Church. This two manual, tubular-penumatic action instrument has since been greatly modified with pipe, action, voicing, and console changes. In 1912, Casavant built two, three-manual organs for Vancouver, Opus 485 of 36 stops for Chalmers Presbyterian (now Holy Trinity Anglican Church) and Opus 501 for the old building of Central Presbyterian Church*. Opus 501 was dismantled before the building was torn down and most of it was incorporated into a new organ at Maranatha Canadian Reformed Church, Surrey in 1977. The oldest extant and very intact tubular-penumatic action organ built by Casavant for the province is the 10-stop, two-manual 1913 Opus 516 built for the Chapel of Ann's Academy in Victoria. There is also a small tubular-penumatic Casavant organ 12-stop Opus 521 instrument built in 1913 for St. David's Anglican Church in Vancouver.

During the period 1920 to 1929, Casavant started building instruments for the north coast and interior regions of the province. Their last tubular-penumatic action organs were also built during this period and the province also acquired theatre-style organs from them. For the first time, tab stops started to be used on their consoles. In 1921, Casavant built their Opus 890 for St. Mary's Anglican Church in Victoria. In 1923, Opus 967, a nine-stop, two-manual tubular-penumatic organ with attached keydesk was built. It has since been modified with an action change and detached console and is presently located at St. Peter's Catholic Church in New Westminster. In 1925, Casavant installed their oldest extant organ in the B.C. interior at First United Church, Kelowna. Opus 1096 of two manuals and 14 stops had tubular-penumatic action but was electrified in 1962 by Stanley Haddon. Later on in 1925, Casavant built an early tab stop example, their Opus 1103, a 16 stop theatre organ for Vancouver's no longer extant Kerrisdale Theatre. In 1958, St. Luke's Anglican Church, Victoria, acquired it. The organ is still there but the percussive effects have been removed.

Casavant's next organ, Opus 1104, was originally built for the University of Alberta in Edmonton. A new console was added in 1947 and Adrian deJong of Abbotsford, bought the entire organ during the 1970s and along with Adrian Koppejan under the name of the Praestant Organ Company, installed 14 ranks of its pipework and a rebuilt two-manual console at the Philadelphia Church of Vancouver, Surrey in 1977. The 1947 three-manual drawstop console and the rest of the organ was installed at Trinity Christian Reformed Church in Clearbook. The organ at Second Church of Christ Scientist in Vancouver, was built by Casavant as Opus 1109 in 1925. Another theatre organ built in 1925 as Opus 1137 for the no longer extant Regent Theatre in Vancouver, was re-installed without percussive effects at the local West Point Grey United Church in 1941 by Stanley Haddon. The original specification is still listed at the console.

During 1926, Casavant installed one of their last tubular-penumatic organs, Opus 1161, at St. Andrew's Anglican Cathedral in Prince Rupert. The instrument's action has since been changed and in about 1960 Jean Girouard of Vancouver substituted the eight foot Oboe with a 5 1/3 mutation stop. Casavant's last theatre organ built for the province as Opus 1167 in 1926 was installed in the no longer extant Windsor Theatre in Vancouver. St. Michael's Anglican Church, Vancouver, obtained it in 1940 and retained the Chimes and Marimba Harp. Casavant's largest contract for the province in this busy year was their Opus 1169, a three-manual, about 30-stop organ at Canadian Memorial United Church in Vancouver. The twin case organ was given a beautiful facade design with dark oak wood and silver painted pipes. Two later rebuilds have changed the organ's original specifications and voicing quite drastically. In 1927, First Church of Christ Scientist in Victoria contracted the firm to build Opus 1180 with three manuals and 27 stops.

From 1930 to 1939, the firm, in an effort to stay competitive and keep costs down, started building instruments with extensive rank borrowing or unification. One advantage of this was a better developed Pedal division specification without having to add complete ranks of additional pipes. After Claver Casavant died in 1933, Stephen Stoot from England became tonal director until 1956. His influence brought about a reform movement in the company toward classical voicing and design for better developed ensemble and clearer sound.

From the depression until 1950, organ building generally went into a slump. A notable exception to this seems to have been the 1932 Opus 1465 organ built for First United Church in Victoria*. With three manuals and 38 stops, this organ is now silent without console, having been replaced by an electronic substitute. Opus 1475 was built for St. Andrew's-Wesley United Church in Vancouver during 1933 but little of the original instrument still remains. In 1934, Casavant built Opus 1497 for St. Saviour's Anglican Pro-Cathedral in Nelson. The two-manual, 11-stop organ was installed in this most elegant stone building by Andrew Chapman, the British Columbia representative for Casavant Frères. This Vancouver resident worked for the firm from about this time until his retirement in 1960. During 1937 and 38, Casavant built several unified type organs for several funeral homes and a hospital in the Vancouver area. These organs had tab stops and, for the most part, were built in chambers with screen fronts. Opus 1543*, possessing 22 stops on two manuals for five ranks of pipes was built for the former Harron Brothers Chapel of Chimes funeral home in Vancouver. Similar instruments to this are Opus 1584 at Westminster Abbey, Mission, the rebuilt organ from Center & Hanna Funeral Chapel now at Gilmore Park United Church, Richmond, Opus 1590 (for St. Margaret's Anglican Church, Vancouver) now at St. Martin's Anglican Church, North Vancouver, and the rebuilt organ (formerly at St. Paul's Hospital) in the rear gallery of Holy Cross Japanese Anglican Church in Vancouver. The major lower mainland installation during this period was the 1939 Opus 1605 organ of three manuals at St. James Anglican Church, Vancouver. It has since been enlarged somewhat to 35 stops controlling 35 ranks of pipes, mostly from the 1939 period. There is much rank extending and borrowing in the Pedal due to a lack of space in the chamber, but the organ possesses a good solid English romantic tonal quality in a room with very reverberant acoustics for its size.

1940 to 1949 shows most Casavant installations following the previous decade's ideas. Installations of Opus 1694 in 1942 at St. Paul's Anglican Church, Nanaimo, Opus 1827 in 1946 at St. Stephen's Anglican Church* (same specification as the 1945 organ at Holy Cross Japanese Anglican Church, Vancouver), West Vancouver, and Opus 1949 in 1949 at Annunciation Catholic Church in Prince Rupert are all unified, have similar stoplists (two manuals, 25 stops, four to five ranks), and do not have any reed pipes. In 1943, new action, chests, and console were added as Opus 1728, to the Fosness organ at the former Holy Trinity Anglican Church in Vancouver. The organ has been relocated to All Saints by the Sea Anglican, Ganges, Saltspring Island. The major installation in the province during this decade was Opus 1954, a three manual, 33 rank, twin case organ built in 1949 at Christ Church Cathedral in Vancouver*. The organ was extensively rebuilt in 1970 and replaced in 2006 by a new Jones Organ which included several Casavant ranks.

In the period 1950 to 1959, prosperity returned to the firm and several major installations in the late romantic voicing style were built for B.C. In 1958, Lawrence Phelps was hired as tonal director to lead the company's transition over to neo-baroque and neo-classical voicing along French and German lines. European companies were bringing in these styles to North America and Casavant was taking a beating in losing several major contract bids for eastern Canadian church organs to them. Mechanical action was also becoming popular again and it soon became imperative that the company change over or go out of business. Neo-classical style voicing was developed at a good time for many organ builders because romantic voicing required a great deal of eight and 16 foot stops, which were more expensive to make. With the depression and war years necessitating cutting corners, the heavy borrowing of ranks, particularly into the Pedal, starved the design idea of its independent divisions. Electronic substitutes for pipes gradually became more competitive to the organ builders as new technological ideas created a need for change. The pipe organ builders re-grouped and decided to market better designs based on the past history of organ building, retaining many of the more successful innovations particularly in the development and substitution of better quality parts in place of conventional ones. At this point, electric and electro-pneumatic action designs were beginning to give a good indication as to their useful life expectancy. Mechanical action was considered to be more reliable and many builders, the smaller shops in particular, started including it in their designs. Some used this type of action exclusively. Baroque and classical style voicing emphasized clarity of tone and great brilliance which incorporated greater use of shorter pipes with simpler voicing than the romantic. The new voicing used this as a basis and retained some of the romantic ideas to encompass all periods of organ literature. Compared with equivalent sized romantic organ specifications, the new voicing style was much easier and less expensive to make and seemed to have even greater presence in sound.

Since the new voicing had a greater dependence on higher pitched sounds, pipe location and room acoustics have become more critical for proper sound deployment. As a result of this, most organs built after 1956 came out from behind the walls in every sense of the word. Designs of completely encased organs with facades of speaking pipes were generally the most successful, as history has proven, but many organs were built on platforms and without cases in order to save expenses. The period from 1956 to the present has seen incredible organ design developments, most of them successful, some of them not, but it has been a growing-pain stage and certainly a most profound one pointing us toward another golden age of organ building.

In 1950, Casavant's first contract in the province that year was Opus 2004, the repairs to and addition of a new console for the 1876 English-made organ at St. Michael & All Angels Anglican Church in Kelowna. Later that year, Opus 2037, a two manual, ten stop organ was installed at Knox United Church in Vancouver. It was enlarged to 17 stops in 1956 and later to 18 stops in 1989 with nine Casavant ranks retained. A small two-manual organ dating from the early 1950s can also be found at St, John's Anglican Church in Ladysmith*. Opus 2108, new action and console were installed at the 1906 Casavant organ at St. Paul's Anglican Church in Vancouver. Chilliwack United Church, (same specification as St. Andrew's Anglican Church, Trail) Chilliwack, had Opus 2223 installed in 1954. A major three-manual installation was Opus 2296 at St.

Mary's Kerrisdale Anglican Church, Vancouver during 1955. Opus 2305 of two manuals and 12 stops was installed later that year at St. Andrew's Anglican Church in Trail.

Another major three manual, 35 stop installation was Opus 2355 at Shaughnessy Heights United Church, Vancouver during 1956. Unlike many of its contemporaries, this organ did not undergo voicing modernization in the 1960s and remains as Casavant's only three-manual, late romantic-voiced organ in the province. The 1958 Opus 2458 organ at Olivet Baptist Church in New Westminster was the last organ built for B.C. before Lawrence Phelps took over as tonal director. Later that year, the 1915 Karn-Warren organ at All Saints Anglican Church in Vernon was rebuilt by the firm and given new action and console as Opus 2485. At the Pemberton Chapel at the Royal Jubilee Hospital, Victoria is a most interesting unenclosed unit organ with a detached console. It was built for John Shaw while he was living in Ontario during 1958 and was one of Lawrence Phelps' first voicing contracts while employed in his new position. The organ has two manuals and 26 stops controlling six ranks of pipes and is voiced in the French neo-classical style. An unusual feature is that the Pedal division has the largest stoplist. Their largest installation in B.C. during that decade was the 1959 Opus 2552 organ at Queens Avenue United Church in New Westminster. It was a hybrid romantic and classically-voiced design of three manuals and 46 stops but further revoicing to neo-classical style was done in 1965. A Resultant Bass 32 was added to the Pedal in 1981.

From the period 1960 to 1970, Casavant built the first fully neo-classically voiced instruments for British Columbia. They were an immediate success and several new installations and revoicings to this type kept the new B.C. representative, J. Jean Girouard, quite busy. B.C.'s first Casavant tracker-action organ, one of their largest of this type in the country, was installed during this period. Casavant's last romantically voiced organ for the province was the 1960 Opus 2584, a two-manual and 16-stop twin-case instrument installed in the rear gallery of Trinity Baptist Church, Vancouver. This was Andrew Chapman's last installation before his retirement. In 1961, Jean Girouard installed the first B.C. contract with the firm for a fully neo-classically voiced organ, Opus 2645 with three manuals and 32 stops at St. Philip's Anglican Church in Vancouver. Later that year for Church of St. John the Divine in Victoria, Casavant built Opus 2694, one of the largest and most complete of the organs in the province, a four-manual 50-stop instrument in three cases. The new organ's voicing is a combined French and German neo-classical style.

In 1964, the 1955 Casavant organ at St. Mary's Kerrisdale Anglican Church in Vancouver was revoiced to neo-classical under the contract Opus 2786. Also in 1964, the well-known recitalist and teacher, Dr. Hugh MacLean, organist at Vancouver's Ryerson United Church, drew up a specification for a new instrument for the church and Casavant was given the contract to build it. With this ambitious project, the church was to have an instrument of four manuals and 67 stops. Funds ran out before the Choir and Gallery divisions were built, but in 2005 the Choir division was completed.

A third contract in 1964 was Opus 2811, a completely exposed, three-manual 31-stop organ on a platform at the sanctuary front of Kerrisdale Presbyterian Church in Vancouver. In 1966, a new four manual, drawstop console was installed at the 1910 Casavant organ in the Victoria Conservatory of Music formerly Metropolitan United Church. In 1968, Opus 2950, a two-manual organ, was installed at New Westminster Christian Reformed Church in Burnaby. Further additions in 1970 and 1975 brought this organ up to 20 Casavant-built stops. During this time, Dr. Hugh MacLean was organ professor at the University of British Columbia in Vancouver. The University contracted Casavant to build another organ of MacLean's specification, this time a mechanical key action (electric stop action) organ of three manuals and 43 stops controlling 64 ranks of pipes. Opus 3055 is Casavant's only intact tracker organ to date in B.C. This was also Jean Girouard's last new organ installation before he left the company in 1972.

The period 1970 to 1984[1] was one of many personnel changes both in the company's executive and its local representatives. Partially as a result of these changes, Casavant lost much of their business in the province, but gained several major contracts in the United States and branched out to do work in Australia and Japan. Only three new Casavant instruments were installed in B.C. between 1970 and 1976. In 1970, the 1949 Casavant organ at Christ Church Cathedral in Vancouver was rebuilt and revoiced by Jean Girouard. The following year, the-1926 Casavant organ at Canadian Memorial United Church, Vancouver, was also rebuilt and revoiced, with a new three-manual, drawstop console added. In 1974, Casavant installed their Opus 3240 in the rear gallery of St. Catherine's Anglican Church in North Vancouver. This organ of two manuals and 13 stops is voiced in the French neo-classical style and is an example of the company's "Modular" series, a pre-specified encased design selection of instruments suggested for smaller locations. They had detached tab stop consoles for the most part and extended ranks for the Pedal division. Another example of this series in the province is Opus 3272, a somewhat smaller instrument than St. Catherine's, installed in 1975 at Vancouver's Christian Apostolic Church, now Bao Lam Buddhist Association, by Jean Girouard's successor, John Darbyshire.

In his brief tenure as the company's B.C. representative, he installed one more contract, a rebuilt and enlarged 1912 Casavant, Opus 501 from Vancouver's old Central Presbyterian Church* at Maranatha Canadian Reformed Church in Surrey. The organ incorporated some Stinkens pipe ranks from another local instrument and a new Casavant three-manual, drawstop console was purchased. It was during this period that Casavant appointed Gerhard Brunzema as their new tonal director. In 1976, Alex Bernhardt, the company's Alberta representative, was given the additional job as B.C. representative and he opened a shop in Vancouver. He installed one instrument in B.C. that year which was Opus 3308, a two manual, 13 stop organ in the new church building at Central Presbyterian Church in Vancouver. Bernhardt resigned in 1981 and Casavant appointed

---

[1] In 1972 Gerhard Brunzema from Germany was appointed tonal director, a position he held until 1979 after which he formed his own organ building company in Fergus, Ontario. He was influential in the further development of Casavant's return to building some new instruments with mechanical action which started in 1960. He also brought about a change to the firm in their approach to older organ rebuilding, to embrace original ideas and restore instruments more carefully and conservatively.

Herbert Huestis, their Washington, and Alaska States' representative to service organs in B.C. as well.

Also in 1981, Jean Louis Coignet from France became Casavant's new tonal director. He brought about a continuation of positive developments in the company's projects with broader design ideas resulting in more eclectic organ designs and a major shift in style towards French symphonic. In 1984, Canadian born Jacquelin Rochette joined Casavant to assist Coignet in pipe voicing.

By 1984, Stephen Miller, Casavant's Alberta representative, took over new organ installations for B.C. and that year installed the last, all new Casavant-design organ in the province for the next 24 years. That was the organ at St. John's Lutheran Church in Vernon.

From 1985 to the present, the company continued to develop. Case facade designs evolved to create a more traditional finished appearance. Casavant became more active in the business of restoring or rebuilding older organs.

In 2000, Stephen Miller worked with the company on the transformation rebuilding of the 1900 Karn-Warren organ at Vancouver's Holy Rosary Cathedral. In 2001 he was also involved in some modifications to the 1906 Casavant organ at St. Paul's Anglican Church in Vancouver. That same year in the same city, Casavant did work on their 1964-built instrument at Ryerson United Church which included voicing adjustments, console upgrades, and a Choir division to finally complete the instrument.

In 2004, Jean Louis-Coignet retired and Jacquelin Rochette took over as tonal director. During this period, the company started building some organs with electric slider pipe and direct electric pipe chests as alternatives to mechanical action and Pitman type electro-pneumatic action.

In May of 2008, Casavant finally installed an all new design instrument in the province for Langley Canadian Reformed Church, Langley.

Throughout Casavant's history, there have been employees who later broke away from the company and formed their own organ building shops. Some even went as far as to start up in the same city. The Companie d'orgues Canadiennes (Canadian Organ Company) of Québec was probably one such builder. They built three instruments in the period 1912 to 1913 for three Victoria Churches. In 1912, they were contracted to build an instrument of four manuals and 45 to 50 stops controlling 47 ranks totalling 3,056 pipes by electro-pneumatic action at the Church of St. John the Divine (Anglican)*. All but the Echo division of the organ was destroyed by fire in 1961. In 1913, two, two-manual organs were built, one of 20 stops, 18 ranks for First Baptist Church and a seven-rank instrument for St. Luke's Church*. The organ in the new First Baptist Church, which was built and installed in 1975 by Hugo Spilker, has much of its pipework from the old Canadian instrument. The St. Luke's instrument was removed and is presently located at the Mennonite Brethern Church* in Matsqui.

Another Québec-based builder to supply an organ for British Columbia was Karl Wilhelm Inc. of Mt. St-Hilaire. Karl Wilhelm, born in Romania but of German ancestry, studied in Europe and in 1960 emigrated to Canada, set up and managed the mechanical action workshop with Casavant Frères before forming his own company in 1966. The firm builds mechanical action organs only, with voicing usually in the German neo-baroque or French neo-classical styles. The casework of their designs were usually made of oak. Over the years, Wilhelm has built several large tracker organs for locations in eastern Canada and the United States. In 1968, they built a small two manual and Pedal practice organ for the University of British Columbia's Music Building* in Vancouver. The organ has three ranks of pipes, one for each division.

The latest Québec-based organ builder to provide instruments for this province has been Wolff & Associés, a prominent mechanical action organ builder from Laval, Québec. The company's founder, Helmut Wolff from Switzerland, studied organ building there with Metzler & Söhne and continued his work studies with builders in Holland, Austria, and the United States including the firms Reiger, Otto Hoffman, and Charles Fisk. Eventually Wolff came to Canada in 1963 and helped Casavant Frères set up their mechanical action workshop. Before leaving the firm in 1965, he largely designed three prominent Casavant organs in eastern Canada. Returning to Switzerland, he continued as a voicer and designer in Geneva. In 1966, he returned to Canada to work with Karl Wilhelm, another ex-Casavant employee, who had just started his own company. In 1968, Wolff moved on and began his own organ-building shop. In 1981, he became incorporated as Hellmuth Wolff & Associés. To date the firm has built 50 instruments and is another top quality Canadian pipe organ builder that is in high demand in this country and the U.S.

The first work this company did in B.C. was providing some woodworking components for the Huestis Pipe Organ Associates of Ladner, rebuilding the organ of Vancouver's St.Andrew's-Wesley United Church. The two expressive divisions' boxes of the 1997-started project are Wolff's work. The firm's first new instrument for the province was Opus 44, the 2001-built portative organ for Early Music Vancouver. This was one of their smallest organs but in late 2005, they installed their largest instrument to date and the largest extant organ in B.C., the 61-stop 85-rank mechanical action organ at Victoria's Christ Church Cathedral.

In 1945, the Acton, Ontario firm of the Keates Organ Co. was formed. Their first B.C. contract was the construction of a large two-manual organ at St. Paul's-Trinity United Church in Nelson during 1969. This organ of 30 stops and about 27 ranks of pipes was voiced in the neo-classical style and is the largest one in the province's interior region. Dietrich Geissler became a partner in the firm and it was renamed The Keates-Geissler Pipe Organ Company Ltd. when, along with John Darbyshire their B.C. representative, they installed a three-manual, 41-stop twin-case organ in 1982 at St. Augustine's Catholic Parish in Vancouver.

In 1915, the firm of Franklin Legge was started in Toronto. They built organs with electro-pneumatic and unified electric action designs. In 1920, they built Opus 57 which can be found at Penticton United Church in Penticton. The two-manual, 20-stop organ has a divided case with four ranks of pipes. In 1948 after Franklin Legge died, the T. Eaton Company department store chain took over the company. The last work done by this shop under the T. Eaton Co. name for B.C. was the Opus 110 rebuild and new console of the organ at St. Andrew's Presbyterian Church in Victoria during 1951. Eaton eventually dropped this line of business and closed down the shop, but William F. Legge, who joined in 1919, continued on his own, eventually being bought out by Franklin Legge's son David. All told, they built about 250 instruments.

Another Ontario builder that did some organ manufacturing during this period was the piano builder Quido. They built a line of smaller unified organs that weren't particularly successful and eventually this company discontinued operations. In 1944, they built Opus 402 for St. Anthony's Catholic Church in Trail. This 29-stop four-rank organ is presently at St. John the Divine Anglican Church in Burnaby.

From 1964-76, the Kitchener, Ontario farm equipment builder turned reed and pipe organ builder, J.C. Hallman Manufacturing Co. made 59 pipe organs. With pipework supplied mainly by Jacques-Stinkens of Zheist, Holland, most of the firm's designs were direct electric action type and unified with four to seven ranks of pipes and sometimes the bass was augmented by electronic sound. The eight foot extended ranks started with a Principal, Stopped Flute, and Salicional, with the Oboe, Krummhorn, and Trumpet added on the better developed instruments. This was usually entirely under expression in a chamber faced with shutter boards. The detached two-manual, tab stop consoles were usually without couplers or pre-set pistons and had between 24 and 32 stops. Several of them also had an Automatic Pedal stop on the Swell manual which brought up the Pedal stops to the bottom notes of the keyboard, a sort of reverse coupler Pedal to Swell. The voicing was usually in a light chiffy neo-classical style. Stan Haddon and later on, John Darbyshire of the BC Pipe Organ Builders Association, represented the firm in B.C. Hallman supplied about 14 organs for them between 1966 and 1969. Not since the Karn-Warren era, had Ontario produced so many instruments for B.C. from one builder.

Organs at Killarney Park Lutheran Church, Vancouver and St. Thomas Anglican Church, Chilliwack had 24 and 32 stops respectively, are representative in their sizes, and have specifications noted in List II. Other Hallman organs of this type were made for Vancouver churches: Dunbar Lutheran*, First German Baptist*, St. Peter and St. Paul Catholic (modified)*; St. Joseph the Worker Catholic Church*, Richmond, St. Paul's Anglican Church*, Powell River, Sisters of the Good Shepherd Catholic Convent*, Surrey, St. Ann's Catholic Church*, (enlarged by Jack Ellis) Abbotsford, Knox United Church*, Prince George and First Presbyterian Church*, Prince Rupert.

The major Hallman installation in B.C. that also was their largest instrument is the organ at St. John's Shaughnessy Anglican Church in Vancouver. With Frederick Carter as the consultant, the firm was contracted to build a 71-stop, 69-rank, three-case organ with two consoles. Three prominent British Columbia-based organ builders will be mentioned next.

Hugo Spilker of Victoria was the busiest installer-technician in the province. A native of Holland, Spilker apprenticed with Stanley Haddon but also learned his trade in Holland by working with Stinkens to voice pipes and hone his building skills with D.A. Flentrop. He started up his business as a technician, organ builder, and voicer in Victoria in 1955. His voicing was in the neo-classical style and most of his designs were for two manual, unified organs with tab stop consoles using a combined electric and electro-pneumatic action. Most of his installations contained some used materials and revoiced pipes. Old wood pipes that are visible from outside the case were usually covered with mahogany veneer in order to present a clean orderly facade. For the most part, case designs and facades were well laid out and placed in favourable speaking positions in their rooms. As a person who believed that a church should not have to spend an excessive amount for a pipe organ, he became a most popular and sought after builder.

Unlike his predecessors, Hugo Spilker avoided installations in chambers and favoured prominent pipe displays. He was also one of the first technicians in recent time to appreciate and retain mechanical action in organs of this type that he serviced, however he didn't appreciate or understand the Victorian romantic voicing of earlier organs and often revoiced or substituted pipes in order to brighten them up.

During the 1960s, Hugo Spilker was Vancouver Island representative for Casavant Frères. While re-building at Church of St. John (Anglican), Victoria in the early 1960s, the church was badly damaged by fire. The organ was severly damaged as a result. Casavant was contracted to build a new instrument and Spilker assisted Jean Girouard, the B.C. mainland representative in the 1964 project. After retiring in the mid 1990s, Hugo Spilker returned to his native Holland.

In his early designs, Spilker used and voiced new pipes from Stinkens. Later on, he branched out to include new pipes from England, Ireland Germany, Belgium and wood pipes from eastern Canada. He also designed and built his own wood pipes in clusters using common pieces on two pipes. Most of his consoles were imported from Europe. As Spilker did not write Opus numbers or dates in his installations, it has been difficult to chronologically list his work, but the following entries from 1955 to 1994 will give a rough idea of most of his work.

1	1955	Residence of A. Highet*	Nanaimo	Custom design unified
2	1955	St. Andrew's United Church	Nanaimo	Action change, enlarged & new console for Karn
3	1960	Church of St. John the Divine Anglican*	Victoria	Rebuild 1912 organ (not completed due to fire)
4	1962	Fairfield United Church*	Victoria	Custom design
5	1962 & 1975	Duncan United Church	Duncan	Action change, 1 rk added and new console to Kimball

6	1962-76	Oak Bay United Church*	Victoria	Rebuild, enlarge and new console for Rutt
7	1962	University of Victoria*	Victoria	Custom design with c. 1890 English-made pipes -tracker
8	1963	St. Mark's Anglican Church*	Victoria	Custom design unified
9	1963	West Vancouver United Church*	West Van.	Custom design with Jean Girouard 3-29
10	1963	St. Michael & All Angels Angl.*	Victoria	Custom design
11	1964	Emmanuel Baptist Church	Victoria	New organ 2-26
12	1964, 1978	Faith Lutheran Church	Surrey	Custom design, enlarged
13	1965	Holy Trinity Anglican Church*	Sooke	Custom design tracker late 1800s English origin
14	1965	St. Peter's Quamichan Anglican*	Duncan	New organ 2 manuals, 3 cases
15	1966	St. Andrew's Catholic Cathedral	Victoria	Rebuilt Casavant and new console
16	1967	Estonian Ev. Luth. Ch. St. Peter	Vancouver	New organ unified
17	1967-68	Queen Margaret's Private School	Duncan	Custom design 2-16
18	1967	Now in Tapestry Church	Richmond	Custom design 2-23
19	1970-71	St. Aidan's United Church	Victoria	New organ unified
20	1972	St. Mark's Evan. Lutheran Church	Vancouver	New organ unified
21	1973	Canadian Reformed Church *	Cloverdale	New organ unitied
22	1973	St. Paul's Anglican Church	Esquimalt	Some pipe redesigning to Conacher tracker
23	1974	Centennial United Church	Victoria	Rebuild, revoice, & new console for Casavant
24	1974	St. Andrew's Presbyterian Church	Victoria	Revoiced and enlarged T. Eaton organ
25	1975	First Baptist Church	Victoria	Custom design, most pipes from 1913 Canadian Organ Company
26	1975	Willowby Christian Reformed Church	Langley	Install rebuilt 1905 Kimball with new console

27	1976	St. Mark's Anglican Church	Qualicum Beach	Custom design unified
28	1978	Canadian Reformed Church	Smithers	New organ unified
29	1978	Ladner Christian Reformed Church	Ladner	Custom design, most pipes from 1933 Woodstock
30	1978	University of Victoria	Victoria	Rebuild & install 1966 Mayer tracker
31	1980	Canadian Reformed Church	Abbotsford	Custom design 2-24
32	1981	Christ Church Cathedral	Victoria	Modified & rebuilt 1856 Bevington tracker
33	1981	Christ Church Cathedral	Victoris	Two rks added to 1927 Harrison & Harrison tracker
34	1981	First Lutheran Church*	Kelowna	New organ unified
35	1981	Colebrook United Church	Surrey	New organ unified
36	1981	St. David's-by-the-Sea Anglican*	Victoria	Custom design
37	1982	Canadian Reformed Church*	Langley	Custom design, some pipes from 1912 Casavant
38	1982	First Lutheran Church	Vancouver	Action rebuild & revoicing of c. 1892 Hinners tracker
39	1994	Good Shepherd Lutheran Church*	Victoria	Custom design

Other Work Done by Hugo Spilker

40	Christian Reformed Church*	Haney	Custom design
41	Christian Reformed Church*	Victoria	Custom design
42	Lutheran Church of the Cross	Victoria	Custom design
43	Hope Lutheran Church*	Port Coquitlam	Custom design
44	Metropolitan United Church*	Victoria	Custom design (in chapel)
45	St. Barnabas Anglican Church*	Victoria	Rebuild & new console to 1916 Karn-Warren
46	St. Joseph's Catholic Church*	Victoria	Custom design
47	St. Matthia's Anglican Church	Victoria	Enlarged 1957 Hill, Norman, & Beard organ

48	St. Paul's Lutheran Church	Nanaimo	Rebuilt, modified, and installed c1900 Lye tracker

* = no specification in List II. Undated organs are not in List I.

The information in List II on the organ at St. Mark's Evangelical Lutheran Church, Vancouver, serves as a detailed typical example of a Spilker unified organ. Most of the extensively unified organs, such as this example, are believed to have been made with all new materials from various sources. Those organs listed as custom designs are usually not as heavily unified and contain some used materials. Hugo Spilker eventually sold his business to Grant Smalley and retired in the mid-1980s after almost 30 years on Vancouver Island. In 1994 he came out of retirement to do one last installation at Good Shepherd Lutheran Church, Victoria.

Probably the most qualified of the B.C. based organ builders has been the Dutch-born Adrian Koppejan who retired in 2001 after spending almost 30 years building instruments from his Chilliwack shop. His career in this field totalled 50 years, 20 of them in Europe starting in his father's shop in Ederveen, Holland, and then with Friedrich Weigle Organ Building in Echterdingen, Germany. He specialised in mechanical action as well as slider chest electric action designs and did restoration work including reed organs. He made his own wooden pipes early in his career, but later concentrated on design, chest, and case construction. Laukhuff of Germany supplied pipes in his earliest designs, but Stinkens of Holland was the most predominant supplier. Koppejan built about 25 all new materials organs from his Canadian shop. These were mainly one and two manual tracker organs destined for Alberta. Over the years he employed up to two people and his first partnership was with Adrian deJong in 1977, where, under the name Praestant Organ Co., they built a custom installation using recycled components for Surrey Christian Reformed (now Philadelphia Church of Vancouver) in Surrey. Their partnership did not last long and he became independent forming the company Adrian Koppejan Pipe Organs. In British Columbia, he did several rebuilds and modifications especially in the Fraser valley region. These included organs at New Westminster Christian Reformed Church, Burnaby, Knox United Church, Vancouver, Free Reformed Church, Abbotsford, and Cooke's Presbyterian Church in Chilliwack. The first all new mechanical action organ built in this province was a one-manual and pedals, six-rank instrument completed in 1982 and displayed at Immanuel Lutheran and later the Free-Reformed Church both in Aldergrove. This organ eventually was sold to a Lutheran Church in Tacoma, Washington. Only three all new materials installations were done in B.C. by Koppejan. These include two tracker organs, one at Gloria Dei Lutheran Church, North Vancouver and a residence organ for Len Noort in New Westminster. One of Koppejan's largest new organs is the 1995 three-manual, 34-stop installation at Good Shepherd Church in Surrey which is the city's finest instrument. Most of Koppejan's work is in Alberta. Organs there include Grace Lutheran, St. Andrew's United, and St. Albert Christian Reformed Church in Edmonton; Hope Lutheran and Emmanuel Christian Reformed Church in Calgary; Bethlehem Lutheran Church in Bruderheim and Redeemer Lutheran Church in Hanna. The most easterly of Koppejan-built organs can be found in St. Paul's Church, Leamington, Ontario. In Washington state two of his instruments are in Tacoma. Besides the organ mentioned earlier at the Lutheran Church, there is a two-manual, 15-stop organ at a Presbyterian church.

Adrian Koppejan Pipe Organs consistently built competitively priced, good quality instruments with neo-classical voicing and slider chest reliability. Although their case designs tended to be simple and without embellishment, they were solidly made and adequately enhanced and focused the sound.

The Victoria organ builder and technician, Grant Smalley, grew up in that city and went to London, Ontario, where he apprenticed with the organ builder Gabriel Kney. In 1981, he returned to Victoria and was hired as Hugo Spilker's assistant. As Spilker approached retirement age, Grant Smalley took over his maintenance contracts and by 1985 became an independent operation. A very capable builder and restorer, Grant Smalley has worked on many of Vancouver Island's pre-1906 tracker organs to undo Hugo Spilker's modernization attempts and returned them to full tonal and action integrity. His work has mainly been on Vancouver Island, but occasionally he has done work on the mainland. In 1996, he partially restored to playing condition, an 1891 two-manual, 18-stop S.R. Warren & Son organ that had been silent for about forty years at Emmanuel Pentecostal Church in New Westminster. He also did partial restoration work on Victoria organs at Church of Our Lord and St. Andrew's Roman Catholic Cathedral. Other Victoria work involving modification and pipework additions were done on organs in St. Luke's Anglican, Centennial United, and St. Matthia's Churches. In 1994, Grant Smalley built a new four-manual drawstop console for the no longer extant, 52-stop Casavant organ at the Stuart Kolbinson residence. His first all new organ contract was in 1991 for a one-manual, four-rank tracker action instrument at Vancouver's Holy Rosary Cathedral. To date he has built a total of seven instruments, four of which were one-manual tracker action portables. Opus 2 was destroyed and 3 and 4 have been loaned out for various musical functions. The tracker organs are totally Grant Smalley's creations with only the keyboards built by an outside source. Other projects that he has done over the years include the enlargement of the 1963 three-rank unit organ of Hugo Spiker's design at St. Michael & All Angels Anglican Church*, Victoria. The rebuild included a new console and four additional ranks of pipes done in 1999. In 2007, he completed a major rebuild on the organ at the Lutheran Church of the Cross, also in Victoria. Grant Smalley's work reflects his skill to produce high quality organs from a B.C. based operation and hopefully we will see more of his work in the future.

Organs From Mainland Europe

The Frankfurt, Germany firm of J.D. Phillips & Sons, established in 1886, manufactured mechanical musical instruments including orchestrions. Orchestrions were music machines incorporating organ pipes, xylophones, pianos, mandolins, and trap effects all activated by pinned cylinders and later by perforated rolls of paper or cardboard. Many had keyboards, as is the case of this B.C. example, enabling it to be played manually. Phillips was a large, well-known builder in Europe and grew steadily in size as it bought out other smaller companies and by 1927 had five factories. Between 1900 and 1920, they built the largest number of orchestrions, with some models using up to 400 organ pipes. Their "Paganini" line of orchestrions were considered as among their best examples. In its construction, they substituted the problems that a mechanically played violin produced, with violin stop pipes. In 1928, R.P. Butchart, founder of

Butchart Gardens, acquired a new Phillips Paganini Style 3 orchestrion from the factory while he was visiting Germany. He had the builder substitute the bevelled mirrors, standard on the model, with wood panels instead. The instrument is still located at Butchart Gardens* in Saanich. Its case is of mahogany and there is a single 84-note keyboard which can manually control a set of violin pipes and a piano. By 1929, Phillips was just about bankrupt. The radio had gained popularity and demand for coin operated orchestrions dropped off. They manufactured radios and cabinets as well as some furniture but the depression finally closed them down.

It wasn't until 1956 that another instrument entirely manufactured in Germany was to arrive in British Columbia. The German born priest at Holy Family German Catholic Parish in Vancouver, took it upon himself to order a two-manual, 16-stop organ from Gebr. Späth of Ennetach-Mengen. The organ, Opus 627, cost $8,000 and arrived in 1956. It is a unique example in that it is the first organ with neo-baroque voicing to come to the province. When G. Herald Keefer saw the organ at the time it was installed, he corresponded with the firm and became their representative for the province. He sold the only other contract for a Späth organ to date for B.C. to St. Mary's Catholic Parish, Vancouver. The organ, built as Opus 662 in 1956, cost $4,999 and was the first tracker action one to arrive in B.C. if not Canada during this period. The two-manual and eight-stop organ was in the rear gallery of Canadian Church of Martyrs in Courtenay. Unfortunately it was eventually removed and dispersed. A smaller German organ builder of the past, Detlef Kleuker built a small two -manual tracker organ in 1988 for the Chinese Petecostal Church, Vancouver.

The Dutch organ builder Verschueren of Heythuysen built two small organs destined by B.C., one of which still exists. In 1959, they built their "Crescendo" model, a 16-stop, three and a half-rank neo-classically voiced electric action unified instrument with two manuals. Costing $3,200, it was installed at St. Andrew's Catholic Church, Vancouver but was destroyed by fire in 1989. Verschueren's only other example in B.C. is one of their "Bach" models, a nine-stop, six-rank organ with one manual and coupled pedal board built in 1963. It is the only Dutch built tracker organ in the province and is located at the Chapel at the Vancouver School of Theology.

In 1970, the Catholic church in Penticton bought a small two-manual, 18-stop three-rank organ for $4,500 from A. deGraaf organ works in Ede, Holland. This unified organ was installed there by Hugo Spilker of Victoria and later moved by him to its present location at Richmond Presbyterian Church in Richmond.

There is a French made organ in B.C. In 1966, Georges Mayer of Sarre-Union built a two-manual, 23-stop organ for the parish of St. Mathias in Arvida, Québec. The organ did not adapt well to that province's climate and soon showed serious action damage from it. The University of Victoria acquired it and brought it out in 1978. The organ's mechanical action was rebuilt and its case re-designed and set up by Hugo Spilker in the recital hall. This unique instrument has voicing in the French neo-classical style.

In the residence of Albert Brennink of Duncan District is a most beautifully crafted mechanical action organ from Switzerland. It was built in 1972 for an international congress of organ builders by a small firm which was known as Ziegler-Heberlein of Uetikon. The two-manual and Pedal six-stop organ was acquired by Brennink from the builder and moved into a specially designed music room where it stands now. The great care and skill that a small builder can possess is evident in this instrument in every respect.

The Danish builder Frobenius Orgelbyggeri which was established in 1909 has been a prominent European organ builder for the last several decades. Since 1944, they have specialized in mechanical action slider chest design instruments. To date they have built over 1,000 instruments. They built in 1968, a small single manual organ which is now at Danish Lutheran Church, Burnaby.

Installer-Technicians in British Columbia

Before an organ builder or parts supplier can be hired to perform their jobs, representatives of these firms must first negotiate with the interested parties toward an agreeable settlement on the cost and many complexities that pipe organs have. The agreed contract will result in that particular party having a unique instrument customized to their needs and preferences. In more cases than not, it is a technician within the province that does the front-line negotiating with the client as well as the after sales service. Most of these technicians have also performed custom installations of their own design, independent of any particular firm, using components from various sources including previous organs. Those self-acclaimed organ builders operating in British Columbia, who for the most part, have installed their own designs using second-hand pipes or components will also be discussed in this chapter. There are also a few self-taught hobbiests who have worked on personal organ building projects, some of which will also be mentioned.

When the first pipe organs arrived in B.C., they had mechanical action, were relatively simple to understand and maintain, and several churches relied on the resources within their own congregation for that maintenance. After this type of action was put aside in favour of more convenient and complicated alternatives, outside professional services became necessary. The future of these services was secured when sleeve tuning replaced the cone tuning required on the more traditional pipe designs and organs needed to be tuned more often.

W.C.S. Seeley of Victoria was the first known serviceman to come to B.C. Whether he had previous training or was self-taught is not known, but he was organist at Durham Cathedral in England before arriving in Victoria in 1858. He became proprietor of the saloon at the Australian House Hotel and set up a small organ repairing business as a sideline. His first contract in 1860-62 was to add a keyboard to the 1858 Bates & Co. of London, England, barrel organ at the local Christ Church Cathedral. He bought the Cathedral's second organ, an 1856 Bevington, after it was salvaged from the fire in 1869 which destroyed the building. He paid $100 for it, erected it in a room adjoining the hotel's bar, and replaced some of the pipes lost in the fire. The front was replaced and composition Pedals were also added.

In 1871, Seeley put the organ up for sale and at the same time publicly announced that he was an "Organ & Pianoforte Builder, Tuner, and Repairer of All Kinds of Musical Instruments". Another instrument that he was known to have extensively worked on is the organ at Church of Our Lord in Victoria. The c. 1827 Appleton organ was in a damaged condition when Sir James Douglas acquired it from the Americans. Seeley was believed to have worked on it before it was installed in Church of Our Lord in 1875. It is believed that most of the organs in Victoria were installed and serviced by him until his death in 1888.

In the early 1900s, Chandos G. Dix and Adolph Fosness operated competing businesses in organ servicing and installations. Dix and his wife were based in New Westminster and were both active in the business. They provided custom design instruments using components supplied mainly by August Laukhuff of Weikersheim, Germany. One such instrument is the 1920 installation at A Masonic Temple in New Westminster. In 1921, they were contracted to electrify the late 1800s English tubular-penumatic action organ at Wesley Methodist Church*, Vancouver (organ is now at St. Michael & All Angels Anglican Church, Kelowna). During 1925, Dix was contracted to enlarge and revoice the Belgian-origin organ at St. Augustine's Catholic Church*, Vancouver. The organ was tracker action but he changed it to tubular-penumatic and installed a new console. A fire destroyed the organ in 1980. Dix and his wife also did extensive work on the organ at St. Francis of Assisi Catholic Church in Vancouver during 1927. In 1929, they did a rebuild to the Walker organ (now gone) at Christ Church Cathedral, Victoria and moved it to their new building. Chandos Dix was one serviceman who took organ pipes in lieu of money for services rendered. This was a commonplace occurrence during the depression and was probably done at the organ in Holy Rosary Cathedral, Vancouver, which he serviced. One of Dix's last known contracts was an unsuccessful action conversion at St. Andrew's Catholic Cathedral in Victoria during the late 1940s.

Adolph Fosness was born in Germany and came to Vancouver in the early 1900s. Like Dix, many of his installations extensively used Laukhuff materials but Fosness made his own wooden pipes and apparently finished them with a varnish that usually never dried properly. Fosness might have been involved with Karn-Warren at one time as his name was mentioned in their installation of a theatre organ at Vancouver's Colonial Theatre* in 1910.

In 1915, Fosness was contracted to virtually replace a Jardine tracker organ with a tubular-penumatic instrument of three manuals and 21 stops at St. Mark's Anglican Church* in Vancouver. The console and many of the components were supplied to Fosness by Laukhuff. In 1924, Fosness installed two new organs of two manuals and tubular-penumatic action in two Vancouver churches: a 13-stop instrument at Mount Pleasant Presbyterian Church* and a 19-stop organ at Holy Trinity Anglican Church (now at All Saints by the Sea Church, Ganges). A two-manual organ of similar size was installed in a joint contract with Chandos Dix in 1928 at Shawnigan Lake Boys School, Shawnigan Lake.

Andrew Chapman, a native of England, became the B.C. representative of Casavant Frères Ltée. in the early 1920s and opened a shop in Vancouver. From this period until his retirement in 1960, he was involved in over 25 Casavant installations and rebuilds in the province. All his work was done under the Casavant name and he never did independent work. One of his apprentices was Stanley Haddon who worked with him from 1926 to 1935. Some of the most notable intact installations that Chapman did in his career were the organs at St. Saviour's Pro-Cathedral, Nelson - 1934, and Shaughnessy Heights United Church, Vancouver - 1956.

As mentioned earlier, Stanley Haddon, a native of Vancouver, apprenticed with Andrew Chapman. In 1936, he started up his own business servicing, rebuilding, and installing custom-design instruments. He was also involved in action conversions in several contracts and at one time was one of the most active serviceman in the province. He obtained parts from such American firms as W.W. Kimball & Co., Chicago, the Toledo Organ Co., Toledo, Ohio, Durst, and American Organ Supply. His early work included assisting in the installation of a new three-manual drawstop Kimball-console at the 1917 Karn-Warren organ at First Church of Christ Scientist (now Coastal Church), Vancouver during 1935 with Kimball's Seattle, Washington representative.

From 1936 to 1943, he removed seven theatre organs from their buildings and converted and installed them in various churches and funeral homes in the lower mainland. In 1936, he moved a 1910 Karn-Warren theatre organ from the Broadway Theatre to the former church building of Shaughnessy Heights United Church* in Vancouver.

In 1937, he was contracted to install, enlarge, and provide a new Toledo Organ Co. console for a 1910 Karn-Warren theatre organ from the Colonial Theatre to Metropolitan Tabernacle (now Church of the Good Shepherd) in the same city of Vancouver. The 1926 Casavant theatre organ at the Windsor Theatre was removed and installed in Vancouver's St. Michael's Anglican Church by Haddon in 1940. Another Casavant theatre organ was pulled out of the Regent Theatre, converted, and installed in West Point Grey United Church, Vancouver the following year. Later on in 1941, Haddon installed a converted 1910 Morton theatre organ from Maple Leaf Theatre into the Roselawn Chapel Funeral Home* in Vancouver. In 1942, Woodlawn, S. Bowell & Sons Funeral Home (now Columbia-Bowell Funeral Chapel) of New Westminster had him install another converted Morton theatre organ, the 1914 instrument from a theatre in Trail. In 1943, he removed a third Morton theatre organ, a 1912 one, originally in Victoria's Piaza Theatre, later moved to a Vancouver residence, converted it and installed it at Mount Pleasant Baptist Church*, Vancouver.

He was contracted to repair and enlarge the fire-damaged 1924 Fosness organ at Mount Pleasant Presbyterian Church* in Vancouver during 1945. In 1949, he was contracted by Marpole United Church in Vancouver to electrify the action of their 1907 Spurdon Rutt tracker organ (now dispersed). Another action conversion was done soon after to the Casavant organ at St. Andrew's Catholic Cathedral in Victoria.

In the early 1950s, he took on an apprentice by the name of Hugo Spilker. This man eventually set up his own business in Victoria and bought Haddon's Vancouver Island service franchise. Haddon also formed a working partnership with Ken Hodgson during this period. In 1955, Haddon installed a 1924 three-manual Möller instrument at Chown Memorial Chinese United Church, Vancouver. In the same year he rebuilt the Kimball organ at Dunbar United Church, Vancouver. In 1956, he removed his Karn-Warren theatre organ installation at Shaughnessy Heights United Church, rebuilt the chests and action, enlarged it, provided a new Hallman console, and installed the instrument in St. James United Church, Vancouver (now dispersed). The Fosness organ at Vancouver's St. Mark's Anglican Church* was given an action change and all re-installed in their new church building during 1956 (the organ is now dispersed).

In the late 1950s, Stan Haddon assisted area representative Harry Gore in the installation of Hill, Norman, and Beard organs for the province. During 1957, Haddon installed a 1920 Möller organ at Highlands United Church in North Vancouver. Fairview United Church, Nelson contracted him in 1958 to electrify the action of their Warren tracker organ and install it in their new building (now dispersed). A new console was installed at the 1912 Casavant organ in. the present Holy Trinity Anglican Church, Vancouver in that year as well.

From 1960 onwards, Haddon started using pipework from Jacques Stinkens of Zeist, Holland and parts from Aug. Laukhuff of Weikersheim, Germany. One custom design of his that included materials from both firms was the 1960 two-manual, 36-stop, and eight-rank unified organ he installed at Our Lady of Sorrows Catholic Church in Vancouver. In 1961, he installed another instrument of his design at St. David's United Church in West Vancouver. This organ has three manuals and 27 stops with 21 ranks of pipes and also uses material from Stinkens and Laukhuff. In 1962, he electrified the action of the tubular-penumatic Casavant organ at First United Church in Kelowna. A custom design instrument was installed by him at St. Thomas Anglican Church*, Vancouver in 1963 and another one in First Christian Reformed Church, Abbotsford in 1964. In 1965, he rebuilt the chests of the late 1800s English-made organ at St. Michael & All Angels Church, Kelowna. During 1966, Haddon installed another of his custom designs at the Christian Reformed Church in Chilliwack. Stan Haddon had a sideline business franchise with J.C. Hallman of Waterloo, Ontario and he sold electronic organs built by them in a store in Vancouver. In 1966, he started installing Hallman's new line of unified two-manual pipe organs with electronic bass. It was during this period that he formed a partnership with John Darbyshire of England. They installed about ten Hallman organs together before Haddon sold off his franchise. Their last installation was the four-manual, 71-stop organ at St. John's Shaughnessy Anglican Church, Vancouver in 1968-70. In 1971, Stan Haddon installed one of his last contracts, the custom designed instrument at St. Andrew's United Church* in Port Moody. In 1975, he retired at the age of 66, after serving 49 years in the business, the longest period for a native of the province to do so. Also during that year, his partners, Ken Hodgson, John Darbyshire and a new apprentice Ted Quinton, joined together to form the British Columbia Pipe Organ Builders Association and established a close liaison with Hugo Spilker of Victoria, Hallman, and the Keates Organ Co. of Acton, Ontario.

G. Herald Keefer of Surrey started his organ-building work in 1956 as a B.C. representative of Gebr. Späth, an organ builder in Ennetach-Mengen, Germany. He brought in only one of Späth's organs before he formed his own firm, G. Herald Keefer & Associates later that year. This one new organ was installed in St. Mary's Catholic Church, Vancouver, and was the first mechanical action organ brought into the province in that century with classical voicing. The organ was later moved to Canadian Church of Martyrs in Courtenay before being removed and dispersed. He had trouble with that organ and never again associated with or preserved mechanical action in any of his later works. With the exception of one brief trip to Europe for further studies, for the most part, Keefer was self-taught. The organs he installed were all rebuilds and modifications of one or several different older instruments and contained some new pipes from Stinkens of Holland, Spain, Portugal, and the United States among other places. Some of his consoles were imported from Balcom & Vaughan of Seattle, Washington. Most of his designs were unified organs with electric or electro-pneumatic action. He was a firm believer in the idea that organs should have sounds derived from a combination of pipes and electronic sources.

Included as Keefer's associates have been Dennis Connorton, who helped him install Opus 15 at St. Andrew's Wesley United*, Vancouver and Anthony J. Ellis, a specialist in electronics and solid state circuitry. Keefer made efforts to label his work quite clearly and this included dates and Opus numbers. From 1956 to 1978, G. Herald Keefer & Associates were involved in 21 projects. Seven of these are still extant in the province and are as follows. His 1956 Opus 1 was the $6,000 rebuilding and re-designing of the 1925 Casavant two-manual, 15-rank Opus 1109 at Second Church of Christ Scientist in Vancouver. In 1964, Opus 12 was completed. It was a two-manual custom design for First United Church* in Vancouver. Their largest project was the re-design enlargement at St. Andrew's-Wesley United Church, Vancouver, of Casavant's Opus 1475 which was a four-manual and 56-stop organ built in 1933. As Opus 15, the organ took four years to complete (1962-1966). Most of the pipework came from Stinkens of Holland and the console came from Balcom & Vaughan in Seattle. That organ has since been rebuilt and the console replaced.

A second organ was installed by the firm in the church's chapel*. The organ had 16 ranks of pipes controlled by a two-manual and 31-stop Balcom & Vaughan console. This organ was later removed and replaced. Keefer completed Opus 17 in 1968 at Holy Trinity Anglican Cathedral, New Westminster, while he was organist there. This organ was originally a two-manual, 20-rank Karn tracker organ built in 1889. Another 1968 project was his custom design two-manual unified organ at North Lonsdale United Church in North Vancouver. He also rebuilt and re-designed a 1954 Balcom & Vaughan organ for West Point Grey Baptist Church* in Vancouver. During 1977 and 1978, he started Opus 21, a rebuild enlargement of a 1951 Möller organ with two manuals at St. Helen's Anglican Church in Vancouver.

Ken Hodgson was quite active as a serviceman for organs in mainland B.C. since he first associated with Stan Haddon in the mid 1950s. He also assisted Haddon in some Hallman Organ Co.

installations including St. John's Shaughnessy Anglican Church in Vancouver, and was one of the founding members of the British Columbia Pipe Organ Builders' Association in 1975.

In 1955, he assisted Stan Haddon in the installation of a 1924 three-manual Möller organ at Chown Memorial United Church in Vancouver. One of his first and few custom installations was the organ at St. Saviour's Anglican Church, Penticton, done in 1961. Also in 1961, he changed the action and installed a Quido organ at St. John the Divine Anglican Church, Burnaby and changed one of its pipe ranks in 1978. In 1972, he converted the action and re-leathered the chests of the 1913 Dix organ at A Masonic Temple in New Westminster. In 1978, he was contracted to lead a project in the restoration of the WurliTzer organ at Vancouver's Orpheum Theatre. One of his last contracts was the 1982-83 installation of another custom design incorporating a 1928 Welte instrument into a three-manual organ at Cedar Grove Baptist Church in Surrey. This organ has since been removed and dispersed. Hodgson served as the last remaining active proponent of romantic voicing among the province's organ servicemen who started in the 1950s.

After Andrew Chapman retired, J. Jean Girouard took over as B.C. representative for Casavant Frères in 1961. A native of Québec, Girouard was trained in organ construction, voicing, and repair at Casavant's factory in Ste.-Hyacinthe. From 1961 until he left the business in 1972, Girouard was involved in six new installations and 11 rebuilds.

Six of these rebuilds were done pretty much on his own. The 1961 Casavant organ at St. Philip's Anglican Church, Vancouver was Girouard's first new installation in the province. Other prominent Casavant ones include the 1964 Ryerson United Church instrument and the 1970 tracker organ at the University of British Columbia, both in Vancouver. The U.B.C. organ was his last installation in the province. He fondly regarded that instrument as "the sports car of organs". On occasion he did tonal refinishing to improve the voicing on some new organs including the one at Kerrisdale Presbyterian Church in Vancouver. Some examples of the organs that he rebuilt can be found at Ruth Morton Baptist Church (1968) and Holy Cross Japanese Anglican Church (1969), both in Vancouver. In 1963, he and Hugo Spilker did a joint rebuild installation of the organ at West Vancouver United Church* in West Vancouver. That organ has since been dispersed. In the late 1960s, Girouard restored the 1907 Casavant Opus 291 of three manuals and 33 stops at St. John's United Church* in Vancouver. Unfortunately, a fire in 1975 gutted the church and most of the organ was destroyed. In 1972, Girouard overhauled the 1939 Casavant organ at St. James Anglican Church, Vancouver. It was his last project in B.C.

In the early 1960s, John Darbyshire, a native of England and a specialist in piano servicing, became a partner of Stan Haddon and Ken Hodgson. He was involved in several Hallman organ installations including St. John's Shaughnessy Anglican Church, Vancouver, until that company closed down. He later became associated with the Keates-Geissler Organ Co. of Acton, Ont. He also became the designer and head voicer of the B.C. Pipe Organ Builders' Association. In 1971, he overhauled and added one rank of pipes to the 1870s English-made organ at St. Michael & All Angels Anglican Church in Kelowna. In 1972, he affected major repairs to the 1900 Karn organ at

Holy Rosary Cathedral* in Vancouver. The organ had been without a console and silent for about five years and a replacement console was also installed. After Jean Girouard's resignation in 1972, Casavant appointed Darbyshire to be their B.C. representative. He hired Ted Quinton of Vancouver as an apprentice, and made two installations under the Casavant name, the two-manual organ at the Christian Apostolic Church (now called the Bao Lam Buddhist Association) in Vancouver and a rebuild enlargement and new console of a 1912 Casavant which was sold and installed at Maranatha Canadian Reformed Church in Surrey.

This three-manual, 41-stop organ remains as one of John Darbyshire's larger installations. In 1976, Darbyshire parted company with Casavant. He then started installing his own custom designs using old and new components from various sources. In 1977, he assisted Bert Blok of Abbotsford in installing a custom design instrument at the Christian Reformed Church at Smithers. It should be added that Bert Blok also installed the 1910 Karn-Warren organ at Second Christian Reformed Church in Abbotsford during 1972. In 1979, Darbyshire assisted the congregation of St. Andrew's United Church in North Vancouver with repairs and revoicing of their 1934 Pilcher organ. In 1980, he installed a custom design organ with 1938 Casavant origins at Gilmore Park United Church in Richmond. During 1981, Darbyshire installed two more custom designs, the organ at St. Andrew's Anglican Church* in Langley and another at All Saint's Ladner Anglican Church* in Ladner which was later removed. In 1982, he secured a contract to install a new three-manual, 41-stop organ of his own design built by Keates-Geissler Pipe Organ Co. for St. Augustine's Catholic Parish in Vancouver.

For a brief period from 1976 until 1982, Alex Bernhardt became the Casavant representative for both Alberta and British Columbia. Because contracts had dropped off in the province, Casavant decided that their future representatives should cover an adjacent territory with B.C. Bernhardt studied with Norman Barr, Casavant's Alberta representative, and took a brief course at the plant before being franchised to represent the firm. He resided and opened a shop in Vancouver, but installed only one Casavant organ during his term, the 1976 instrument at Central Presbyterian Church in Vancouver. He gained a few service contracts in the lower mainland area and in 1981, installed a Resultant 32 in the Pedal of the Casavant organ at Queen's Avenue United Church in New Westminster. His last contract before his resignation in 1982 was the action rebuild of the Fosness organ at St. Mark's Anglican Church* in Vancouver. That organ is no longer extant.

In 1982, Casavant appointed Herb Huestis, the Washington and Alaska representative to service B.C. as well. Since this appointment was made, he revoiced and overhauled the Casavant organs at Christ Church Cathedral and the University of British Columbia in Vancouver as well as the Girouard-Spilker organ at West Vancouver United Church* in West Vancouver. In early 1983, he and his wife moved to the lower mainland from Washington.[2]

---

[2] In 1985, Alberta representative Steve Miller took over as sales and installer rep. for B.C.. Herb and Marianne Huestis then became somewhat independent of Casavant but continued to service organs in B.C. in their name. Before Herb Huestis retired from active pipe organ servicing, he was contracted under

Another technician that has been active in the province has been Jack Ellis under the name Anthony John Ellis Church Organs. He has an electronics background and once worked with G. Herald Keefer and learned pipe organ building from him. All Ellis' work has been in the lower mainland. He has installed custom instruments of new and used components with pipe and electronic derived sounds. Instruments at St. Anthony's Catholic Church*, (1990) Vancouver, St. Michael's Church*, (an enlargement of the 1960s Keefer organ from St. Andrew's-Wesley United Church chapel) Burnaby, St. Ann's Catholic Church*, (Hallman organ enlarged) Abbotsford, and Yarrow Mennonite Brethern Church*, (his first pipe organ installation) Chilliwack, are examples of his work.

There have been a handful of organ enthusiasts in the province who, beyond listening, playing, or owning a factory-made pipe organ, succeeded in designing and building their own instruments. There are a few extant examples of these projects that will be mentioned here. They represent varying degrees of success but all are most unique.

In 1962, a fellow by the name of Mr. Chadwick built a small two-manual, five-rank organ. Much of it he made himself, including the wood pipes of Douglas fir. The organ was installed at Willingdon Heights United Church* in Burnaby.

During 1965, Graham Anderson, assisted by Hugo Spilker, re-designed and enlarged the two-manual Fosness-Dix organ built in 1928. They retained five ranks of the original Laukhuff pipework and added an additional six ranks of Stinkens pipes. The organ is at the chapel of Shawnigan Lake Boys' School in Shawnigan Lake and has been enlarged since that time.

In 1970, Surrey resident Norman Starr designed and built a two-manual, six-rank unified organ for his residence. With Jean Girouard as his consultant, he purchased and voiced metal pipes from Stinkens and made his own wood pipes. He also built the drawstop console which is panelled in solid walnut. In 1982, he installed the organ in a rear chamber at St. Helen's Anglican Church, Surrey. This organ remains as one of the most successful home-built instruments in the province.

Steen Larsen, a native of Denmark and a resident of North Vancouver, could hardly be considered a self-taught hobbiest. He spent several years apprenticing with the Copenhagen tracker organ builder Krühn before moving to this province. In 1980, he designed and built a two rank portable hand pumped barrel organ for street use. The organ has mechanical action with 72 flute and violin pipes. The rotating pegged barrel played six melodies on a 41-note scale. In 2005, Steen supervised the installation of a 1968 Frobermus five rank tracker action organ at

---

the name Huestis Pipe Organ Associates of Ladner to do a major rebuild of the main organ at St. Andrew's-Wesley United Church, Vancouver. This lasted from 1994 to 2001 and resulted in a very successful transformation of the instrument. Marianne Huestis has continued on as a very busy organ technician both in B.C. and Washington State.

Danish Lutheran Church of Vancouver in Burnaby. He enlarged it to have one Pedal stop. He acquired a pedalboard, action components and made the wood sub-bass pipes himself.

Summary

When compared with many other provinces and countries, the history of B.C.'s extant organs may seem rather short and trivial, but it is, nevertheless, a significant one. In terms of expectation towards size and numbers, perhaps one's sights need to be lowered, but a well-built organ doesn't necessarily have to be a large one, nor are all large organs well-built. Since the mid-1800s, churches, universities, theatres, funeral homes, and residences in British Columbia have acquired a most interesting cross section of various types and makes of organs. It is surprising to note how inconsistent with one another the churches have been when selecting their instruments. Some of the most unusual organs have been placed in some of the most unlikely locations. At present, B.C. has a few internationally historic instruments and several more potentially historic and quite unique organs. Some of these instruments have been rebuilt or enlarged, and from a historian's point of view, this can be all right provided that the original builder's pipes, voicing, and successful action ideas can be left intact wherever possible. There are some historic instruments that badly need proper restoration and unfortunately several examples that have been changed all too often to the latest trends by committees and builders who do not appreciate what they have. Sometimes a lack of funds is a good thing for the sake of the preservation of older organs. Temptation to change may be stifled and if they were well-built to begin with, occasional trouble-shooting and minor repairs may be all that is necessary to set things right. All too often, well-built examples of man's ingenuity have succumbed to modernization or destruction for the sake of change. Only within the past few years, have some people realized and been effective in saving a little of this heritage. Regardless of how short this heritage might have been, I believe it is our obligation to preserve some concrete examples of it for future generations to understand and appreciate.

The original designs of these examples I believe are just as effective in today's church music as the day they were created, and do not need to succomb to change. Even though the earliest organs to arrive in the province were not Canadian built, Vancouver Island now has one of the largest concentrations of old English built tracker organs outside of England. This fact needs to be recognized and those concerned should be made aware of the most fortunate responsibility they have as caretakers of this heritage. This province also purchased several organs from three early Ontario organ builders. Precious few of these still exist in restorable condition. There are also some good examples of most of Casavant's different voicing ideas since 1905.

In my opinion, the following Victorian and late romantic period organs in British Columbia churches are historic or have potential historic significance:

- c. 1827 origin Thomas Appleton of Boston tracker organ at Church of Our Lord, Victoria.
- 1859 J.W. Walker of England tracker organ at St. John's Anglican Church, Duncan.
- 1870 A. Pease of England tracker organ at St. Saviour's Anglican Church, Victoria.
- c. 1878 A. Hunter of England tracker organ at Cumberland United Church, Cumberland.
- c. 1878 Unknown builder, residence of N. Kobald, Langley.
- 1890 P. Conacher of England tracker organ at St. Paul's Anglican Church, Esquimalt.
- 1891 S.R. Warren of Toronto tracker organ at Emmanuel Pentecostal Church, New Westminster.
- c. 1900 Edward Lye of Toronto, tracker organ at Lakeside Presbyterian Church, Summerland.
- 1901 Lye & Sons of Toronto tracker organ at St. Paul's Lutheran Church, Nanaimo.
- 1906 Casavant organ at St. Paul's Anglican Church, Vancouver.
- 1910 Casavant organ at Victoria Conservatory of Music, Victoria.
- 1913 Casavant tubular-pneumatic organ at St. Ann's Chapel Museum, Victoria
- 1913 Casavant tubular-pneumatic organ at St. David's Anglican Church, Vancouver.
- 1927 Harrison & Harrison of England tracker organ at Christ Church Cathedral, Victoria.
- 1956 Casavant organ at Shaughnessy Heights United Church, Vancouver

These irreplaceable examples of our heritage should be retained and preserved. Any future work done on them should be done with respect to the original design idea. The restoration and preservation of these organs will give us and those after us, an idea of how organ design affected the instruments in the province and will serve as an interesting comparison with present and future innovations.

The pipe organ buying trend in British Columbia has slowed down since 1970. Over this same period, the State of Washington has been undergoing the exact opposite. B.C.'s first pipe organs were mainly brought in for Anglican, Methodist and Presbyterian churches. These and other established faiths dwindled to some extent as people started turning to more evangelical faiths. The trend continues today with the Dutch and German origin faiths now taking the lead in buying pipe organs. Washington State has undergone a resurgence back to mechanical action designs and have supported the development of several small, but high quality builders in the Pacific Northwest. Some of these builders have designed organs that attempt to duplicate the 16th and 17th century European builders, not just in pipe construction and voicing, but in action, case, and keydesk design as well.

One of the few secondary industries in Canada from which people have bought more products than imports, has been the pipe organ building industry. Canada has gained an international reputation in organ building. Some of the finest organ builders in the world are based in this country. Only two of these Canadian builders have contributed a representative number of organs to the province.

The future potential for other firms will largely depend on our knowledge of and attitudes toward them.

Some people have accused me of being pro-Casavant, pro-tracker action, and pro-recital organ design. It is true that I have drawn people's attention to some of Casavant's better examples in an effort to make them aware of examples of better calibre designs. I admire most of what this company has done, but not all Casavant installations have been completely successful and under certain circumstances some have been less than desirable. On the other hand it would be difficult to voice legitimate complaints about their console set ups, action designs and reliability, and pipe construction. Even criticisms against their voicing ideas have been largely subjective and with little understanding. At any rate, Casavant has become well-known for their high level of quality and there are some other Canadian builders who have equivalent quality as well. I support any builder that meets or exceeds this standard. Yes, I am pro-tracker action. It is not an earth shaking personal revelation that this kind of action is the best and most reliable type to date. It is a proven fact and more builders are returning to it. For the first 60 years from the beginning of the 20th century, the trend was for organ builders to use any alternative to mechanical action. For the sake of initial savings in labour and materials and design flexibility, these organs were produced. Experimenting replaced tradition to the point of disastrous consequences.

More firms are now returning to mechanical action. As far as I am aware of, all of Canada's best organ builders have used this action and some use it exclusively in the keyboard. For greater flexibility in combination action, many of these designs use electric stop action which is a compromise to its reliability, but perhaps a necessary one for our time. With regard to so-called recital organ stoplists, any half decent church music organ worth its salt can also be a recital organ. From the organ builder's point of view, the terms are pretty much synonymous these days. Most of the compositions written for organ have been written by God-fearing Christians for church services or under this influence. A well-made nine rank pipe organ can effectively be used to play hymns and some recital compositions for organ and/or various instruments. The largest organ in the world cannot effectively be used to play every work the way it was intended by the composers. It appears that most future churches that are built will be smaller suburban ones. So too, a smaller organ can most effectively serve this size of church for generations to come.

For Those Concerned With Buying or Having an Organ Rebuilt or Serviced

Purchasing a pipe organ is a major undertaking and for those planning on doing so, I offer the following suggestions. An organ is usually the most expensive piece of equipment in a church, home, or music hall. To get the best sound from it, place it in a good location that is higher than and directly facing the listeners. The room should be designed to enhance the organ's sound and have a reverberance level of somewhere between that of a carpet shop and a railway station. The rule of thumb for a good acoustic design is to have a room with fairly lofty walls, with few surface breaks. Organ location seems best in a relatively shallow and wide rear gallery where the sound will directly speak from behind and over the audience's heads. This can work from the front of the room too as long as it speaks from a high location down the centre axis. Avoid placing the organ in a chamber, it really needs an integral hardwood case to enhance and focus the sound. It would be ideal to design a room for the organ, but all too often it ends up the other way around. If the room has too much reverberation in it, sound clarity will suffer. If it doesn't have any at all, the sound will be quickly absorbed as it travels to the opposite end. Acoustic quality of rooms has been more critical for neo-classical voicing than with romantic voicing. With rooms of little acoustic life, it was often necessary to add more or beef up existing stops with romantically voiced organs than with more favourable environments. Neo-classical voicing will not work very well in rooms with lifeless acoustics. To help alleviate this problem, avoid heavy carpeting, padding on pews and acoustic tiles.

The organ should be placed in a location away from draughts, direct sunlight, and potentially leaky windows. They seem to work best under fairly stable temperature and humidity conditions. The humidity of the province's climate along the coast has been favourable for most organs.

For churches that are considering purchasing an organ, I strongly recommend that any tradition of autocratic power on the clergy or organist's part be put aside in favour of a democratic decision made by a committee. Several minds can work to a better end than one or two, and these people should share a responsibility in the research and decision making. As financial supporters of the project, the congregation should be made aware of and become involved with it. In forming a music committee, I believe its membership should include the clergy, the organist and possible assistants, representatives of the choir, financial committee spokespersons, anyone in the congregation involved with organ building (keeping their preferences, and the reasons for them in mind), carpenters, electricians, and those who are simply interested in the organ itself. Usually the organist of the church is the consultant, but sometimes an outside person is hired for the job. A consultant is a person with a background in this area who will act as a source of information and should give impartial advice.

Don't rush into any quick decisions. Most people know very little about pipe organs and find it quite overwhelming. Take matters one step at a time and methodically list items of interest and information. Learn as much as possible about the instrument. One can never be over qualified in this area and there are few experts. The decision that will be made should have a favourable influence on the church's music and result in an exciting organ that will be enjoyed as much by future generations as those who are present. Unlike electronic instruments, pipe organs can not easily be brought in for demonstration. Some builders are also so busy that it may take a few years to have an organ installed in your church. The wait could be very well worth it.

Visit neighbouring congregations to find what they have for an instrument. Compare examples of various builders. Most knowledge must be gained by going out and discovering for yourself. Compare the various designs, sounds, console and case arrangements and note any defects as well as outstanding advantages. Decide whether or not you have seen enough to make a responsible decision. Sometimes it will be necessary to travel further than convenient to seek out new and better examples or builders.

Choose at least three companies for final bid proposals. In approaching these firms, draw up a budget, list basic requirements, a stoplist proposal, and any other pertinent information. If you are convinced by a builder to change parts of your proposal, be fair to the other bidders and let them know of and comment on these changes.

The sales approach of pipe organ builders can be quite different than that of the electronic instrument builders. Some of the best pipe organ builders do not hire aggressive sales people or offer fancy colourful pamphlets including lists of "happy" customers. In many cases you have to seek them out. Most of their business comes by word of mouth, referrals, or as a result of their established reputation, and better builders have been kept quite busy without having to resort to hard sell or devious tactics. Personality evaluations should mean little to an informed music committee beyond expecting direct answers to all questions. The objective here is to obtain the most suitable organ for your needs and obtain help from the representative towards that goal, rather than to evaluate this person's mannerisms. If the representative will be in charge of the installation, check his ability by getting information about his past work, both favourable and otherwise. A friendly and agreeable representative could quite easily be incompetent and a quiet, self-conscious, nervous mumbler could be the most capable.

For the sake of expense, quality of construction and life expectancy, I believe that it is worth the price to obtain a well-built organ instead of the alternatives. There is an alternative to buying a new pipe organ – buying a used one. Many of the suggestions about buying a new instrument apply here too, but the builder might be unavailable.

Find a reputable technician that is familiar with the type of organ you are interested in, to advise you on its condition. Used instruments give better indications of how well designed, constructed, and serviced they have been. Insist on a signed agreement for any work to be performed or conditions for the sale of the instrument.

I believe one of the best sources for a used instrument are the many Victorian style tracker organs mostly found in the United States. For the most part, these organs have been discarded by churches that have closed down or wanted to "modernize". These organs are available in various states of condition, from dismantled and requiring repair and action rebuilding, to fully operational, and have been sold for between $500 and about $100,000.

For the number of pipes that they contain, these organs have quite large cases and require appropriate space for them. This is a potential affordable alternative that could last many years. The organ at First Lutheran Church in Vancouver was purchased as a result of this idea.

If you are involved in a church that is considering rebuilding its organ, determine the feasibility and your objective in the project. I am a preservationist by nature, but even preservation has a reasonable limit. If the instrument in your church is one that I have listed in the historical organs list, I strongly urge that you restore the organ by finding a repair technician who respects the original designer's ideas. If the organ is not considered historic, take a long hard look at what you have. If it has been rebuilt several times, it is possible that more damage than good has been done over the years or that the original design wasn't a particularly good one. I don't think there is much point wasting more money on it under these circumstances, and perhaps it should be replaced or some of its pipes incorporated into a better design. If the organ has lasted 50 to 60 years since major work was last done, it may be to your best interest to have it rebuilt or restored. Most technicians like adding, replacing, or revoicing pipes in rebuild contracts. Be aware of this fact and ask them why they think these changes should be made. Try to get at least three different outside opinions before making a decision.

If you are trying to find a qualified technician to service your present instrument, find out who is available and get information on their training, skills, and expertise. Ask other organists their opinions on these service people.

Another thing to consider is the technician's availability for emergency repair. Another problem arises in that the technician who is more available, might not fix the problem as effectively as the other one who is not as easily reached. The second technician may suggest or implement more effective preventative action so the problems do not occur as often. Consult with other organists on these matters and look at the overall condition of the instruments they are playing. In all likelihood, before the technician submits a service contract bid, he or she may wish to inspect your instrument. After they do so, they may not wish to service it, not because of lack of qualifications for the type, but because of its current state of condition. Some technicians will service and do make-shift repairs on just about anything, while others may suggest rebuilding or replacement of the organ before they will become involved. Consider all that they have to say very carefully. Much can be learned here.

The greatest advocates of pipe organs are usually the organists themselves. They are all too often a much taken for granted and underpaid lot. British Columbia has several recital level organists who have made commendable efforts in attempting to develop greater public awareness of the instrument's potential. Because the organ has had a tradition of church-centred activity, the secular public is largely unaware of its greatness. The organ and its music can be a key toward ecumanism beyond the various faiths and into the world community through culture. In this instrument, that I love so dearly, has come one of our greatest creations. For many hundreds of years, it has sounded its testimony for music and has survived through adverse weather conditions, wars, and ever changing technology. This book was written about the organs of British Columbia in the hope that more people will become aware of and involved with them. I have done much travelling to tell you what I know and have given you a key to better understanding of them. The best way to experience them is to go out and hear for yourself.

The Future of the Pipe Organ

Over the past several years, there have been remarks made by individuals that the future of the pipe organ does not bode well. There are predictions by some that this instrument is heading to its demise, like the reed organ, and will be obsolete because of our modern technological innovations being able to create replacements that are easier to maintain, take up less space, are more versatile and simply cost less. Some believe that in the future pipe organs will only be built for really large churches and concert halls. It also seems that fewer and fewer people know about the sounds made by pipe organs. They aren't used as much as in the past and our radio and TV broadcasters seem to air their sound less these days despite the fact that more music was written for the pipe organ than any other instrument. There is also a stigma about pipe organs by many non-church going folks about its religious and death connection. Yes, it seems the future of the pipe organ that once was a highly respected, commonly used instrument, will dwindle to near oblivian.

But let us examine the pipe organ for what it is. It is a very large and complex mechanical musical instrument that goes back in history over one thousand years. Innovations in organ design have expanded the options of how to activate its voices, but it still essentially uses wind in order to create its sound. In the wonderful world of electronics, sound reproduction, amplification and projection, many changes have evolved to make things more portable, convenient, immediate, versatile, compact and inexpensive. More people than ever have personal electrical sound reproducing equipment because costs have gone down and equipment is more convenient and compact. We have been conditioned to listen to more and more reproduced music through speakers and accept this, yet often these speakers do not give us accurate full frequency sound reproduction. The sound source may even be compressed to give more time play at the expense of lost music detail. So compromises have been made and quality has been sacrificed for convenience and cost. Pipe organs have been brought into this age with electrical innovations too. Current organ designs have incorporated electrical conveniences for the instrument player's benefit in organ operation. Electrical innovation in reproductive technology has also been used to substitute pipe sound with speaker-generated sound from sampled pipe sources. Again this is a space and cost saving convenience. But it is conditioning people to accept sound through speakers and not air blowing through pipes.

Today the pipe organ is mostly found and used for service playing in churches. Its primary function is to support congregational singing. There are many similarities between pipe organs and people in sound production. In order to create sound, pipe organs like people, need to store air and support and give it adequate pressure to flow past shaped hard surfaces to emit sound. We both need to move this sound, resonate it and project it.

I have been in places with pipe organs, and while participating in singing, have felt the presence of the instrument around me, embracing me with its sound and seemingly gently wrapping its arms around me and squeezing my lungs to coax song out of me. I don't believe I'll ever experience that sensation from a set of speakers or any other sound source. It seems that our technology of change has been working on separating us from this commonality with the pipe organ. The marriage of people and pipe organs that has worked for hundreds of years, is being substituted by other "conveniences."

There are still composers who write wonderful music for the pipe organ. No other single musical instrument can effectively support a large gathering of singers. No matter where it is located, the organ is its own entity. It's not an instrument to be used only for one exclusive purpose or cause. Pipe organs have been used as street instruments and as theatre instruments to give sound effects for film and stage. They have been used alone and with other instruments in many styles of music including rock and jazz. Many are permanently mounted in churches, but these organs do not represent any particular religion. They do not speak words to convert wandering souls to a particular faith. Rather they speak sounds of the universal language of music to inspire and move people to greater awareness and a more fulfilling life.

List I: Chronology of Pipe Organs Built in British Columbia

The following list of extant instruments as of 2009 have designated year entry determined by the majority of the oldest pipework in each case. Because of several rebuilds, there are a few organs with undetermined assembly dates. These are added to the end of the list. Those marked with ' c ' are believed assembled within ten years of the date. Action abbreviations are as follows: T = tracker key and stop action, AU = Austin Universal action, TP = tubular-penumatic action, EP = electro-pneumatic action, ES = electric controlled slider chest action, E = direct electric action, E/P = combined direct electric and electro-pneumatic controlled pipe chests, TE = tracker key action, electric controlled stop action.

	Year	Name	Location	Builder	Manuals & Stops	Ranks	Action
1	c. 1827	Church of Our Lord Ref. Episc.	Victoria	Appleton, Hamill	2 - 21	20	T
2	1859	St. John's Anglican Church	Duncan	J.W. Walker	1 -10	12	T
3	1870	St. Saviour's Anglican Church	Victoria	A. Pease	2 - 11	10	T
4	c. 1876	St. Michael & All Angels Angl.	Kelowna	(English), Casavant	3 - 23	23	EP
5	c. 1878	Cumberland United Church	Cumberland	Hunter	1 - 7	7	T
6	1878	Residence of M. & N. Kobald	Langley	?, Koppejan	1 - 9	5	T
7	1889	Holy Trinity Anglican Cathedral	New Westminster	Warren, Keefer	3 - 45	20	EP
8	1890	St. Paul's Anglican Church	Esquimalt	Conacher, Spilker	3 - 24	27	T
9	1891	Emmanuel Pentecostal Church	New Westminster	S.R.Warren	2 - 18	18	T
10	c. 1892	First Lutheran Church	Vancouver	Hinners & Albertson	2 - 13	13	T
11	1893	St. Andrew's United Church	Nanaimo	Karn, Spilker	2 - 14	13	AU
12	c. 1900	Lakeside Presbyterian Church	Summerland	Lye	2 - 13	13	T
13	c. 1901	St. Paul's Lutheran Church	Nanaimo	Lye, Spilker	2 - 11	12	T
14	1905	Willoughby Christian Reformed Church	Langley	Kimball, Spilker	2 - 11	12	EP
15	1906	St. Paul's Anglican Church	Vancouver	Casavant	2 - 21	20	EP
16	1907	St. Andrew's Cathedral (RC)	Victoria	Casavant, Spilker	3 - 26	26	EP
17	1907	Paroisse Notre Dames de Lourde	Maillardville	Karn-Warren	2 - 7	7	AU
18	c. 1910	Duncan United Church	Duncan	Kimball, Spilker	2 - 8	8	EP
19	1910	Westminster Abbey	Mission	Casavant	3 - 41	39	EP
20	1910	Victoria Conservatory of Music	Victoria	Casavant	4 - 56	54	EP

	Year	Name	Location	Builder	Manuals & Stops	Ranks	Action
21	1910	Living Hope Christian Reformed Church	Abbotsford	Karn-Warren	2 - 8	8	EP
22	1910	Church of The Good Shepherd (Anglican)	Vancouver	Karn-Warren	2 - 20	18	EP
23	1912	Holy Trinity Anglican Church	Vancouver	Casavant, Haddon	3 - 37	40	EP
24	1912	Maranatha Canadian Reformed Church	Surrey	Casavant, Darby-shire, Smalley	3 -41	44	EP
25	1913	St. Ann's Chapel Museum	Victoria	Casavant	2 - 10	9	TP
26	c. 1913	South Abbotsford Mennonite Ch.	Matsqui	Canada Organ Com-pany	2 -	7	EP
27	1913	A Masonic Temple	New Westminster	Chandos Dix	2 - 12	11	EP
28	1913	St. David's Anglican Church	Vancouver	Casavant	2 - 11	11	TP
29	1913	First Baptist Church	Victoria	Canada, Spilker	2 - 22	16	E/P
30	1913	Cooke's Presbyterian Church	Chilliwack	Karn-Warren, Koppe-jan	2 - 18	20	ES
31	c. 1914	Columbia-Bowell Funeral Chapel	New Westminster	Morton	2 - 19	4	EP
32	1915	All Saints Anglican Church	Vernon	Karn-Warren, Dix, Casavant	2 - 14	14	EP
33	1917	Coastal Church	Vancouver	Karn-Warren, Kim-ball	3 - 35	20	EP
34	c. 1919	Ruth Morton Baptist Church	Vancouver	Karn-Warren, Casa-vant	2 - 19	17	EP
35	1920	Highlands United Church	North Vancouver	Möller	2 - 18	17	EP
36	1920	Butchart Gardens	Brentwood Bay	Aeolian	2	16	
37	1923	St. Peter's Catholic Church	New Westminster	Casavant	2 - 9	9	EP
38	1924	Chown Memorial & Chinese United Church	Vancouver	Möller	3 - 26	24	E
39	1924	All Saints by the Sea Anglican Church	Ganges	Fosness, Casavant, D.Quinton	3 - 29	27	EP
40	1925	First United Church	Kelowna	Casavant	2 - 14	12	EP
41	1925	St. Luke's Anglican Church	Victoria	Casavant,Smalley	2 - 22	23	EP
42	1925	Trinity Christian Reformed Church	Clearbrook	Casavant, Koppejan	3 - 36	35	EP
43	1925	2nd Church of Christ Scientist	Vancouver	Casavant, Keefer	2 - 31	11	EP

	Year	Name	Location	Builder	Manuals & Stops	Ranks	Action
44	1926	West Point Grey United Church	Vancouver	Casavant	2 - 15	14	EP
45	1926	St. Andrew's Anglican Cathedral	Prince Rupert	Casavant	2 - 8	8	EP
46	1926	St. Michael's Anglican Church	Vancouver	Casavant	2 - 15	15	EP
47	1927	Christ Church Cathedral (Angl.)	Victoria	Harrison & Harrison	2 - 13	12	T
48	1927	1st Church of Christ Scientist	Victoria	Casavant	3 - 27	29	EP
49	1927	Residence of Jimmy Tarling	Burnaby	WurliTzer	3 - 77	15	EP
50	1927	Orpheum Theatre	Vancouver	WurliTzer	3 - 70	13	EP
51	1928	Canadian Memorial United Ch.	Vancouver	Casavant	3 - 36	44	EP
52	1928	Penticton United Church	Penticton	Franklin Legge	2 - 20	4	E
53	1928	Butchart Gardens	Brentwood Bay	J.D. Phillips & Sons	1	2	
54	1932	Sands Memorial Chapel of Chimes	Victoria	Kimball	2 - 22	3	EP
55	1933	Ladner Christian Reformed Ch.	Delta	Woodstock, Spilker	2 - 17	17	EP
56	1933	Christian Reformed Church	Smithers	Woodstock, Blok	2 - 16	19	EP
57	1934	St. Andrew's United Church	North Vancouver	Pilcher, Darbyshire	3 - 47	34	EP
58	1934	St. Saviour's Pro-Cathedral (Ang)	Nelson	Casavant	2 - 11	10	EP
59	1937	Terrace Christian Reformed Ch.	Terrace	Kimball	2 - 20	3	E
60	1938	Westminster Abbey (RC)	Mission	Casavant	2 - 23	5	EP
61	1938	Gilmore Park United Church	Richmond	Casavant, Darbyshire	2 - 22	4	EP
62	1938	St. Martin's Anglican Church	North Vancouver	Casavant	2 - 25	7	EP
63	1938	St. James' Anglican Church	Vancouver	Casavant	3 - 35	35	EP
64	1942	St. Paul's Anglican Church	Nanaimo	Casavant	2 - 24	5	EP
65	1944	St. John the Divine Anglican Ch.	Burnaby	Quido	2 - 29	4	EP
66	1945	Holy Cross Japanese Anglican Church	Vancouver	Casavant	2 - 25	5	EP
67	1945	St. Mary's R.C. Church	Ladysmith	Casavant	2 - 16	2	EP
68	1946	St. Stephen's Anglican Church	West Vancouver	Casavant	2 - 25	5	EP
69	1949	Annunciation R.C. Church	Prince Rupert	Casavant	2 - 25	5	EP
70	1954	Chilliwack United Church	Chilliwack	Casavant	2 - 12	11	EP
71	1954	West Point Grey Baptist Church	Vancouver	Balcom & Vaughan, Keefer	2 -	4	E
72	1955	St. Andrew's Anglican Church	Trail	Casavant	2 - 12	12	EP

	Year	Name	Location	Builder	Manuals & Stops	Ranks	Action
73	1955	St. Mary's Anglican Church	Vancouver	Casavant	3 - 41	47	EP
74	1955	Dunbar United Church	Vancouver	Möller	2 - 21	18	E
75	1956	Holy Family German R.C. Parish	Vancouver	Späth	2 - 16	22	ES
76	1956	Shaughnessy Heights United Ch.	Vancouver	Casavant	3 - 35	33	EP
77	1956	Residence of Dorothy Barrs	Victoria	A.K. Smalley	4 - 41	37	EP
78	1957	Centennial United Church	Victoria	Casavant; Hill, Norman & Beard;Smalley	3 - 30	28	EP
79	1957	St. Andrew's Presbyterian Church	Victoria	Warren; Eaton; Spilker; Hill, Norman, & Beard; Smalley	3 - 35	39	EP
80	1957	St. Matthia's Anglican Church	Victoria	Hill, Norman, & Beard; Spilker; Huestis; Smalley	2 - 20	16	EP
81	1958	Olivet Baptist Church	New Westminster	Casavant	2 - 13	15	EP
82	1958	Pemberton Chapel, Royal Jubilee Hospital	Victoria	Casavant	2 - 29	7	EP
83	1959	Queens Avenue United Church	New Westminster	Casavant	3 - 47	45	EP
84	c. 1960	St. David by The Sea Angl. Ch.	Victoria	Spilker, Smalley	2 - 19	4	E/P
85	c. 1960	St. Martin's in The Field Angl. Ch.	Victoria	Hugo Spilker	2 -	2	E/P
86	c. 1960	Grace Lutheran Church	Victoria	Hugo Spilker	2 -	4	E/P
87	1960	Our Lady of Sorrows R.C. Ch.	Vancouver	Stan Haddon	2 - 36	8	EP
88	1960	Trinity Baptist Church	Vancouver	Casavant	2 - 16	15	EP
89	1961	St. Philip's Anglican Church	Vancouver	Casavant	3 - 33	41	EP
90	1961	Church of St. John the Divine Anglican	Victoria	Casavant	4 - 53	65	EP
91	1961	St. David's United Church	West Vancouver	Stan Haddon	3 - 27	22	EP
92	1961	St. Saviour's Anglican Church	Penticton	Ken Hodgson	2 - 29	5	EP
93	1962	Fairfield United Church	Victoria	Hugo Spilker	2 -		E/P
94	1962	Marpole United Church	Vancouver	J.W. Walker	2 - 18	4	EP
95	1962	University of Victoria	Victoria	(English), Spilker	1 - 3	3	T
96	1963	St. Thomas Anglican Church	Vancouver	Stan Haddon	2 -	7	EP
97	1963	St. Mark's Anglican Church	Victoria	Hugo Spilker	2 - 20		E/P

	Year	Name	Location	Builder	Manuals & Stops	Ranks	Action
98	1963	Vancouver School of Theology Chapel	Vancouver	Verscheuren	1 - 9	6	T
99	1963	St. Michael & All Angels Ang. Ch	Victoria	Hugo Spilker	2 -		E/P
100	1963	St. Christopher's Anglican Church	West Vancouver	Hill, Norman, & Beard	2 - 14	10	EP
101	1964	First Christian Reformed Church	Abbotsford	Stan Haddon	2 - 21	17	EP
102	1964	Emmanuel Baptist Church	Victoria	Hugo Spilker	2 - 26	12	E/P
103	1964	First United Church	Vancouver	Warren, Casavant, Keefer	2 - 20	10	E
104	1964	Kerrisdale Presbyterian Church	Vancouver	Casavant	3 - 31	39	EP
105	1964	Ryerson United Church	Vancouver	Casavant	4 - 74	78	EP
106	1965	St. Peter's Quamichan Angl. Ch.	Duncan	Hugo Spilker	2 - 22	7	E/P
107	1966	Knox United Church	Prince George	J.C. Hallman	2 -	4	E
108	1966	St. Paul's Anglican Church	Powell River	J.C. Hallman	2 -	6	E
109	1966	University of Victoria	Victoria	Mayer; Spilker	2 - 24	35	T
110	1967	New Westminster Christian Reformed Church	Burnaby	Casavant; Koppejan	3 - 31	32	EP, ES
111	1967	Estonian Evangelical Church of St. Peter	Vancouver	Hugo Spilker	2 - 21	6	E/P
112	1967	Tapestry Church (CRC)	Richmond	Hugo Spilker	2 - 23	20	E/P
113	1967	Queen Margaret's Private School	Duncan	Hugo Spilker	2 - 16	2	E/P
114	1967	St. Joseph The Worker R.C. Ch.	Richmond	J.C. Hallman	2 -	4	E
115	1968	North Lonsdale United Church	North Vancouver	Morton; Keefer	2 - 53	8	E
116	1968	Danish Lutheran Church of Vancouver	Burnaby	Frobenius; Larsen	1 - 6	6	T
117	1968	St. John's Shaughnessy Angl. Ch.	Vancouver	J.C. Hallman	4 - 71	69	E
118	1968	First Presbyterian Church	Prince Rupert	J.C. Hallman	2 - 24	4	E
119	1968	St. Peter & St. Paul R.C. Church	Vancouver	Hallman; D. Quinton	2 - 30		E
120	1968	Sisters of the Good Shepherd R.C. Convent	Surrey	J.C. Hallman	2 -	3	E
121	1968	St. Ann's R.C. Church	Abbotsford	J.C. Hallman	2 -	3	E
122	1968	St. Thomas Anglican Church	Chilliwack	J.C. Hallman	2 - 32	4	E

	Year	Name	Location	Builder	Manuals & Stops	Ranks	Action
123	1968	Killarney Park Lutheran Church	Vancouver	J.C. Hallman	2 - 30	4	E
124	1968	University of British Columbia	Vancouver	Karl Wilhelm	2 - 3	3	T
125	1969	First German Baptist Church	Vancouver	J.C. Hallman	2 -	7	E
126	1969	Nelson United Church	Nelson	Keates	2 - 30	27	EP
127	1970	St. Aidan's United Church	Victoria	Hugo Spilker	2 - 21	8	E/P
128	1970	St. Helen's Anglican Church	Surrey	Norm Starr	2 - 21	6	EP
129	1970	University of British Columbia	Vancouver	Casavant	3 - 43	64	TE
130	1970	Richmond Presbyterian Church	Richmond	Albert de Graaf	2 - 18	3	EP
131	1971	St. Andrew's United Church	Port Moody	WurliTzer; Haddon	2 - 20	4	EP
132	1972	St. Mark's Evangelical Lutheran Church	Vancouver	Hugo Spilker	2 - 21	7	E/P
133	1972	Residence of Albert Brennink	Duncan District	Ziegler	2 - 6	8	T
134	1974	St. Catherine's Anglican Church	North Vancouver	Casavant	2 - 13	17	EP
135	1975	Bao Lam Buddhist Association	Vancouver	Casavant; Keates	2 - 16	14	EP
136	1975	Trinity Lutheran Church	Richmond	Wicks	2 - 21	10	E
137	1976	Central Presbyterian Church	Vancouver	Casavant	2 - 13	15	EP
138	1976	St. Mark's Anglican Church	Qualicum Beach	Hugo Spilker	2 - 18	4	E/P
139	1977	St. Helen's Anglican Church	Vancouver	Möller; Keefer	2 - 33	10	E
140	1977	Philadelphia Church of Vancouver	Surrey	Casavant, Praestant	2 - 18	14	EP
141	1978	Canadian Reformed Church	Smithers	Hugo Spilker	2 - 23		E/P
142	1978	Faith Lutheran Church	Surrey	Hugo Spilker	2 - 22	7	E/P
143	1979	Trinity Western University	Langley	Casavant; Koppejan	2 - 12	12	T
144	c. 1980	Hope Lutheran Church	Victoria	Hugo Spilker	2 -	7	E/P
145	1980	Canadian Reformed Church	Abbotsford	Woodstock; Spilker	2 - 24		E/P
146	1980	Residence of Steen Larsen	North Vancouver	Steen Larsen		2	T
147	1981	St. Andrew's Anglican Church	Langley	John Darbyshire	2 - 24		E
148	1981	Colebrook United Church	Surrey	Hugo Spilker	2 - 21	6	E/P
149	1982	Christ Church Cathedral (Angl.)	Victoria	Bevington; Spilker	1 - 5	5	T
150	1982	St. Augustine's R.C. Parish	Vancouver	Keates	3 - 41	31	EP
151	1984	St. John's Lutheran Church	Vernon	Casavant	2 – 20	20	EP
152	1985	Gloria Dei Lutheran Church	North Vancouver	Adrian Koppejan	2 – 8	10	T

	Year	Name	Location	Builder	Manuals & Stops	Ranks	Action
153	1985	Holy Rosary Cathedral (RC)	Vancouver	Grant Smalley	1 - 4	4	T
154	1986	St. Andrew's-Wesley United Ch.	Vancouver	Goetze & Gwynn	1 - 13	11	T
155	1986	St. Mary's Anglican Church	Victoria	Casavant; Huestis	2 - 20	25	EP
156	1988	Chinese Pentecostal Church	Vancouver	Detlef Kleuker	2 - 13	17	T
157	1989	Knox United Church	Vancouver	Casavant; Koppejan	2 - 18	20	EP
158	c. 1990	Chemainus United Church	Chemainus	Wicks; Smalley	2 -	8	E/P
159	1990	Church of St. Barnabas (Angl.)	Victoria	John Brombaugh	1 - 6	7	T
160	1991	Residence of Leonard Noort	New Westminster	Adrian Koppejan	2 - 10	10	T
161	1992	St. Andrew's Anglican Church	Kelowna	Leonard Zack	1 - 8	6	T
162	1994	Good Shepherd Lutheran Church	Victoria	Hugo Spilker	2 -	2	E/P
163	1995	Good Shepherd Church (RC)	Surrey	Adrian Koppejan	3 - 34	33	ES
164	1995	First Christian Reformed Church	Chilliwack	Haddon; Koppejan	2 - 26	11	EP
165	1995	Built by Grant Smalley	Victoria ·	Grant Smalley	1 - 4	4	T
166	1997	Built by Grant Smalley	Victoria	Grant Smalley	1 - 5	5	T
167	1998	West Vancouver United Church	West Vancouver	Martin Pasi	2 - 31	36	T
168	1998	St. Michael & All Angels Ang. Ch	Victoria	Spilker; Smalley	2 - 24	7	EP
169	2000	Holy Rosary Cathedral (RC)	Vancouver	Karn-Warren; Casavant	3 - 48	51	EP
170	2001	Early Music Vancouver	Vancouver	Hellmuth Wolff	1 - 4	5	T
171	2004	Christ Church Cathedral (Angl.)	Vancouver	Casavant; Jones	3 - 39	45	TE, EP
172	2005	Christ Church Cathedral (Angl.)	Victoria	Hellmuth Wolff	4 - 61	85	TE
173	2007	Lutheran Church of The Cross	Victoria	Spilker; Smalley	2 - 17	10	EP
174	2008	Langley Canadian Reformed Ch.	Langley	Casavant	2 - 22	22	ES
175	2008	Cathedral Church of St. John The Evangelist (Anglican)	Victoria	Grant Smalley	2 - 23	15	EP
176	*1909, 1932, 1966	St. Andrew's-Wesley United Church	Vancouver	Casavant, Stinkens, Pasi, Huestis	3 - 59	66	EP
177	*1928, 1965, 2004	Shawnigan Lake School	Shawnigan Lake	Fosness; Anderson; Spilker; Smalley	2 - 29	25	EP

List II: Alphabetical Order of Pipe Organs in British Columbia

Not every organ with pipes has been documented with detailed specifications. There are many unit organs in the province and references are made to their locations with a few detailed specifications as examples. There are a few small custom installation organs of mixed origins and heavy unification that have not been covered in detail. One is an older four-rank, two-manual unit organ at St. Andrew's United Church in Port Moody. Lower mainland organ technician, Jack Ellis has built some unit organs and there is passing reference to some of his work. Also not included are hybrid combination pipe and electronically derived sound organs where speaker systems generate most of the voices. One exception is the organ at St. Andrew's Presbyterian Church in Victoria. It has sufficient pipes and is of enough historic significance to warrant a listing of its pipework specification only. Also not included in this book are details of some privately owned organs because they are not as easily accessible.

A Masonic Temple, New Westminster, B.C. (12 stops, 11 ranks)

The instrument here is the only remaining pipe organ in a Masonic Temple in the lower mainland. It was manufactured in 1913 by Aug. Laukhuff, Weikersheim, West Germany, and installed here by Chandos G. Dix of New Westminster in about 1920. It was dedicated as a war memorial in 1927. In 1961, Stan Haddon of Vancouver affected major repairs to it and in 1972, Ken Hodgson renewed the leathers and changed the action from tubular to electro-pneumatic. The organ is located at the west end of the 1911 building, in a chamber about 15 feet above the floor. The silver painted dummy facade pipes are arranged simply on a lip extension from the wall. The European style two-manual 30-note Pedal console is situated below the case and faces away from it. The console has tab stops with pre-set finger pistons which, when pressed, activates the stop names to rise on cards along a window over the tabs of the respective names. The Crescendo and Swell Pedals are also in reverse order to conventional consoles.

Specifications:

SWELL		GREAT		PEDAL	
Bourdon	16	Open Diapason	8	Sub Bass	16
Rohr Gedact	8	Stopped Diapason	8	Bass Flute	8
Oboe Gamba	8	Dulciana	8		
Aeoline	8	Principal	4		
Vox Celeste	8	Great Super			
Flute	4				
Tremulant					

COUPLERS

Swell Sub to Great Sub
Swell to Great
Swell to Great Super
Swell to Pedal
Great to Pedal

ACCESSORIES

Finger Pistons:
  Manual I – P-F-T-off Pre-select
  Manual II – P-F-T-off Pre-select
Swell Shutter Pedal
Crescendo Pedal

All Saints Anglican Church, Vernon, B.C. (14 stops & ranks)

In 1915, Karn-Warren of Woodstock, Ontario built this organ with romantic voicing and tubular-penumatic action. Andrew Chapman of Vancouver installed a new Casavant two-manual drawstop console and changed the action to electro-pneumatic in 1958. The changes were listed as Casavant's Opus 2485. The pipes are located in a corner at the right side of the front and speak out through a facade into the chancel and a screen into the nave. The console is at the opposite side of the chancel facing the pipe facade.

Specifications:

SWELL		GREAT		PEDAL	
Open Diapason	8	Open Diapason	8	Bourdon	16
Stopped Diapason	8	Melodia	8	Bass Flute	8
Gamba	8	Dulciana	8		
Aeoline	8	Principal	4		
Celeste	8	Waldflöte	4		
Flauto Traverso	4				
Oboe	8				
Swell Sub					
Swell Super					
Swell Unison Off					
Tremulant					

COUPLERS

Swell Sub to Great
Swell to Great
Swell Super to Great
Swell to Pedal
Swell Super to Pedal
Great to Pedal
Great Super to Pedal

ACCESSORIES

Finger Pistons:
Manual I – 4 Great Pre-select
4 General Pre-select
Manual II – 4 Swell Pre-select
Great to Pedal Toe Stud
4 General Pre-select Toe Pistons
Full Organ Toe Stud
Swell Shutter Pedal
Crescendo Pedal

All Saints By The Sea Church (Anglican), Ganges, B.C. (29 stops, 27 ranks)

In 1924, Adolf Fosness of Vancouver installed a new organ believed manufactured by Aug. Laukhuff, Weikersheim, West Germany, for Holy Trinity Anglican Church in Vancouver. In 1943, for the sum of $10,000, Casavant Frères installed new electro-pneumatic action, chests, and a two-manual drawstop console and called it Opus 1728. In 1977 a Trumpet rank was provided by Durst Organ Supply Co., Erie, Pennsylvania. In 1993, it was later removed just prior to the building being demolished and the organ was dismantled and sold to St. George's Anglican church. In 1994, that building was moved across the street, re-configured, and re-named All Saints by The Sea. The organ was installed there by David Quinton, son of retired organ technician, Ted Quinton. More recently, the organ has been undergoing alteration and enlargement by David Quinton with a third manual added to the existing console and additional pipes and components from Victoria Churches St. Andrew's Presbyterian and Christ Church Cathedral. The organ is located in a chamber at the front of the church above the sacristy. There is a screen front with a simple facade of one flat of pipes. The console is located at the back of the church.

Specifications:

SWELL

Bourdon	16
Röhr Flute	8
Gamba	8
Voix Celeste	8
Traverso Flute	4
Nazard	2 2/3
Piccolo	2
Tierce	1 3/5
Oboe	8
Clarion +	4
Chimes	
Tremulant	
Swell 16	
Swell 4	

PEDAL

Bourdon	16
Lieblich Bourdon (Sw)	16
Gedeckt	8
Viole (Pos)	8
Gemshorn (Pos)	4

GREAT

Open Diapason	8
Flute	8
Salicional	8
Principal	4
Harmonic Flute	4
Fifteenth	2
Scharff +	II rks
Trumpet +	8

COUPLERS

Positiv to Swell
Positiv to Great
Positiv to Pedal
Positiv 4 to Pedal
Swell to Great
Swell 4 to Great
Great to Pedal
Great 4 to Pedal

POSITIV

Stopped Diapason +	8
Viole +	8
Flute +	4
Gemshorn +	4
Flageolet +	2
Clarinet (From Swell)	8

ACCESSORIES

Thumb Pistons:
- Manual I –
  - 4 Great Pre-select
- Manual II –
  - 4 Swell Pre-select
- Manual III –
  - 4 Positiv Pre-select
  - 4 General Pre-select Toe Studs

Full Organ Toe Stud
Swell Shutter Pedal
Crescendo Pedal

Annunciation Catholic Church, Prince Rupert, B.C. (25 stops, 5 ranks)

The organ in this church was built as Opus 1949 by Casavant et Frères of St. Hyacinthe, Québec in 1949. It is situated in an integral case with a detached two-manual and Pedals tab stop console in the rear gallery. The instrument is an example of Casavant's unified style of stoplist disposition and has electro-pneumatic action. The five extended ranks of pipes are entirely enclosed in a swell box.

Specifications:

SWELL		GREAT		PEDAL	
Contra Dulciana	16	Lieblich Gedeckt	16	Bourdon	16
Rohrflöte	8	Open Diapason	8	Octave	8
Viola di Gamba	8	Rohrflöte	8	Stopped Flute	8
Dulciana	8	Viola di Gamba	8	Cello	8
Voix Celeste	8	Dulciana	8	Dulcet	4
Lieblich Flöte	4	Lieblich Flöte	4		
Violina	4	Dulcet	4		
Dulcet	4	Nazard	2 2/3		
Nazard	2 2/3	Fifteenth	2		
Piccolo	2				
Tierce	1 3/5				
Tremulant					

COUPLERS

Swell to Great
Swell to Pedal
Great to Pedal

ACCESSORIES

Finger Pistons:
  Manual I – 3 Great Pre-select
  Manual II – 3 Swell Pre-select
Expression Pedal (entire organ)
Crescendo Pedal

Bao Lam Buddhist Association, Vancouver, B.C. (16 stops, 14 ranks)

In 1975, Casavant Frères was awarded the contract to build a new organ for this church which was Christian Apostolic at the time. The building was modified and acoustically improved to accommodate the organ which was installed as Opus 3272 by John Darbyshire during his tenure as the company's B.C. representative. The organ is a modern romantic voiced example of Casavant's modular series, a grouping of various suggested stoplists on a standard size predesigned electro-pneumatic action pipechest and case for smaller churches. St. Catherines Anglican Church in North Vancouver is the only other B.C. example of this series but voiced in French Classical style. In 1991 the Ontario builder Keates-Geissler installed a four rank Antiphonal section on a fully exposed pipe chest extended off the rear gallery. The main organ case is centred in the front of the sanctuary with the facade partially concealed behind a screen. The detached two-manual tab stop console is located in the rear gallery.

Specifications:

SWELL

Stopped Diapason	8
Salicional	8
Flute	4
Trumpet	8

GREAT

Principal	8
Chimney Flute	8
Principal	4
Octave	2

ANTIPHONAL

Gedackt	8
Quint	5 1/3
Gemshorn	4
Octave	2

PEDAL

Bourdon	16
Principal	8
Chimney Flute (Gr.)	8
Octave (Gr.)	4

COUPLERS

Antiphonal to Swell
Antiphonal to Great
Swell to Great
Antiphonal to Pedal
Swell to Pedal
Great to Pedal

ACCESSORIES

Chimes
Swell Shutter Pedal
Crescendo Pedal

Built by Grant Smalley, Victoria, B.C. (4 stops, 3 ½ ranks and 5 stops, 4 ½ ranks)

In 1995, the Victoria organ builder Grant Smalley completed his Opus 3, a portable organ with integral case and keyboard with mechanical action. All components except the keys were built by him including the all wood specification pipes. The stops are lever type mechanisms with extensions for double activation. The single manual without pedal board has a 51-note compass. In 1997, Smalley also built Opus 4, a similar organ with an added reed stop and all wood pipes. These two organs have been used for various musical functions in Victoria and the lower mainland by being put up for rent by the builder.

Specifications:

Opus 3 Manual

Diapason (mc)	8
Gedeckt	8
Rohrflute	4
Principal	2

Opus 4 Manual

Gedeckt	8
Rohrflute	4
Quint (mc)	2 2/3
Principal	2
Regal	8

Canadian Memorial United Church, Vancouver, B.C. (36 stops, 44 ranks)

Casavant Frères built this twin case organ in 1928 as Opus 1269, the funds for which were provided by the Americans as a war memorial, in the sum of $10,000. In 1960, a Trumpet stop was added for $750. In 1960, Hill, Norman & Beard of London, England was paid $22,500 to replace the console and add a few more ranks of pipes. The console only lasted 10 years before wearing out and in 1971, J. Jean Girouard of Casavant rebuilt the organ, installed a new console and had the organ revoiced from romantic to neo-classic style under the direction of Lawrence Phelps. The ornately decorated dark oak cases with facades of silver coloured dummy pipes are in chambers at both sides of the choir. The Choir division is at the left and the rest in the right side.

Specifications:

SWELL		GREAT		CHOIR	
Gedackt	8	Quintaden	16	Holtz Gedackt	8
Salizional	8	Prinzipal	8	Gemshorn	4
Vox Coelestis	8	Rohr Flöte	8	Nasat	2 2/3
Prinzipal	4	Oktav	4	Klein Prinzipal	2
Nachthorn	4	Spitz Flöte	4	Terz	1 3/5
Bach Flöte	2	Oktav	2	Sifflöte	1
Mixtur	III rks	Mixtur	IV rks	Zimbel	III rks
Fagott	16	Trompette	8	Krummhorn	8
Trompette	8	Chimes		Trumulant	
Oboe	4				
Tremulant					

Canadian Memorial United Church, Vancouver, B.C. Continued

COUPLERS

Swell to Great
Swell to Choir
Choir to Great
Swell to Pedal
Great to Pedal
Choir to Pedal

PEDAL

Prinzipal	16
Subbass	16
Quintaden (Great)	16
Oktav	8
Pommer Gedackt	8
Oktav	4
Mixtur	III rks
Posaune	16
Trompette	8
Schalmei	4

ACCESSORIES

Finger Pistons:
Manual I – Choir to Pedal
  5 Choir Pre-select
Manual II – Swell to Great
  Choir to Great
  Great to Pedal
  5 Great/Pedal Pre-select
  5 Pedal Pre-select
Manual III – Swell to Pedal
  5 Swell Pre-select
Swell to Pedal Toe Stud
Great to Pedal Toe Stud
Choir to Pedal Toe Stud
5 General Pre-select Toe Pistons
Full Organ Toe Stud
Swell & Choir Shutter Pedals
Crescendo Pedal

Canadian Reformed Church, Abbotsford, B.C. (24 stops)

This organ was installed here at the beginning of 1980 by Hugo Spilker of Victoria with Dirk Jansz Zwart as consultant. The case is situated on a platform at the front of the church and the console is detached and at the left front side. The organ has two manuals and Pedal with electro-pneumatic action. The wind chests and some of the pipes are from a 1933 Woodstock Organ Co. instrument that was at First Baptist Church in Vancouver. Stinkens of Holland supplied additional pipes.

<u>**Specifications:**</u>

SWELL		GREAT		PEDAL	
Gedeckt	8	Bourdon	16	Subbass	16
Salicional	8	Principal	8	Bourdon	16
Celeste	8	Rohr Flöte	8	Octave Bass	8
Open Flute	4	Octave	4	Bass Flute	8
Nasard	2 2/3	Stopped Flute	4	Choral Bass	4
Gemshorn	2	Super Octave	2	Posaune	16
Cymbel	II rks	Mixture	IV rks	Trumpet	4
Krummhorn	8	Sesquialtera	II rks		
Tremolo		Trumpet	8		
		Tremolo			

COUPLERS

Swell to Great
Swell to Pedal
Great to Pedal

Centennial United Church, Victoria, B.C. (30 stops, 28 ranks)

This former Methodist church had several small organs at different times before members of the congregation agreed to form a company within the church to raise $4,131 to purchase a new Casavant Frères instru-ment in 1910. Opus 403 was a two-manual 22-stop organ with tubular-penumatic action. In the late 1950s its action was changed to electro-pneumatic. During 1974, Hugo Spilker changed the pipework somewhat with alterations, revoicing, and additions including new Stinkens made pipes. He also provided a new console. In 1993, Grant Smalley replaced that console with a larger rebuilt three-manual second-hand drawstop design of the 1950s made by Aeolian-Skinner which originally came from a location in Missouri. A third manual four-stop Positiv division was added to it. The additional ranks comprised of re-worked older pipes and a new Principal 2 made by B.C. pipe maker Jack Pearson. He also added the Pedal reed extended rank which are 1957 Hill, Norman & Beard pipes from Victoria's Christ Church Cathedral's old organ. The Swell Trumpet also had most of its pipes replaced by new one's made by Orgues Létourneau Limitée of Québec. The original ornately painted facade also had extensions appropriately made by Grant Smalley as well. This organ stands across the front of the elegant old sanctuary with the detached console below and facing the choir stalls and organ case. This instrument is the largest active pipe organ in a United Church on Vancouver Island.

Centennial United Church, Victoria, B.C. Continued

Specifications:

SWELL

Gedackt	16
Open Diapason	8
Stopped Diapason	8
Gamba	8
Gamba Celeste (tc)	8
Principal *	4
Transverse Flute	4
Harmonic Piccolo	2
Sesquialtera	II rks
Trumpet * ++	8
Oboe	8
Tremolo	
Swell to Swell 4	
Swell Unison Off	

* = Relocated/modified by Hugo Spilker 1974
+ = Stinkens pipes added by Hugo Spilker 1974
++ = added by Grant Smalley 1993

GREAT

Principal	8
Rohr Flute *+	8
Gemshorn *	8
Octave	4
Prestant	4
Open Flute *	4
Fifteenth +	2
Mixture +	II rks
Great to Great 4	
Great Unison Off	

COUPLERS

Swell to Pedal 8
Swell to Pedal 4
Great to Pedal 8
Great to Pedal 4
Positiv to Pedal 8
Swell to Great 8
Swell to Great 4
Positiv to Great 8
Swell to Positiv 8

POSITIV

Bourdon ++	8
Principal ++	4
Principal ++	2
Quinte ++	1 1/3

PEDAL

Open Diapason	16
Bourdon	16
Gedackt (Sw)	16
Bass Flute (ext)	8
Trombone ++	16
Trumpet (ext) ++	8
Clarion (ext) ++	4

ACCESSORIES

Thumb Pistons:
- Manual I –
  - Positiv to Great
  - 5 Positiv Pre-select
- Manual II –
  - Great to Pedal
  - 5 Great Pre-select
  - 5 General Pre-select
- Manual III –
  - 5 Swell Pre-select
  - Full Organ

5 Pedal Pre-select Toe Pistons
5 General Pre-sel. Toe Pistons
Swell Shutter Pedal
Crescendo Pedal

Central Presbyterian Church, Vancouver, B.C. (13 stops, 15 ranks)

In 1976 Casavant Frères Ltée. built their Opus 3308 for this church. The two-manual tab stop organ was installed on a platform at the front left side in the sanctuary by their B.C. and Alberta representative, Alex Bernhardt. The design of the instrument is with neo-classical voicing and completely exposed pipework. This new building replaces the larger previous one that was across the street. It too had a Casavant organ in it, which was sold to and incorporated within a custom design installation at Maranatha Canadian Reformed Church in Surrey.

Specifications:

SWELL		GREAT		PEDAL	
Stopped Diapason	8	Principal	8	Bourdon	16
Viole De Gambe	8	Chimney Flute	8	Principal	8
Spire Flute	4	Octave	4	Chimney Flute (Great)	8
Principal	2	Mixture	IV rks	Octave	4
Trumpet	8	Chimes			
Tremulant					

COUPLERS

Swell Sub to Great
Swell to Great
Swell to Pedal
Swell Super to Pedal
Great to Pedal

ACCESSORIES

Finger Pistons:
Manual I – 3 Great Pre-select
3 Pedal Pre-select Toe Pistons
Manual II – 3 Swell Pre-select
3 General Preselect
Swell Shutter Pedal
Crescendo Pedal

Chilliwack United Church, Chilliwack, B.C. (12 stops, 11 ranks)

The organ here was built by Casavant Frères in 1954 as Opus 2223 and installed by Andrew Chapman. It is located in a chamber behind a screen in the front right corner of the sanctuary. The detached two-manual tab stop console with pedal board is on the same side facing frontwards. The instrument has neo-romantic pipe voicing and electro-pneumatic action.

Specifications:

SWELL

Principal	8
Stopped Diapason	8
Viola da Gamba	8
Voix Celeste	8
Harmonic Flute	4
Oboe	8
Tremulant	
Swell Sub	
Swell Super	

GREAT

Open Diapason	8
Melodia`	8
Dulciana	8
Principal	4
Great Super	

COUPLERS

Swell Sub to Great
Swell to Great
Swell Super to Great
Swell to Pedal
Swell Super to Pedal
Great to Pedal
Great Super to Pedal

PEDAL

Bourdon	16
Stopped Flute (ext.)	8

ACCESSORIES

Thumb Pistons:
- Manual I –
  - 3 Great & Pedal Pre-select
- Manual II –
  - 3 Swell Pre-select

Great to Pedal Toe Piston
3 General Pre-select Toe Pistons
Swell Shutter Pedal
Crescendo Pedal

Chinese Pentecostal Church, Vancouver, B.C. (13 stops, 17 ranks)

The organ in this church is a smaller version of an instrument by the same builder made for the older sister church in Hong Kong, China. After many of the members emigrated to this area, they chose the same builder, Detlef Kleuker of Brackwede /Westfalia, Germany, to design and install the organ for this contemporary freeform ceiling building. The 1988 work is a neo-classically voiced tracker action organ of modern styling with polished tin face pipes enclosed in a dark red mahogany case. The organ is located in the front centre of the sanctuary. Although predominately German in voicing style, there is some ancient Chinese instrument sound influence in the organ particularly in the Hautbois stop. There are two 61-note manuals and a 30-note AGO pedal board.

Chinese Pentecostal Church, Vancouver, B.C. Continued

Specifications:

SWELLWERK		HAUPTWERK		PEDAL	
Metal-Gedackt	8	Principal	8	Subbass	16
Rohrflöte	4	Flute	8	Spitzflöte	8
Principal	2	Octave	4	Choralbass	4
Quinte	1 1/3	Mixture	IV rks		
Sesquialtera	II rks	Hautbois	8		
Tremolo					

COUPLERS	ACCESSORIES
I/II Toe iron	Swell Shutter Pedal
I/Pedal Toe iron	
II/Pedal Toe Iron	

Chown Memorial & Chinese United Church, Vancouver, B.C. (26 stops, 24 ranks)

In 1924, M.P. Möller Pipe Organ Co. of Hagarstown, Maryland built their Opus 3597 instrument for First Baptist Church, Hoboken, N.J. It was later moved to a Seattle, Wa. church before being brought up and installed at Chown in 1955 by Stan Haddon and Ken Hodgson. With the possible exception of the console, the organ is as originally built and is the largest most intact example of a Möller organ in B.C. The instrument is entirely enclosed in expression boxes behind a screen front chamber on the north chancel side. The pitch set at A435 is another indication of theatre organ influence in the design. The detached three-manual tab stop console is connected by electric action. Most of the pipe ranks extend beyond the 61 note manual compass to effectively accommodate the sub and super couplers bringing the pipe total to 1556.

Specifications:

SWELL

Bourdon	16
Open Diapason	8
Gedeckt	8
Salicional	8
Viol d'Orchestre	8
Voix Celeste (tc)	8
Harmonic Flute	4
Cornopean	8
Oboe	8
Vox Humana	8
Tremulant	
Swell 16	
Swell 4	
Swell Unison Off	

GREAT

Open Diapason	8
Doppel Flute	8
Gamba	8
Gemshorn	8
Wald Flute	4
Cathedral Chimes	
Great 4	

PEDAL

Double Open Diapason	16
Bourdon	16
Lieb. Gedeckt (Sw)	16
Octave Bass	8
Bourdon (ext)	8
Dolce	8
Pedal 4	

CHOIR

English Open Diapason	8
Melodia	8
Dulciana	8
Flute	4
Clarinet	8
Choir 16	
Choir 4	
Choir Unison Off	

Chown Memorial & Chinese United Church, Vancouver, B.C. Continued

COUPLERS

Swell Sub to Great
Swell to Great
Swell Super to Great
Swell Sub to Choir
Swell to Choir
Swell Super to Choir
Choir Sub to Great
Choir to Great
Choir Super to Great
Choir Sub to Swell
Choir to Swell
Choir Super to Swell
Swell to Pedal
Swell Super to Pedal
Great to Pedal
Great Super to Pedal
Choir to Pedal

ACCESSORIES

Finger Pistons:
- Manual I –
  - 4 Choir / Pedal Pre-select
- Manual II –
  - 6 Great / Pedal Pre-select
  - 6 General Pre-select
- Manual III –
  - 6 Swell / Pedal Pre-select

Swell to Pedal Toe Stud
Great to Pedal Toe Stud
Sforzando Hitchdown
Swell Shutter Pedal
Great / Choir Shutter Pedal
Crescendo Pedal

Christ Church Cathedral, Vancouver, B.C. (39 stops, 45 ranks)

Christ Church's building interior has recently been extensively rebuilt and modified and during this process the choir & organ loft have been relocated from the front to the newly built rear gallery. The Bray, Ireland firm of Kenneth Jones Pipe Organs Ltd. was contracted for just under $1 million to design and build a new organ incorporating and revoicing approximately 19 ranks of Christ Church's 1949 Casavant Opus 1954 as well as four other used ranks. The rest of the materials were new creating a freestanding case of three modules with flamed copper and polished tin speaking pipe facade and a detached three 58-note manuals, 32-note pedal board drawstop console facing the choir and organ case from the gallery rail. The action is mechanical keyboard, electro-pneumatic pedal board, and electric stop. There is a 99-memory level combination system as well as floppy-disc memory storage. The bottom 20 notes of both 32′ stops are electrically generated sounds. The first Irish built organ in B.C., its voicing could be considered as neo-romantic.

<u>**Specifications:**</u>

SWELL		GREAT		POSITIVE	
Violin Diapason	8	Principal	16	Principal	8
Stopped Diapason	8	Octave	8	Rohrflute	8
Viola da Gamba	8	Harmonic Flute	8	Salicional	8
Voix Celeste (tc)	8	Gamba	8	Octave	4
Principal	4	Octave	4	Spitzflute	4
Nason Flute	4	Mixture	IV rks	Nazard	2 2/3
Fifteenth	2	Cymbal	II rks	Superoctave	2
Mixture	IV rks	Trumpet (en chamade)	8	Nachthorn	2
Contra Trumpet	16	Clarinet	8	Tierce	1 3/5
Cornopean	8	Cimbelstern		Mixture	IV rks
Oboe	8			Trumpet	8
Tremulant				Tremulant	

Christ Church Cathedral, Vancouver, B.C. Continued

PEDAL

Major Bass (ext)	32
Subbass (ext)	32
Open Diapason	16
Open Wood	16
Subbass	16
Octave (ext)	8
Bass Flute (ext)	8
Trombone	16

COUPLERS

Swell to Great
Swell to Positive
Positive to Great
Swell to Pedal
Great to Pedal
Positive to Pedal

ACCESSORIES

Finger Pistons:
- Swell to Great
- Swell to Positive
- Positive to Great
- Swell to Pedal
- Great to Pedal
- Positive to Pedal
- 8 General Pre-select
- Manual I – 8 Positive Pre-select
- Manual II – 8 Great Pre-select
- Manual III – 8 Swell Pre-select

Swell to Great Toe Stud
Great to Pedal Toe Stud
8 Divisional Pre-select Toe Studs to Pedal
8 General Pre-select Toe Studs
Swell Shutter Pedal

Christ Church Cathedral, Victoria, B.C. (13 stops, 12 ranks)

The second largest of three organs in Christ Church is this unique tracker action organ built in 1927 by Messrs. Harrison & Harrison of Durham, England. It was built for the residence of W.N. Mitchell, Halsway Manor, Somerset, England. In 1938, it changed hands and was shipped to the Fairbridge Society at the Prince of Wales Farm School, Cowichan, Vancouver Island where it was placed in the chapel. Christ Church acquired it in 1980, installed it in the rear gallery, and used it for church services while the main organ was being rebuilt and prepared for rear gallery installation. The smaller organ was then relocated to a platform at the right side of the chancel. In 1980, Keates Geissler removed the Great Contra Dulcian 16 and placed it in the main organ. Between 1981 and 1986, Hugo Spilker removed other pipes including a Rohr Flöte 8, Viola da Gamba 8, Harmonic Flute 4, and Principal 2 from the original design. He added four ranks which included old revoiced pipes and pipework made by Geiske as well as Batz from Holland. He also revoiced the Swell Echo Salicional into a Celeste. Since then, Grant Smalley rebuilt the organ's action. The organ is enclosed in a wood case with two simple flats of pipes in the facade.

Specifications:

SWELL

Lieblich Gedackt	8
Vox Angelica	8
Celeste	8
Principal +	4
Nasard +	2 2/3
Trumpet	8
Tremolo (na)	

+ = Added by Hugo Spilker 1981 - 86

GREAT

Open Diapason	8
Claribel Flute	8
Octave	4
Rohr Flute +	4
Flute +	2

COUPLERS

Swell to Great
Swell to Pedal
Great to Pedal

PEDAL

Sub-bass	16
Flute (ext)	8

ACCESSORIES

Great to Pedal Toe Piston
3 Swell Pre-select Toe Pistons
3 Great Pre-select Toe Pistons
Swell Shutter Pedal

Christ Church Cathedral, Victoria, B.C. (5 stops & ranks)

The second organ of the cathedral was built in 1856 by Bevington & Sons, Soho, England. In 1862, it was presented to the church by Baroness Burdett Coutts. In 1869, the cathedral burnt down but two priests saved most of the organ. It was then purchased for $100 by W.C.S. Seeley of Seeley's Saloon, Australian Hotel, James Bay Bridge, and erected in a room adjoining the bar. Seeley repaired the organ, replaced several flute pipes, added composition Pedals, and a gold painted front. He sold it to St. Andrew's Cathedral in 1873 where it remained until 1884 when it was transferred to a temporary pro-cathedral, later the Institute Hall on View St. In 1892, St. Ann's Academy acquired it and then St. Mark's Anglican had it in 1913. In 1953, Mr. Dallymore of Dundas St., Esquimalt, bought it. It was then sold to Hugo Spilker in in 1962 who then sold it back and installed it in the rear gallery of Christ Church just under 100 years after it had left that congregation. Modifications by Spilker in the 1980's changed it further from original but a more recent restoration by Grant Smalley was more in line with the original. The action is still mechanical with a 54 note single keyboard. Much of the facade is from original 8 ft. Diapason later cut down by Spilker but only 12 pipes of the Flute 8, 42 pipes of the Principal 4, and the top half of the Claribel 2 are Bevington's work. The organ is located on the main floor of the nave on the left side towards the front.

__Specifications:__

MANUAL (1961)		MANUAL (1981)		MANUAL (2001)	
Claribel -	8	Stopped Bass (12n)	8	Flute *	8
Dulciana	8	Chimney Flute (tc) -	8	Principal	4
Flute +	4	Principal	4	Claribel -	2
Nasat +	2 2/3	Flageolet	2	Quint ++	1 1/3
Principal	2	Nineteenth ++	1 1/3	Twenty-second ++	1
		Twenty-second ++	1		

- = many pipes added by Seeley in 1870
+ = non-original addition
++ = added by Spilker in 1982
* = most pipes added by Spilker in 1980's from cathedral's 1927 Harrison & Harrison organ

Christ Church Cathedral, Victoria, B.C. (61 stops, 85 ranks)

The organ that is located in the west gallery of this cathedral is a dream come true for the musical director, Michael Gormley, and all those who supported the project. The largest of three pipe organs in the sanctuary, it replaced a mainly 1957 Hill, Norman & Beard instrument unsuccessfully rebuilt in 1980 by Keates Geissler. The Laval, Québec firm of Hellmuth Wolff & Associes was contracted to create a unique eclectically-designed organ based on French and South German classical styles with some Italian romantic influence as well. The largest organ project to date by Wolff, organ technician Herb Huestis was hired to assist in voicing the reed pipes. After 30 months of work, the installation of Opus 47 was completed on October of 2005. With over 4,300 pipes, this $2.2 million organ includes gallery modifications and is the largest and most expensive instrument in B.C. It is also considered one of the finest instruments of its voicing style and design in the world.

Christ Church Cathedral, Victoria, B.C. Continued

The instrument has freestanding cases of solid mahogany and mahogany veneered wood. An earthquake resistant steel frame structure supports the main case. The case design is contemporary with many flats of polished high tin content speaking Principal pipes in the façade. The disposition of divisions starts with the Unterwerk at the base with façade pipes from the Oberwerk which stand above it. The Hauptwerk is arranged at both sides of the Oberwerk and the Pedal division is split and located at impost level adjacent to the outer sides of the Hauptwerk. A separately encased Rückpositiv stands at the gallery rail. The detached four 58-note manuals, 30-note straight-flat pedal board console with curved and terraced stop jambs faces the choir stalls and main organ case. Its keys use tracker action to connect to the pipes and the stops use electric action to activate the ranks. The manual keys' natural notes are capped in ox-bone with arcaded nosings of padouk wood. The sharps are solid ebony. The pedal board naturals are white oak and the sharps are capped with rose-wood. There is a multilevel capture combination system with 256 levels of memory and a sequencer. These are six pre-set pistons for each of the five divisions and 12 general pre-select pistons. The wind system is by a Ventus blower feeding two parallel-ford bellows. This system can be modified by winkers which can engage pipe chest concussion bellows as needed. In a word this is a "magnificent" instrument appropriate for a grand cathedral.

Specifications:

OBERWERK		UNTERWERK (Swell)		HAUPTWERK	
Suavial	8	Lieblich Gedackt	16	Praestant	16
Copula major	8	Principal	8	Octave	8
Quintadena	8	Bordun	8	Spitzflöt	8
Octava	4	Salicional	8	Slöt travers	8
Copula minor	4	Unda Maris	8	Octave	4
Violetta	4	Octava	4	Hohlflöt	4
Fletl	2	Nachthorn	4	Quint	2 2/3
Oberquinte	1 1/3	Flagiolet	2	Superoctave	2
Mixtur	IV rks	Mixtur	V rks	Mixtur	V-VI rks
Hörnli	II rks	Basson	16	Cornet	Vrks
Trompete	8	Trompette	8	Fagott	16
Vox Humana	8	Oboe	8	Trompette	8
		Clairon	4	Tremulant	
		Tremulant			

Christ Church Cathedral, Victoria, B.C. Continued

RÜCKPOSITIV

Quintadena	16
Principal	8
Rohrflöt	8
Octave	4
Koppelflöt	4
Nasat	2 2/3
Superoctave	2
Terz	1 3/5
Mixtur	V rks
Dulcian	16
Trompete	8
Krummhorn	8
Tremulant	

PEDALWERK

Bordun	32
Principalbass	16
Subbass	16
Octavbass	8
Flötbass	8
Choralbass	4
Rauschpfeife	V rks
Kontraposaune	32
Posaunenbass	16
Trompetenbass	8
Trompette	8
Schalmey	4

COUPLES

Oberwerk to Hauptwerk
Unterwerk to Hauptwerk
Rückpositiv to Hauptwerk
Oberwerk to Manual I
Unterwerk to Manual I
Oberwerk to Pedal
Unterwerk to Pedal
Hauptwerk to Pedal
Rückpositiv to Pedal

ACCESSORIES

Rückpositiv Tacet
Unterwerk Shutter Pedal
Unison Off Manual I
Stabilizer wind (winkers)
Echo (open Unterwerk rear louvers)
Nachtigall
Zimbelstern

Christian Reformed Church, Smithers, B.C. (16 stops, 14 ranks)

The organ here was installed by John Darbyshire and Bert Blok of Abbotsford in 1977. Many of the pipes came from a 1933 Woodstock Organ Co. instrument that was in Vancouver's First Baptist Church. They have been crammed in a rather cluttered way into a low ceiling rear gallery. Even some of the Pedal Bourdon pipes against the wall extend into the attic above the ceiling. The console, from the United States, was made by Reisner and had three manuals which was reduced to two and also has tab stops. It is located at the front left of the church and because of its distance from the pipes, causes sound delay problems for the organist. There is very little borrowing in the ranks which are voiced in the romantic style, a bit unusual for a Christian Reformed Church. There are not 1 but 2 Celestes in the two manual divisions.

Specifications:

SWELL		GREAT		PEDAL	
Open Diapason	8	Open Diapason	8	Bourdon	16
Stopped Diapason	8	Medodia	8	Gedeckt	16
Salicional	8	Gemshorn	8	Bass Flute	8
Voix Celeste	8	Celeste	8		
Flute Harmonic	4	Octave	4		
Flautina	2	Rohr Flute	4		
Clarinet	8	Great Super			
Tremolo					
Swell Super					

COUPLERS

Swell to Great
Swell Super to Great
Swell to Pedal
Swell Super to Pedal
Great to Pedal
Great Super to Pedal

ACCESSORIES

Finger Pistons:
Manual I – Swell to Great
Great to Pedal
4 Great Pre-select
Manual II – Swell to Pedal
4 Swell to Pre-select
Swell to Pedal Toe Stud
Great to Pedal Toe Stud
Sforzando Toe Stud
Swell Shutter Pedal
Crescendo Pedal

Church of Our Lord (Reformed Episcopal), Victoria, B.C. (21 stops, 20 ranks)

The oldest extant organ in B.C. stands in the chancel of this building where it has been since 1876 or 77. It was originally built as a two-manual with short compass Swell instrument in about 1827 by the famous Boston, Mass. cabinet maker turned organ builder Thomas Appleton for St. Paul's Episcopal Church, Wilamantic, Connecticut at a cost of approximately $5,000. In 1867, S.S. Hamill was contracted to modify the organ somewhat which included extending the Swell division to full compass by making a new chest, adding another rank of pipes and providing a new expression box for it. At one point in time it is believed that this organ was located in a church in Baltimore, Maryland. Eventually it came to this coast transported aboard a sailing ship and was destined for a probable third home in a church in Oregon. Unfortunately the vessel ran aground and was wrecked off San Fransisco, California. The organ, however, was salvaged and later acquired by Sir James Douglas who was one-time Governor of the colony of British Columbia as well as a member of this church's congregation. He had the organ shipped up to Victoria where it was repaired by W.C.S. Seeley. After the present structure of Church of Our Lord was completed in 1875, Douglas donated the organ to the church and John Bergstrom of San Francisco installed the organ there. Over the years, the care of the organ was entrusted to various technicians including Vancouver's Chandos G. Dix who did work on it in the 1940s and probably early 50s. It was believed that at this time the Hamill added Swell rank, the Bourdon 16, was replaced with a Celeste 8. Also done was the installation of a replacement Swell expression box and extension of the Pedal Diapason, which is actually a Bourdon, from 27 notes to 30 notes with a replacement concave radiating pedal board added. The action at this time to the Pedal was tubular-penumatic which could have been Dix's work as well. The Great Trumpet rank was also removed between 1948 and 1957. In 1986, area technician Grant Smalley took over the care of the instrument. Since that time, he installed a new 8′ Trumpet rank that was made in Ireland and also made some restoration in respect to the original design including replacement of the pneumatic pulldowns with tracker action to the Pedal pipes. Despite the alterations over the years a great deal of the original Appleton made pipes and components are still there. The organ is encased in a medium dark stained pine gothic style cabinet with a facade of gold painted speaking Diapason pipes. The keydesk has two 54-note manuals and 30-note pedal board.

Specifications:

SWELL

Open Diapason	8
Stopped Diapason Bass	8
Stopped Diapason Treble	8
Viol di Gamba	8
Celeste Bass +	8
Celeste Treble +	8
Principal	4
Mixture	III rks
Bassoon Bass +	8
Hautboy Treble +	8
Tremulant	

GREAT

Open Diapason	8
Stopped Diapason Bass	8
Stopped Diapason Treble	8
Dulciana (tc)	8
Principal	4
Flute (tc)	4
Twelfth +	2 2/3
Fifteenth	2
Mixture	II rks
Trumpet ++	8

PEDAL

Diapason	16

COUPLERS

Great & Swell
Pedal & Keys
Pedals to Swell

ACCESSORY

Swell Shutter Pedal

+ = Not from original pipework
++ = Added by Grant Smalley

Church of St. Barnabas Anglican, Victoria, B.C. (6 stops, 7 ranks)

In the rear gallery of this church is found a most interesting small tracker action organ made by the prominent American builder, John Brombaugh of Eugene, Oregon. Brombaugh was an innovative organ builder who expanded quite effectively on 18th century German organ design ideas. This instrument with its bold bright singing sound is a modest example typical of his work. Built in 1990, Opus 31F was the last of six identical stock designed ones and was purchased by the church from him for $85,000. The organ, enclosed in a fumed oak and cedar case, has a polished high tin content façade of speaking Principal pipes with carved oak pipe shades. The attached keydesk has a single 50-note manual made with bone covered naturals and ebony sharps. The 26-note straight flat pedal board has maple wood with rosewood sharps. The Quint is part of the Mixture III and is activated by pulling the draw stop half way out. The temperament is Kellner's "Bach" type.

Specifications:

MANUAL		PEDAL		COUPLER
Gedackt	8	Subbass (ext)	16	Manual to Pedal
Praestant	4			
Flute	4			
Quinte	3			
Octave	2			
Mixture	III rks			
Tremulant				

Church of St. John the Divine (Anglican), Victoria, B.C. (53 stops, 65 ranks)

In 1912, a new four manual 50 stop, 47 rank organ was built by the Companie d'Orgues Canadiennes (Canadian Organ Company) of St. Hyacinthe, Québec and installed in the present building after it was newly erected. The organ had 20 couplers at the console and three different wind pressures controlling some 3.056 pipes including a 32-foot Pedal Open Diapason and, apart from the main case in the front, an Echo division in a chamber at the rear left side of the nave. In 1960, while Victoria organ builder Hugo Spilker was in the midst of rebuilding the organ, a fire severely damaged the church, and destroyed all but the echo division of the organ. In 1961, the church hired Casavant Fréres to build their opus 2694 and their B.C. representative, J. Jean Girouard supervised the installation assisted by Hugo Spilker who temporarily represented the firm for Vancouver Island at that time. The instrument, voiced in neo-classical style under Lawrence Phelps' supervision and costing $52,515 to build, is his only example built for Vancouver Island, the first new Casavant organ there since 1943. Only one other example of Casavant's revival period has since been relocated to the island, namely the small organ at Victoria's Royal Jubilee Hospital Chapel. St. John's organ has since undergone some alterations since 2000, both the Swell and Great Trumpets have been rebuilt, the Choir Krummhorn was replaced with a new Casavant Crommorne, and Victoria organ builder Great Smalley replaced the Choir Cymbal III with a Scharf III. He also undertook the removal of the old Echo division and provided three replacement circa 1970 Casavant pipe chests to enlarge that division. He then mounted a new Principal 8 rank from Québec organ builder Letourneau and 11 ranks of 1974 Casavant pipework acquired from Ontario's Islington United Church. This organ is currently the second largest four-manual Casavant organ of this voicing period in a church in B.C. and the second largest organ on Vancouver Island.

Church of St. John the Divine (Anglican), Victoria, B.C. Continued

Specifications:

ANTIPHONAL

Principal	8
Harmonic Flute (prep)	8
Bourdon	8
Octave	4
Rohrflöte	4
Blockflöte	2
Fourniture 1 1/3	IV rks
Sesquialtera 2 2/3	II rks
Festival Trumpet (prep)	8
Rohrschalmei	8
Tremulant	

CHOIR (unencl.)

Gedeckt	8
Erzähler	8
Erzähler Celeste	8
Praestant	4
Koppelflöte	4
Blockflöte	2
Quintflöte	1 1/3
Scharff 1	III rks
Sesquialtera 2 2/3	II rks
Crommorne	8
Antiphonal Chimes	
Tremulant	
Choir 16	
Choir Unison off	
Choir 4	

COUPLERS

Antiphonal 8 to Great
Swell 8 to Great

SWELL

Principal Etroit	8
Viole de Gambe	8
Cor de Nuit	8
Voix Celeste	8
Octave	4
Flute Harmonique	4
Nazard	2 2/3
Octavin	2
Plein Jeu 1	IV rks
Basson	16
Trompette	8
Hautbois	8
Clairon	4
Tremulant	
Swell 16	
Swell Unison Off	
Swell 4	

PEDAL

Contrabass	16
Bourdon	16
Quintaton (Gr)	16
Principal	8
Rohr Gedeckt	8
Choralbass	4
Nachthorn	2
Mixture 2 2/3	IV rks
Posaune	16
Basson (Sw)	16
Trompette (ext)	8
Basson (Sw)	8
Schalmei	4
Antiphonal Chimes	

GREAT

Quintaton	16
Diapason	8
Rohrflöte	8
Gemshorn	8
Octave	4
Spitzflöte	4
Superoctave	2
Fourniture 1 1/3	IV rks
Trumpet	8

ACCESSORIES

Thumb Pistons:
- Manual I -
  - Choir to Pedal
  - 5 Choir Pre-select
- Manual II -
  - Antiphonal to Great
  - Swell to Great
  - Choir to Great
  - Great to Pedal
  - 5 Great/Pedal Pre-select
  - 5 Pedal Pre-select
- Manual III -
  - Swell to Pedal
  - 5 Swell Pre-select
  - 6 General Pre-select
- Manual IV -
  - Antiphonal to Pedal
  - 3 Antiphonal Pre-select

Great to Pedal Toe Stud
Full Organ Toe Stud

Church of St. John the Divine (Anglican), Victoria, B.C. Continued

COUPLERS

Swell 4 to Great
Choir 16 to Great
Choir 8 to Great
Antiphonal 8 to Choir
Swell 16 to Choir
Swell 8 to Choir
Swell 4 to Choir
Antiphonal 8 to Pedal
Swell 8 to Pedal
Great 8 to Pedal
Choir 8 to Pedal
Choir 4 to Pedal

ACCESSORIES

6 General Pre-select
Toe Pistons
Antiphonal Shutter Pedal
Crescendo Pedal

Church of The Good Shepherd (Anglican), Vancouver, B.C. (20 stops, 18 ranks)

Vancouver's no longer extant Colonial Theatre had Adolph Fosness install a 17-rank with draw-stop console Karn-Warren organ in 1910. In 1937, Metropolitan Tabernacle bought it for $2,800 and had Stan Haddon of Vancouver install and enlarge it and provide a new tab stop console of two manuals from the Toledo Pipe Organ Co. Inc., Toledo, Ohio. Several years ago the Metropolitan congregation moved out and this Anglican group is presently using the building. With the exception of the Haddon added Great Salicional, this organ has identical specifications to the similar vintage Karn-Warren organ at Vancouver's Ruth Morton Baptist Church. The Good Shepherd Church organ's pipes and chests are in a chamber at the upper front of the room with a down facing screen facade extension from the wall. The room has good acoustics but the tonal egress of the organ pipes is too hampered by the chamber arrangement to make unamplified sound effective. The console is located at the front right side facing left on a platform below the organ. The instrument's Swell division is quite large compared with the rest and as is common with romantically voiced organs the Pedal division is under developed. A Pedal Super coupler, however, is available here to alleviate the problem somewhat.

Specifications:

SWELL

Bourdon	16
Stopped Diapason	8
Viol d'Gamba	8
Quintadena	8
Aeoline	8
Voix Celeste	8
Flauto Traverso	4
Piccolo	2
Oboe Gamba	8
Vox Humana	8
Chimes	
Tremolo	
Swell Sub	
Swell Super	
Swell Unison Off	

GREAT

Contra Viole	16
Open Diapason	8
Doppel Flute	8
Salicional +	8
Dulciana	8
Principal	4
Clarinet	8
Tremolo	
Great Super	
Great Unison Off	

COUPLERS

Swell Sub to Great
Swell to Great
Swell Super to Great
Swell to Pedal
Great to Pedal

PEDAL

Bourdon	16
Lieblich Gedeckt (Sw)	16
Violone (Gr)	16
Pedal Super	

ACCESSORIES

Thumb Pistons:
- Manual I –
  - 4 Great Pre-select
  - 4 General Pre-select
- Manual II –
  - 4 Swell Pre-select

6 Pre-select Toe Studs
Swell Shutter Pedal
Crescendo Pedal

+ = added in 1937 by Stan Haddon

Coastal Church, Vancouver, B.C. (35 stops, 20 ranks)

In 1918, the previous owners of this building, First Church of Christ Scientist, purchased their first pipe organ from the Ontario builder, Karn-Warren. Chandos Dix serviced the organ in its early days and at one point removed a rank of pipes from it; the Choir division French Horn 8. In 1935, the Seattle representative of the W.W. Kimball & Co., Chicago, Illinois, Mr. Longmore assisted by Vancouver technician Stan Haddon provided a new three-manual drawstop console, installed new relay action, and put the Great division under expression. Since 2001, the congregation moved out of the building and the Coastal Church commenced services there. The organ is still being used from time to time. It is the largest extant example in B.C. of Karn-Warren's work. Most of the pipe chests are of 73 pipes per rank to accommodate super coupling more effectively and there is some unification as well. The organ is in a chamber at the front of the sanctuary. The facade is an elegant colonial style screen. The detached console is in front facing the chamber and it controls approximately 1,224 pipes with electro-pneumatic action.

Coastal Church, Vancouver, B.C. Continued

Specifications:

SWELL

Violin Diapason (tc)	16
Horn Diapason	8
Gross Flute	8
Viol d'Orchestra	8
Wald Flute (ext)	4
Violina (ext)	4
Contra Fagotto (tc)	16
Vox Humana (tc)	16
Cornopean	8
Oboe	8
Vox Humana	8
Octave Cornopean (ext)	4
Vox Humana (ext)	4
Tremulant	
Swell Sub	
Swell Super	

ACCESSORIES

Thumb Pistons:
- Manual I –
  - 6 Choir Pre-select
- Manual II –
  - Great to Pedal
  - 6 Great / Pedal Pre-select
  - Nos. 5 - 8 General Pre-select
- Manual III –
  - Swell to Pedal
  - 8 Swell Pre-select
  - Nos. 1 - 4 General Pre-select

Swell to Pedal Toe Stud
Great to Pedal Toe Stud
6 General Pre-select Toe Studs
Sforzando Toe Stud
Swell Shutter Pedal
Great Shutter Pedal
Choir Shutter Pedal
Crescendo Pedal

GREAT

Open Diapason	8
Doppel Flute	8
Violoncello	8
Gemshorn (Ch)	8
Octave (ext)	4
Stopped Flute (ext)	4
Bass Tuba	16
Tuba (ext)	8
Harp	
Tremulant	
Great Sub	
Great Super	

PEDAL

Sub Bass (Gr O.D. ext)	16
Violone (Gr ext)	16
Lieblich Gedeckt	16
Flute (Ch)	8
Violoncello (Gr)	8

CHOIR

Concert Flute	8
Viol d'Gamba	8
Gemshorn	8
Quintadena	8
Harmonic Flute	4
Zart Flute (ext)	4
Piccolo (49 notes)	2
Bass Clarinet (tc)	16
Clarinet	8
Chimes	
Tremulant	
Choir Sub	

COUPLERS

Swell Sub to Great
Swell to Great
Swell Super to Great
Swell Sub to Choir
Swell to Choir
Swell Super to Choir
Choir Sub to Great
Choir to Great
Choir Super to Great
Choir to Swell
Swell to Pedal
Great to Pedal
Great Super to Pedal
Choir to Pedal

Colebrook United Church, Surrey, B.C. (21 stops, 6 ranks)

Hugo Spilker of Victoria built and installed the organ here in 1981. He incorporated and adapted the Hallman Organ Company console of the church's previous instrument which had electronic generated voices. On pipechests with direct electric action he used neo-classically voiced pipes obtained from Belgium, Germany, and England. The organ was placed on two levels behind a wooden screen in the front. The detached two-manual console has tab stops with a unified set up without couplers or pre-set pistons. This is a typical example of the builder's work although the sound seems a bit mellow and throttled back compared with others. The room. however has favourable acoustics and the organ's position in it permits an ample projection of its sound.

Specifications:

SWELL		GREAT		PEDAL	
Gedeckt	8	Principal	8	Bourdon	16
Gemshorn	8	Bourdon	8	Bass Flute	8
Flute	4	Octave	4	Gemshorn	8
Spitz Quinte	2 2/3	Gemshorn	4	Choral Bass	4
Gemshorn	2	Super Octave	2	Gemshorn	4
Tierce	1 3/5	Mixture	II rks	Twenty Second	2
Clarinet (synthetic)	8	Scharff	II rks	Mixture	II rks
Vibrato					

ACCESSORIES

Swell Shutter Pedal
Crescendo Pedal

Columbia Bowell Funeral Chapel, New Westminster, B.C. (19 stops, 4 ranks)

In about 1914, the Van Nuys, California firm of Robert Morton built a theatre organ that spent several years in the Bijou or Tivoli Theatre in Trail, B.C. At one time it was moved to a Masonic Temple in New Westminster before being sold to this funeral home for $1,200 in 1942 and installed by Stan Haddon of Vancouver. All the percussive effects were removed except the chimes and the organ has a Violin Diapason rank from the 1914 Karn Warren organ that was at Vancouver's Strand Theatre. The organ is fully under expression in a chamber at the back of the chapel. The detached two-manual theatre-style console in the rear gallery is the original Morton one.

Specifications:

SOLO

Bass Flute	16
Violin (Tenor C)	16
Concert Flute	8
Violin	8
Orchestral Flute	4
Violin	4
Vox Humana (Tenor C)	8
Chimes	

ACCOMPANIMENT

Concert Flute	8
Violin	8
Orchestral Flute	4
Violina	4
Vox Humana (Tenor C)	8
Tremolo	

ACCOMPANIMENT TRAPS

Violoin Diapason	8
Principal	4

PEDAL

Bass Flute	16
Flute	8
Viola	8
Violin Cello	8
Octave	4

ACCESSORIES

Expression Pedal
Ccrescendo Pedal

Cooke's Presbyterian Church, Chilliwack, B.C. (18 stops, 20 ranks)

This instrument is the largest one in Chilliwack and is derived from a 1913 Karn-Warren theatre organ. In 1988, Adrian Koppejan, whose organ building shop was nearby, was contracted to do a major rebuild and enlargement of the organ at a cost of $50,000. The old electro-pneumatic pipe chests were largely replaced by electric slider type. The old console shell was retained and largely re-constructed. Of the 13 original Karn-Warren ranks, nine were retained. The rest were mainly new ones except for a revoiced Trumpet rank. The organ is situated in a wide shallow chamber behind a screen at the front of the sanctuary. The detached drawstop console of two manuals and 30-note Pedal is at the right front side.

Specifications:

SWELL

Gedackt	8
Viola di Gamba	8
Voix Celeste	8
Principal +	4
Rohrflöte	4
Nasard +	2 2/3
Waldflöte +	2
Tierce +	1 3/5
Oboe	8
Tremulant	
Swell Sub	
Swell Super	

GREAT

Principal +	8
Doppelflöte	8
Octave +	4
Super Octave +	2
Mixture +	III rks
Trumpet +	8
Great Super	

COUPLERS

Swell Sub to Great
Swell to Great
Swell Super to Great
Swell to Pedal
Great to Pedal

PEDAL

Bourdon	16
Open Diapason	8
Choral Bass	4

ACCESSORIES

2 Pre-select Toe Studs
Swell Shutter Pedal
Crescendo Pedal

+ = Added by Adrian Koppejan in 1988

Cumberland United Church, Cumberland, B.C. (7 stops & ranks)

The organ here was built for St. Paul's Naval Church by Albert Hunter, 379 Kennington Road, London, England. It was brought to this coast by sailing ship via Cape Horn and installed in St. Paul's Naval Church, Victoria, in 1878. It was sent to Comox in 1912 and installed in St. George's United Church, Courtenay. It is believed that at this time its wind chests were supplied air with the help of a Ford Model T car engine. In 1951, the church purchased an electronic substitute and the organ was moved to Cumberland United Church, where it has remained ever since. In the early 1960s, Hugo Spilker of Victoria did some work to it, however the pipes are believed to be unchanged for the most part and the organ serves as a good example of English Romantic voicing. The organ is situated in the centre of the interior. The Front pipes were painted, but Hugo Spilker steel wooled them. The case is made of polished 50/50 metal speaking Open Diapason pipes for the facade, wood Bourdon pipes forming the sides, and mustard stained wood for the panelling. The pipework is entirely enclosed, except the Open Diapason 8 and the keydesk is attached with a single 56-note manual and a 27-note straight flat pedal board.

Specifications:

MANUAL		PEDAL		COUPLER
Open Diapason	8	Bourdon	16	Manual to Pedals
Stopped Diapason	8			
Dulciana (T.C.)	8	**ACCESSORY**		
Principal	4			
Flute	4	Hitchdown Swell Shutter		
Fifteenth	2			

Danish Lutheran Church of Vancouver, Burnaby, B.C. (6 stops and ranks)

The instrument in the rear gallery of this church was originally built for and eventually donated to this congregation by Resen Church near Skive, Denmark. Built as Opus 727 in 1968 by Frobenius Orgelbyggeri, Kongens Lyngby, Denmark, this organ had a single keyboard without Pedal and five ranks of pipes. Local organ builder, Steen Larsen, who apprenticed with Frobenius, went to the factory in Denmark with the idea of building the church an organ from a set of Frobenius designed plans. Opus 727 was available instead and was suitable for the church. By February of 2004, Steen Larsen and company completed the relocation of the organ. In 2005 a Frobenius made 27-note straight flat pedal board was added to accompany the 56-note keyboard. Steen Larsen added a Subbass that he built along with the pipe chest and electric action. The case is a simple design with painted wood and a single flat facade of Principal 4 based polished high tin content speaking pipes. This is the only Danish built pipe organ in the province. The voicing is neo-classical and the instrument speaks out well in this barrel shaped ceiling room of favourable acoustics. The keyboard and stop action of this organ is mechanical.

Specifications:

MANUAL		PEDAL	
Gedakt	8	Subbass	16
Principal	4		
Rørfløjte	4		
Spidsfløjte	2		
Oktav	1		

Dunbar Heights United Church, Vancouver, B.C. (21 stops, 18 ranks)

In 1955, Vancouver organ builder Stan Haddon was contracted to install an organ in a chamber behind the right side wall of the chancel of this building. He provided a 1937 vintage detached two 61-note manuals and 32-note AGO Pedal drawstop console built by the Toledo Organ Co., Toledo, Ohio and new pipework by M.P. Moller, of Hagarstown, Maryland. The organ has a screen and simple three dummy pipe triple cluster in its facade which faces a duplicate screen on the other side of the chancel. The expression box is for the whole organ and the action is believed to be electric. Two unusual ranks of pipes that are rare in the province are this instrument's Vox Atheria and French Horn.

Specifications:

SWELL		GREAT		PEDAL	
Open Diapason	8	Open Diapason	8	Bourdon	16
Flute	8	Concert Flute	8	Lieblich Gedeckt	16
Salicional	8	Melodia	8	Flute (ext.)	8
Vox Atheria (tc)	8	Gamba	8	Flute (ext.)	4
Aeoline	8	Dulciana	8		
Oboe	8	Octave (ext.)	4		
Vox Humana (tc)	8	Fern Flute	4		
French Horn	8	Nazard	2 2/3		
Tremulant I		Clarinet	8		
Tremulant II					

ACCESSORIES

Finger Pistons:
- Manual I –
  - 3 General Pre-select
  - 3 Great Pre-select
- Manual II –
  - 3 Swell Pre-select

3 General Pre-select Toe Pistons
Sforzando Toe Stud
Expression Pedal
Crescendo Pedal

COUPLERS

Swell to Pedal 8
Swell to Pedal 4
Great to Pedal 8
Swell to Great 16
Swell to Great 8
Swell to Great 4
Great to Great 4
Great Unison Cancel
Swell to Swell 16
Swell to Swell 4
Swell Unison Cancel

Duncan United Church, Duncan, B.C. (8 stops & ranks)

The organ here was originally built in c1910 by W.W. Kimball & Co. of Chicago, Illinois for a private home. It was later moved to the Royal Victoria Theatre in Victoria, and then to First United Church in Victoria. In 1931, David Ford brought it up to Duncan where it was placed in the front of this building's sanctuary. Hugo Spilker of Victoria changed the action from tubular to electro-pneumatic and added a Nazard 2 2/3 in 1962 and in 1975 he installed a new two-manual tab stop console. The entire organ (except for the first 24 notes of the Great Diapason), Pedal Bourdon, and Chimes are enclosed in an expression box.

__Specifications:__

SWELL

Stopped Diapason	8
Gamba	8
Flute d'Amour	4
Nazard*	2 2/3
Chimes	
Tremolo	
Swell Super	

GREAT

Diapason	8
Dulciana	8
Open Flute	4
Great Super	

COUPLERS

Swell to Great Sub
Swell to Great
Swell to Great Super
Swell to Pedal
Swell to Pedal Super
Great to Pedal

PEDAL

Bourdon	16

ACCESSORIES

Mech. Expression Shutter Pedal
Crescendo Pedal

* = Added in 1962 by Hugo Spilker – in place of Vox 8 in a rear shuttered box (extension of Swell Box rear wall).

Early Music Vancouver, Vancouver, B.C. (4 stops, 5 ranks)

In 2001, Early Music Vancouver acquired for approximately $50,000 a mechanical action portative organ made for them by Hellmuth Wolff & Associès of Laval, Québec. The organ, Opus 44, is completely enclosed in oak wood panelling and under expression. There is no pipework facade but there are two star motive opening cut outs in front with rotating shutters behind controlled by a lever over the keyboard. This gives progressive volume control. The top panel can also be latched open for additional volume. The instrument was designed and voiced by Hellmuth Wolff. The windchest and soft maple wood pipes were made by John Schreiner. The metal pipes were made by Luc Ladurantaye. The reverse colour single manual keydesk without pedal board has 53 keys. The key compass can be transposed to play four temperments from meantone to equal: 392, 415, 440, and 465 hertz. All four brass side push stop levers on the right side are double draw to partially or fully activate the pipe ranks that they control on the split bass & treble keyboard. Stop #4 partial is a Quinte and full draw activates a second rank to become a Sesquialtera. This is one of Hellmuth Wolffe's smallest organs at 310 lbs. It measures 43″ high, 44″ wide, and, including keyboard, 24 1/2″ deep. The voicing is sweet, clear, and not overly loud in volume. This is the first Wolff organ to arrive in British Columbia.

Early Music Vancouver, Vancouver, B.C. Continued

Specifications:

MANUAL

Bourdon	8
Bourdon (Treble)	8
Flûte à Cheminée	8
Flûte à Cheminée (Bass)	8
Quinte (Treble)	2 2/3
Doublette	2
Doublette (Bass)	2
Sesquialtera (Treble)	II rks

Emmanuel Baptist Church, Victoria, B.C. (26 stops, 12 ranks approx.)

In 1964, Hugo Spilker was contracted to build an organ for the former building of this congregation. The organ was later enlarged and moved into the front of the present building. It is a unified type instrument with combined electric and electro-pneumatic action comprised of pipes from Stinkens of Holland. There is a detached two-manual tab stop console that has a pedal board with an unusual shape to the sharp note keys. The voicing is neo-classical style with a pleasant sounding rank of string pipes, however inadequate wind pressure in the reservoir can make the upper register notes sound shakey at times.

Specifications:

SWELL		GREAT		PEDAL	
Gedackt	8	Principal	8	Bourdon	16
Salicional	8	Rohr Flöte	8	Octave Bass	8
Celest T.C.	8	Dulciana (Swell)	8	Bass Flute	8
Gedackt (from 8)	4	Octave	4	Choral Bass	4
Salicet (from 8)	4	Gedackt (Swell)	4	Choral Flute	4
Quint (T.C.)	2 2/3	Super Octave (from 4′)	2	Mixture	III rks
Piccolo (from 8)	2	Mixture 1 ½′	III rks	Contra Fagott 1-12	16
Tierce (T.C.)	1 3/5	Oboe (Swell)	8	Oboe (Swell)	8
Oboe	8			Schalmei (Swell)	4
Tremolo					

ACCESSORIES

Finger Pistons:
Manual I – 5 Swell Pre-select – detached setter board
Manual II – 5 Great Pre-select
5 General Pre-select
Swell Shutter Pedal
Crescendo Pedal

Emmanuel Pentecostal Church, New Westminster, B.C. (18 stops and ranks)

The organ that stands in the front of the sanctuary at this church was one of the first Canadian built instruments shipped by train to B.C. It is the oldest extant original location organ in the province. It was built in 1891 at a cost of about $10,000 by S.R. Warren & Sons of Toronto for this building which was St Andrew's Presbyterian Church. The original blower was driven by a water motor on two feeders but by 1910 the bellows were driven by electric motor and some collapsed pipes were replaced. The congregation maintained the organ themselves, the most prominent of them being a Mr. Robins. After the United Church of Canada was formed in 1925, the congregation dwindled and eventually they sold the property to the Pentecostals. The organ was neglected and vandalized somewhat over the years to the point of being unplayable by the 1950s. In the 1970s, they restored the decorative design of the facade pipes. Through my efforts, finally in 1996, Grant Smalley was hired to restore the organ. In the first stage of work he restored the keydesk, action, wind system, and some of the pipe ranks to playable condition. Much more needs to be done. The organ measures 26′ high, 30′ wide, and 8′ deep with a facade of 50 Great and Pedal speaking Open Diapason pipes

Emmanuel Pentecostal Church, New Westminster, B.C. Continued

mounted on an elegant oak case front. The attached drawstop keydesk has two 58-note manuals, 27-note flat pedal board, and tracker action throughout. The Swell box is mounted in the middle behind the facade with split Great & Pedal divisions. The stop jamb and pipe chests were prepared to have a Great Trumpet 8 but boards covering the toe holes indicate that one was never supplied.

Specifications:

SWELL

Open Diapason (tc)	8
Stopped Dia. (Bass)	8
Stopped Dia. (Treb)	8
Salicional	8
Aeoline	8
Traverse Flute	4
Viola	4
Oboe	8
Tremolo	

COUPLERS

Swell to Great
Swell to Pedal
Great to Pedal

GREAT

Open Diapason (tc)	8
Stopped Dia. (Bass)	8
Melodia (tc)	8
Dulciana (tc)	8
Principal	4
Harmonic Flute	4
Fifteen	2
Mixture	III rks
Trumpet (prep)	8

PEDAL

Double Open Diapason	16
Bourdon	16

ACCESSORIES

2 Swell Pre-select Hitchdowns
2 Great Pre-select Hitchdowns
Full Organ Hitchdown
Swell Shutter Pedal

Estonian Evangelical Lutheran Church of St. Peter, Vancouver, B.C. (21 stops, 6 ranks)

This organ was built in 1967 by Hugo Spilker of Victoria. It is situated in two cases in the rear gallery of this A-frame building. The organ is unified with electric action, electro-pneumatic Pedal controlling 378 pipes from a two-manual 30-note Pedal detached tab stop console. The pipework is unenclosed except for the Oboe which is in an expression box at the left side case. The bottom octave of the Principal forms a bridge between the two cases. There are no couplers or pre-set pistons.

Specifications:

SWELL		GREAT		PEDAL	
Rohr Flute	8	Bourdon	16	Bourdon	16
Rohr Gedackt	4	Principal	8	Octave Bass	8
Spitz Flöte	2	Bourdon	8	Bass Flute	8
Larigot	1 1/3	Octave	4	Choral Bass	4
Oboe	8	Flute D'Amour	4	Choral Flute	4
		Quinte Flute	2 2/3	Cymbel	II rks
		Super Octave	2	Oboe	4
		Cymbel	II rks		
		Oboe	8		

ACCESSORIES

Expression Pedal
Crescendo Pedal

Faith Lutheran Church, Surrey, B.C. (22 stops, 7 ranks)

In 1964, Hugo Spilker of Victoria installed a 3 1/2 rank organ in the congregation's old building. In 1978, Spilker was again contracted to build a larger instrument for their new building. He installed a unified organ with combined electric and electro-pneumatic action using some pipes from the previous instrument. It is situated on a platform over the entrance to the sanctuary at the right rear in a striking contemporary concrete building with good acoustics. The case is completely exposed with a facade of speaking Principal pipes with mahogany veneered Pedal Bourdon pipes at each side. The detached two 56-note manuals 30-note Pedal tab stop console is at the other side at the back. There aren't any couplers or pre-set pistons on the console.

Specifications:

SWELL		GREAT		PEDAL	
Gedeckt	8	Principal	8	Bourdon	16
Gemshorn	8	Bourdon	8	Octave Bass	8
Flute	4	Principal	4	Bass Flute	8
Gemshorn	4	Gemshorn	4	Choral Bass	4
Quint	2 2/3	Super Octave	2	Choral Flute	4
Gemshorn	2	Mixture	II rks	Twenty Second	2
Oboe	8	Oboe	8	Mixture	II rks
				Oboe	4

ACCESSORY

Swell Shutter Pedal
(for Gedeckt, Gemshorn, & Oboe)

First Baptist Church, Victoria, B.C. (22 stops, 16 ranks approx.)

In 1913, the Canadian Pipe Organ Company of St. Hyacinthe, Québec built a two manual organ of 20 stops, 18 ranks for the old building of First Baptist. In 1975, the congregation moved to a new building and Hugo Spilker rebuilt, revoiced, and installed the organ in the rear of the sanctuary. He provided a new case and facade design along with a detached two manual stop tab console located in the front left of the room. The action is combined electric and electro-pneumatic and there is some borrowing and unification in the disposition.

Specifications:

SWELL

Gedackt	8
Gamba	8
Celest (T.C.)	8
Principal	4
Open Flute	4
Nazard +	2 2/3
Gemshorn +	2
Tierce +	1 3/5
Trumpet (Ex. Gt.)	8
Oboe	8

GREAT

Diapason	8
Bourdon	8
Dulciana (T.C.)	8
Octave	4
Rohr Flute	4
Super Octave	2
Mixture 1 ½′ +	III rks

COUPLERS

Swell Sub to Great
Swell to Great
Swell Super to Great
Swell to Pedal
Swell Super to Pedal
Great to Pedal

PEDAL

Bourdon	16
Gedeckt	16
Octave Bass (Gr.)	8
Bass Flute (Ext.)	8
Choral Bass (Gr.)	4

ACCESSORIES

Finger Pistons:
  Manual I – 4 Swell Pre-select
  Manual II – 4 Great Pre-select
General Pre-select
Great to Pedal Toe Stud
4 General Pre-select Toe Pistons
Swell Shutter Pedal

+ added by Hugo Spilker in 1975.

First Christian Reformed Church, Abbotsford, B.C. (21 stops, 17 ranks)

The organ here was built in about 1964 by Stan Haddon using the wind chest, pipe chests, Subbass 16, and console from the organ at the Strand Theatre in Vancouver which was built in about 1914 by Karn-Warren. He also put in pipes from Stinkens of Holland. In 1975, Balcom & Vaughan Pipe Organ Co. of Seattle, Washington installed a new two manual tab stop console, a Gemshorn 8, and Bill Bunch tonally modified the organ. The instrument is located in a chamber in the front with a black cloth screen and some silver coloured pipe clusters mounted as a facade.

Specifications :

SWELL

Rohr Flöte	8
Gemshorn	8
Gemshorn Celeste	8
Koppel Flöte	4
Octave	2
Nasat	1 1/3
Fagott	8
Tremulant	
Swell Sub	
Swell Super	

COUPLERS

Swell Sub to Great
Swell to Great
Swell Super to Great
Swell to Pedal
Swell Super to Pedal
Great to Pedal
Great Super to Pedal

GREAT

Principal	8
Singend Gedackt	8
Prestant	4
Spill Flöte	2
Flach Flöte	2
Mixture	II rks
Fagott (Swell)	8
Fagott (ext.)	4
Great Sub	
Great Super	
Great Unison Off	

PEDAL

Sub Bass	16
Sanft Bass	16
Principal (Great)	8
Bass Flute (ext.)	8
Oktav	4
Fagott (Swell)	8

ACCESSORIES

Finger Pistons:
Manual I – Great to Pedal
3 Great Pre-select
3 Pedal Pre-select
Manual II – Swell to Pedal
3 Swell Pre-select
6 General Pre-select
Great to Pedal Toe Stud
3 Pedal Pre-select Toe Pistons
6 General Pre-select Toe Pistons
Sforzando Toe Stud
Swell Shutter Pedal
Crescendo Pedal

First Christian Reformed Church, Chilliwack, B.C. (26 stops, 11 ranks)

The organ in this church was installed in 1966 by Stanley Haddon of Vancouver. Additional ranks of pipes were added in 1975 by congregation member Anton Bestebroer. A German made Trumpet 8 was added in 1976 by Ken Hodgson. The organ wasn't made of high quality components and so proceeded to deteriorate over the years until 1995 when Adrian Koppejan was contracted to rebuild and enlarge it and provide a new two-manual tab stop console. He also provided a new facade of polished metal Principal speaking pipes in front of the enclosure situated at the front over the pulpit. The detached console is at the left. The organ, as was the case before, is comprised of moderate unification throughout but has a much improved more cohesive sound.

Specifications:

SWELL

Open Diapason	8
Bourdon	8
Gamba (Gr)	8
Principal (ext.)	4
Rohr Flute	4
Violone (ext.)	4
Nazard	2 2/3
Piccolo (ext.)	2
Vox Humana	8
Tremulant	
Swell to Swell 16	
Swell to Swell 4	

+ = added by Adrian Koppejan in 1995

GREAT

Bourdon (ext.)	16
Principal +	8
Gedeckt	8
Gamba	8
Octave (ext.)	4
Open Flute +	4
Quint	2 2/3
Super Octave (ext.)	2
Mixture +	IV rks
Trumpet	8
Great to Great 4	

COUPLERS

Swell to Great	16
Swell to Great	8
Swell to Great	4
Swell to Pedal	8
Great to Pedal	8
Great to Pedal	4

PEDAL

Sub Bass	16
Octave (Gr)	8
Gedeckt (Gr)	8
Choral Bass (ext.)	4
Flute (ext.)	4
Trumpet (ext.)	16
Trumpet (Gr)	8

ACCESSORIES

Finger Pistons:
- Manual I – Great to Pedal
  - 4 Great Pre-select
  - 4 General Pre-select
- Manual II – Swell to Pedal
  - 4 Swell Pre-select

4 General Pre-select Toe Studs
Swell Shutter Pedal
Crescendo Pedal

First Church of Christ Scientist, Victoria, B.C. (27 stops, 29 ranks)

In 1927, Casavant Frères built their Opus #1180 for this church. The pipes and chests are situated behind a screen front chamber at the front of the church. The three-manual drawstop console is close by and connected by electro-pneumatic action. The action was rebuilt by Hugo Spilker of Victoria and he also, at one time, replaced Trumpet 8 in the Great with a three-rank mixture and moved that rank to the Swell.

Specifications:

SWELL

Bourdon	16
Open Diapason	8
Stopped Diapason	8
Viola di Gamba	8
Aeoline	8
Voix Celeste	8
Principal	4
Dolce Cornet	III rks
Trumpet *	8
Oboe	8
Tremulant	
Swell Sub	
Swell Super	

COUPLERS

Swell Sub to Great
Swell to Great
Swell Super to Great
Swell Sub to Choir
Swell to Choir
Swell Super to Choir
Choir Sub to Great
Choir to Great
Choir Super to Great
Swell to Pedal
Swell Super to Pedal
Great to Pedal
Choir to Pedal

GREAT

Open Diapason	8
Hohl Flöte	8
Salicional	8
Octave	4
Harmonic Flute	4
Fifteenth	2
Mixture + (1 1/3)	III rks

PEDAL

Open Diapason	16
Bourdon	16
Gedeckt	16
Octave (ext)	8
Stopped Flute (ext)	8

CHOIR

Violin Diapason	8
Melodia	8
Dulciana	8
Wald Flöte	4
Clarinet	8
Tremulant	
Choir Sub	
Choir Super	

ACCESSORIES

Finger Pistons:
Manual I – Swell to Choir
Choir to Pedal
2 Choir Pre-select
Manual II – Swell to Great
Choir to Great
Great to Pedal
3 Great Pre-select
2 Pedal Pre-select
Manual III – Swell to Pedal
4 Sell Pre-select
Great to Pedal Toe Stud
4 General Pre-select Toe Pistons
Full Organ Toe Stud
Swell Shutter Pedal
Choir Shutter Pedal
Crescendo Pedal

+ Added by Hugo Spilker * Moved to Swell

First Lutheran Church, Vancouver, B.C. (13 stops and ranks)

In British Columbia there are several establishments that have obtained pipe organs that were designed and built for different venues but for some reason were no longer needed and offered up for re-location. This arrangement, although cost saving over purchasing an all new custom design, has resulted in varying degrees of success. These instruments have been made available through the owners themselves, technicians turned organ builder, established new organ design builders, and listing agencies representing owners such as in this relocation at First Lutheran. The Organ Clearing House of Harrisville, New Hampshire was founded in 1959 by the late Alan Laufman and has provided a consultation and support service including instrument removal and relocation. An organs available list was obtained from them and without further consultation those involved in the project took it on themselves to shop for and obtain something available that was suitable. An organ was found and purchased from a private source in Los Angeles, California in 1981. It turned out that the instrument was missing much of its action and the vendor did not give the assistance in setting up the organ that was assumed. The organ was a mechanical action design built in about 1892 by Hinners & Albertson of Pekin, Illinois. In 1910, it was rebuilt by this firm's successor, Hinners Organ Co. Victoria Organ builder Hugo Spilker was hired to replace the missing action parts, provide a new blower motor and change the pipework somewhat to brighten it up. In 1994, Ladner organ technician Herb Huestis was paid $8,000 to repair and restore back the romantically voiced character the organ was designed to be. Only the Flute 2 of Spilker's pipe changes remained in place of a removed Aeoline 8 in the Swell. Originally the Great division was enclosed with the Swell except for the the Open Diapason 8 included in the facade prospect and Octave 4, but now the entire organ is unenclosed. The organ is located in the rear gallery. With an oak case it measures about 12 ½' wide, 14' tall, and 11' deep with a drawstop keydesk of two 61-note manuals and a 27-note flat straight pedal board.

First Lutheran Church, Vancouver, B.C. Continued

Specifications:

SWELL		GREAT		PEDAL	
Violin Diapason (tc)	8	Open Diapason	8	Bourdon	16
Stopped Diapason	8	Melodia	8		
Salicional (1st oct. St.Dia.)	8	Dulciana	8		
Flute D'Amour	4	Principal	4	**COUPLERS**	
Flute (ensc. Quinte 2 2/3)	2	Twelfth	2 2/3		
Oboe-Gamba	8	Super Octave	2	Swell to Great	
Tremulant				Swell to Pedal	
				Great to Pedal	

First United Church, Kelowna, B.C. (14 stops, 12 ranks)

The oldest Casavant organ in the B.C. interior is this instrument built in 1925 as Opus 1096. It had tubular-penumatic action but was was modified to electro-pneumatc type by Stan Haddon of Vancouver. For many years there was a screen covering a pipe facade but in 1993 the polished metal facade was restored after the screen was removed. The instrument is located front and centre in this room of good acoustics the detached two-manual drawstop console is nearby and faces the back of the room. The organ has English romantic style voicing which is quite solid and majestic for its small size.

First United Church, Kelowna, B.C. Continued

Specifications:

SWELL

Violin Diapason	8
Stopped Diapason	8
Viola da Gamba	8
Voix Celeste	8
Flauto Traverso	4
Nazat	2 2/3
Piccolo	2
Oboe	8
Tremulant	
Swell Sub	
Swell Super	

GREAT

Open Diapason	8
Melodia	8
Dulciana	8
Principal	4
Great Super	

COUPLERS

Swell Sub to Great
Swell to Great
Swell Super to Great
Swell to Pedal
Swell Super to Pedal
Great to Pedal
Great Super to Pedal

PEDAL

Bourdon	16
Flute	8

ACCESSORIES

Thumb Pistons:
- Manual I –
  - Great to Pedal
  - 2 Great Pre-select
- Manual II –
  - 4 Swell Pre-select

Swell Shutter Pedal
Crescendo Pedal

Gilmore Park United Church, Richmond, B.C. (22 stops, 4 ranks)

In 1938, Casavant Frères built Opus 1584, a four-rank unit organ for Center & Hanna Funeral Chapel in Vancouver. The home went bankrupt in 1966 and the organ was eventually sold to this congregation in 1970. In 1980-81, John Darbyshire of Abbotsford rebuilt the organ, replacing several pipes with others of various vintages. The console was also replaced by an older rebuilt one, Casavant's Opus 1109, from the 1925 organ at Second Church of Christ Scientist in Vancouver, which was made available after its organ was rebuilt by G. Herald Keefer. In 1999, the organ was moved into Gilmore Park United Church's new building. The organ is still unified with 4 ranks comprised of Principal 85 pipes, Flute 85 pipes, String 61 pipes, and Oboe 61 pipes. The organ is located in a chamber at the front of the sanctuary. There is a facade of dark brown lacquered speaking Principal pipes and the rest of the organ is under expression. The detached two-manual tab stop console is at the front right side facing toward the back. There aren't any couplers or pre-set pistons at the console.

Specifications:

SWELL

Geigen Principal	8
Lieblich Gedeckt	8
Dulciana	8
Octave	4
Lieblich Flute	4
Dulcet	4
Dulcet	2
Oboe	8

GREAT

Bourdon	16
Geigen Principal	8
Lieblich Gedeckt	8
Dulciana	8
Octave	4
Lieblich Flute	4
Dulcet	4
Twelfth	2 2/3
Super Octave	2

PEDAL

Bourdon	16
Diapason	8
Gedeckt	8
Geigen	4
Flute	4

ACCESSORIES

Expression Shutter Pedal
Crescendo Pedal

Gloria Dei Lutheran Church, North Vancouver, B.C. (8 stops, 10 ranks)

In 1985 this church contracted Adrian Koppejan of Chilliwack to build them a seven-stop mechanical action instrument for the front of the sanctuary. The Positiv Dulzian, which was prepared for on the pipechest, was added by Koppejan a few years later. In 1992, after the completion of their new church building, the organ was moved to one side near the front of the room. It is free standing in an oak wood case with a facade of polished metal Principal 4 speaking pipes. The rest of the pipes are within the case except the Bourdon 16 which is mounted behind it. The attached drawstop keydesk has two 56-note manuals and a 30-note concave radiating pedal board. The organ speaks quite clearly and effectively in a room with good acoustics.

Specifications:

POSITIV		GREAT		PEDAL	
Quintadena	8	Holzgedackt	8	Bourdon	16
Rohrflöte	8	Prinzipal	4		
Praestant	2	Mixtur	III rks		
Dulzian	8				
Tremulant					

COUPLERS

Positiv to Great
Positiv to Pedal
Great to Pedal

Good Shepherd Church (RC), Surrey, B.C. (34 stops, 33 ranks)

In the south side of the chancel of this contemporary design radiating style sanctuary is found the 1995 built Adrian Koppejan organ, Opus 20. Adrian Koppejan of Chilliwack, B.C.,was the largest organ builder in the province. He made well priced good quality tracker and electric-slider action neo-classically voiced organs for the past 25 years in B.C. and has installed them in Western Canada and Washington State. Opus 20 is his largest all new organ design installed in B.C. and is a good example of his work. The electric-slider action instrument here has a detached drawstop console with three 61-note manuals and a 32-note AGO pedal board. It is located at the left side convergence of the chancel and nave. The facade is of bleached oak panelling interspersed with small flats of polished metal pipes. The organ has a very fine tone with neo-classical voicing. It is evident that a great deal of effort and expense was made in the constructing of this high quality building but unfortunately the acoustics are plain and don't enhance the organ's sound.

Specifications:

SWELL

Bourdon	16
Gedeckt	8
Salicional	8
Voix Celeste	8
Principal	4
Chimney Flute	4
Quint	2 2/3
Flachflöte	2
Tierce	1 3/5
Cimball	II rks
Oboe	8
Tremolo	
Swell to Swell	16
Swell to Swell	4

GREAT

Principal	8
Stopped Flute	8
Octave	4
Open Flute	4
Super Octave	2
Mixture	IV rks
Trumpet	8
Chimes	
Auto Pedal to Great	

POSITIV

Chimney Flute	8
Prestant	4
Koppel Flute	4
Nasard	2 2/3
Gemshorn	2
Sifflet	1
Dulzian	8
Tremolo	
Positiv to Positiv	16
Positiv to Positiv	4

PEDAL

Open Diapason	16
Subbass	16
Gedeckt Bass (ext.)	16
Octave	8
Gedeckt Flute (Sw.)	8
Choral Bass (ext.)	4
Trombone (ext.)	16
Trumpet	8
Clarion (ext.)	4

Good Shepherd Church (RC), Surrey, B.C. Continued

COUPLERS

Swell to Great	16
Swell to Great	8
Swell to Great	4
Positiv to Great	8
Swell to Positiv	8
Swell to Pedal	8
Swell to Pedal	4
Great to Pedal	8
Great to Pedal	4
Positiv to Pedal	8

ACCESSORIES

Finger Pistons:
- Manual I – 5 Positiv Pre-select
- Manual II – 5 General Pre-select
  - 5 Great Pre-select
  - Full Organ
  - Midi 1 – 4 Cancel
- Manual III – 5 Swell Pre-select

Great to Pedal Toe Stud
5 General Pre-select Toe Studs
Sforzando Toe Stud
Swell Shutter Pedal
Crescendo Pedal

Highlands United Church, North Vancouver, B.C. (18 stops, 17 ranks)

In about 1920, the Möller Organ Company of Hagerstown, Maryland built an instrument for a church in Iowa. In the late 1950's, the organ was put up for sale and purchased by Highlands United Church and installed in about 1957 by Stan Haddon of Vancouver. The organ was later moved to the new church building and an Octave 4 and Fifteenth 2 added to the Great division to brighten up the stoplist. The organ is presently located behind a screen in a chamber at the front of the sanctuary. The detached two-manual tab stop console faces it from the right front side and the action is electro-pneumatic. The best features of the organ's sound lie in the string, Celeste, and flute stops.

Specifications:

SWELL

Bourdon	16
Violin Diapason	8
Stopped Diapason	8
Salicional	8
Voix Celeste	8
Flute D'amour	4
Flautina	2
Oboe Bassoon	8
Tremolo	
Swell Sub	
Swell Super	
Swell Unison Off	

+ = added since 1957

GREAT

Open Diapason	8
Doppel Flute	8
Melodia	8
Viol D'Gamba	8
Octave +	4
Flute Traverso	4
Fifteenth +	2
Great Super	
Great Unison Off	

COUPLERS

Swell Super to Great
Swell to Great
Swell Sub to Great
Swell to Pedal
Great to Pedal

PEDAL

Bourdon (Swell)	16
Lieblich Gedackt	16
Bass Flute	8

ACCESSORIES

Chimes
Finger Pistons:
Manual I – 3 Great Pre-select
Manual II – 3 Swell Pre-select
Swell Shutter Pedal
Crescendo Pedal

Holy Cross Japanese Canadian Anglican Church, Vancouver, B.C. (25 stops, 5 ranks)

The organ in the rear gallery of this contemporary design A-frame church was built in 1945 as Opus 1768 by Casavant Frères Ltée. of St. Hyacinthe, Que. It spent several years in the chapel of St. Paul's Hospital in Vancouver prior to being purchased in 1969 and moved here which was formerly St. Peter's Anglican Church. Jean Girouard, the Casavant area representative at the time, was contracted to move and rebuild the organ for them. The organ is a typical example of Casavant's post Depression era cost cutting unified organ design. During World War II, restrictions on building material and metal use forced organ builders to cut back production. Unit organ designs were an expedient way to reduce the backlog of waiting contracts. This organ is pretty much as original with an integral oak panelled case and screen front with a simple single flat of gold painted non-speaking pipes. The detached console with full compass two manuals and AGO pedal board has tab stops. It is located beside the case but facing the opposite side of the gallery and connected to the pipework by electric action.

Specifications:

SWELL

Contra Dulciana (tc)	16
Rohr Flöte	8
Salicional	8
Dulciana	8
Lieblich Flöte	4
Salicet	4
Dulcet	4
Nazard	2 2/3
Piccolo	2
Tierce	1 3/5
Tremulant	

GREAT

Lieblich Gedeckt (tc)	16
Open Diapason	8
Rohr Flöte	8
Salicional	8
Dulciana	8
Octave	4
Lieblich Flöte	4
Dulcet	4
Nazard	2 2/3
Fifteenth	2

COUPLERS

Swell to Great
Swell to Pedal
Great to Pedal

PEDAL

Bourdon	16
Octave	8
Stopped Flute	8
Cello	8
Dulcet	4

ACCESSORIES

Expression Pedal
Crescendo Pedal

Holy Family German Catholic Parish, Vancouver, B.C. (16 stops, 22 ranks)

The organ in this church was built for them in 1956 by Gebr. Späth, Ennetach-Mengen, Germany and cost $8,000. It was originally located in the front but in 1961, it was moved to the rear gallery by Stan Haddon. It is the first example of German neo-classical voicing and the only extant Späth organ in the province. Opus 627 does not have an expressive division but does have a plain single flat facade of speaking Prinzipal pipes in front. The detached two manual tab stop console faces the case and is connected by electro-slider action. The pre-set system is in European style with two sets of toggle switches over the stops for two different stop arrangements which are activated by pre-set push knobs. The organ has a strong bright sound that fills the room quite adequately.

Specifications:

SCHWELLWERK

Gedackt	8
Salicional	8
Prinzipal	4
Rohrflöte	4
Flageolet	2
Scharff	III rks
Sesquialter	II rks
Tremolo	

HAUPTWERK

Prinzipal	8
Holzflöte	8
Octave	4
Nachthorn	2
Mixtur	IV rks
Trompete	8

KOPPELN

Manual I 16′ to Manual II
Manual I to Manual II
Manual I 4′ to Manual II
Manual I to Pedal
Manual II to Pedal

PEDAL

Subbass	16
Octavbass	8
Stillposaune	16

ACCESSORIES

Finger Pistons:
- Hand Regulated Piston
- Combination I
- Combination II
- Tutti (full organ)

Crescendo Lever & Pedal

Holy Rosary Cathedral (R.C.), Vancouver, B.C. (48 stops, 51 ranks)

In 1900, the Woodstock, Ontario firm of Karn-Warren built a three-manual 40-stop 43-rank organ in the rear gallery of the new cathedral building. It cost $7,500 and included new pipework made by S.R. Warren of Toronto, Ontario and an Austin-Universal action with components provided by the American firm Austin Organ Co. The voicing was influenced by the French romantic style. Over the years, the instrument suffered under the hands of inexperienced second-rate organ technicians and inadequate funding for proper maintenance. Chandos Dix serviced the organ during the Depression and in lieu of payment it is believed that he took out the eight ranks of pipes missing from the original specification. Stan Haddon also serviced and altered the organ somewhat from 1956 – 60. In the late 1960s, the console was removed for some reason and the organ was silent for five years and further damaged by rain water leaks. In 1972, John Darbyshire was hired to make it work again and this included providing a 1925 Kilgen Organ Co. tab stop console, however, the organ continued to be plagued with problems. The need to properly restore the organ by respecting the original design was expressed by several concerned people to the clergy, but instead, the Québec firm of Casavant Frères Ltée. was hired in 1998 to build a new organ which was to include much of the old

Holy Rosary Cathedral (R.C.), Vancouver, B.C. Continued

pipework plus 20 new ranks bringing the pipe count to 2,899. In 2000, 100 years after the original organ was installed, Opus 3787 was installed in the rear gallery by Casavant's western Canada representative Steve Miller & Associates and was the firm's first major contract in the province in about 15 years. Costing about $480,000, only about 19 of the 31 saved old pipe ranks were left intact with only minor repair or augmentation. Everything else was new including the Swell box, electro-pneumatic action Pitman pipechests, and three-manual full-compass drawstop console. The one thing that was restored back to original was the stencilling on the Open Diapason speaking pipe facade which had been painted over for many years. The old organ which spoke into the room with a gentler easy driven wooly sound has been replaced with a horse of a different colour. This new design reflects the French symphonic influence but is a hi-breed reflecting the current trend to cover as much organ literature as possible. Some of the old is still there but now the sound is much more driven with a lot more brightness in the upper pitches and fiery reeds. The acoustics in this building are magnificent and easily enhance this organ's capabilities.

Specifications:

SWELL		GREAT		CHOIR	
Bourdon	16	Double Open Dia.	16	Geigen Principal +	8
Open Diapason	8	Open Diapason +	8	Melodia	8
Stopped Diapason	8	Principal *	8	Gamba *	8
Salicional *	8	Doppel Flute	8	Dulciana	8
Viola di Gamba	8	Dolce	8	Fugara @-	4
Voix Celeste TC	8	Principal +	4	Harmonic Flute	4
Principal -	4	Wald Flute	4	Harmonic Piccolo +	2
Flauto Dolce +	4	Twelfth	2 2/3	Quinte Flute @	1 1/3
Flautino +	2	Fifteenth +	2	Clarinet @	8
Mixture +	V rks	Mixture +	IV-V rks	Tremulant	
Cornet +	II rks	Trumpet @	8	Choir 16	
Bassoon (ext) +	16	Clarion +	4	Choir 4	
Cornopean @	8				
Oboe @	8				

Holy Rosary Cathedral (R.C.), Vancouver, B.C. Continued

Vox Humana *@	8
Clarion +*	4
Tremulant	
Swell 16	
Swell Unison Off	
Swell 4	

PEDAL

Resultant (prep.)	32
Open Diapason	16
Contrabass	16
Subbass	16
Bourdon (Sw.)	16
Octave Bass -	8
Bass Flute	8
Octave (ext) -	4
Trombone *@	16
Bassoon (Sw.)	16
Trumpet (Gr.)	8
Oboe (Sw.)	4

- = Ranks relocated from original layout to another division
* = Used rank added since 1900
@ = Pre-1998 ranks that have been re-voiced; reeds with new shallots and some old resonators replaced
+* = Re-voiced used ranks added by Casavant in 2000
+ = New ranks added by Casavant in 2000

Holy Rosary Cathedral Chancel, Vancouver, B.C. (4 stops & ranks)

In 1991, Victoria organ builder Grant Smalley built a new tracker action one for this church. It was his first new organ contract for a church and is a good example of the high level of quality in materials and skill that he learned from his apprenticeship with Ontario,organ builder, Gabriel Kney. The organ, which is located on the chancel right side behind a screen, is self-contained in an oak case with a speaking pipe facade of two flats. The organ has a single reverse key colour manual of 56 notes. The stops are not divided and there is no pedal board. The instrument was completed at a cost of $25,000. The stops are activated by foot-operated pull-down levers. This organ is Grant Smalley's Opus 1.

Specifications:

MANUAL

Stopped Flute	8
Flute	4
Principal	2
Quint	1 1/3

Holy Trinity Anglican Church, Vancouver, B.C. (37 stops, 40 ranks approx.)

The organ here in the former Chalmers United originally Presbyterian Church was built as Opus 485 by Casavant Frères in 1912. In 1958, the original console was replaced by one supplied through Durst Organ Supply of Erie, Pa. and installed by Stan Haddon of Vancouver at a total cost of $7,000. When Holy Trinity took over the premises they renovated the building's interior and changed the room shape and configuration. The organ's location is the same but is at the rear of the seating area. The facade has glossy silver coloured speaking pipes and the detached three-manual drawstop console is located at the chancel right side and faces toward the front middle. It was not fully functional in 2008 but there was enough working to show many of the romantically voiced stops in this domed room of very good acoustics.

Holy Trinity Anglican Church, Vancouver, B.C. Continued

Specifications:

SWELL

Bourdon	16
Principal	8
Stopped Diapason	8
Viol d'Gamba	8
Aeoline	8
Voix Celeste	8
Harmonic Flute	4
Piccolo	2
Dolce Cornet	III rks
Cornopean	8
Oboe	8
Tremolo	
Swell Sub	
Swell Super	

COUPLERS

Swell to Great 16
Swell to Great 8
Swell to Great 4
Swell to Choir 16
Swell to Choir 8
Swell to Choir 4
Choir to Great 16
Choir to Great 8
Choir to Great 4
Swell to Pedal 8
Swell to Pedal 4
Great to Pedal 8
Great to Pedal 4
Choir to Pedal 8
Choir to Pedal 4

GREAT

Open Diapason	16
Open Diapason	8
Violin Diapason	8
Doppel Flöte	8
Salicional	8
Principal	4
Harmonic Flute	4
Super Octave	2
Mixture	III rks
Trumpet	8
Great Super	

PEDAL

Double Open Diapason	16
Bourdon	16
Gedeckt	16
Open Flute	8
Bass Flute	8
Cello	8
Trombone	16
Contra Trompette	16
Trompette	8
Clairon	4

CHOIR

Open Diapason	8
Melodia	8
Dulciana	8
Wald Flute	4
Flute	2
Clarinet	8
Tremolo	
Choir Sub	
Choir Super	

ACCESSORIES

Thumb Pistons:
- Manual I –
  - Swell to Choir
  - Choir to Pedal
  - 5 Choir Pre-select
- Manual II –
  - Swell to Great
  - Choir to Great
  - 5 Great Pre-select
  - 5 Pedal Pre-select
- Manual III –
  - Swell to Pedal
  - 5 Swell Pre-select
  - 6 General Pre-select

5 General Pre-select Toe Pistons
Sforzando Toe Stud
Swell Shutter Pedal
Choir Shutter Pedal
Crescendo Pedal

Holy Trinity Cathedral (Anglican), New Westminster, B.C. (45 stops, 20 ranks)

The organ here was originally a two manual 20 rank S.R.Warren built in 1889, part of which came from Vancouver's Rex Theatre. In 1956, Stan Haddon electrified the action and installed a new Reuter built console which he obtained from Balcom & Vaughan in Seattle. In 1968, G. Herald Keefer was contracted to rebuild the organ for $19,000. He replaced some of the original pipes with ones brought in from England, Spain, and Stinkens of Holland and added electrically generated sound in the 32-foot ranks. His Opus 17 instrument contains moderate unification in the stoplist. The cases are at both sides of the chancel and the three-manual console is at the left.

Specifications:

SWELL		GREAT		POSITIV	
Wald Flute	8	Diapason	8	Wald Flute (Swell)	8
Salicional	8	Rohr Flute	8	Gedect	8
Erzähler	8	Hohl Flute	8	Quintadena	8
Celeste II	8	Principal	4	Doppel Flute (Swell)	4
Principal	4	Harmonique Flute	4	Flöte	4
Flute	4	Fifteenth	2	Quinte	4
Salicet	4	Spillflute	2	Blockflute	2
Flauto	2	Fife	1	Acuta	III rks
Harmonic Flute	1	Harmonique	III rks	Zimbel	II rks
Fagott	16	Bassoon (Solo)	16	Cor Anglais (Solo)	8
Trompette	8	Trumpet (Swell)	8	Trumpet Magna (Swell)	4
Oboe	8	Krummhorn (Pos,)	8	Krummhorn	4
Vox	8	Great Super		Carillon Bells	
Swell Sub					
Swell Super					

Holy Trinity Cathedral (Anglican), New Westminster, B.C. Continued

COUPLERS

Swell to Great
Swell Super to Great
Swell to Positiv
Swell Super to Positiv
Positiv to Great
Swell to Pedal
Great to Pedal
Positiv to Pedal

PEDAL

Resultant	32
Open Wood	16
Bourdon	16
Flute	8
Choral Bass	4
Bombarde (Swell)	32
Contra Bassoon (Solo)	16
Trumpet (Swell)	8

ACCESSORIES

Thumb Pistons:
- Manual III – Swell to Pedal
  - 5 Swell Pre-select
    - Pedal to Manual Pre-select
- Manual II – Great to Pedal
  - 5 Great Pre-select
  - 5 Pedal Pre-select
  - Pedal to Manual coupler
  - Sforzando
- Manual I – Positiv to Pedal
  - 5 General Pre-select
  - Pedal to Manual Coupler
  - 5 General Pre-select Toe Pistons
  - Sforzando Toe Stud
  - Solo & Swell Shutter Pedals
  - Crescendo Pedal

Kerrisdale Presbyterian Church, Vancouver, B.C. (31 stops, 39 ranks)

This organ, built in 1964 by Casavant and installed by J. Jean Girouard, is an example of a fully exposed organ without face pipes or screen. It is located on a platform in the front of the church. The action is electro-pneumatic and the detached three manual and pedals drawstop console is located in the right facing the front. The voicing is neo-classical and was done by Lawrence Phelps with Jean Girouard doing some additional final voicing. The Opus is 2811.

Specifications:

SWELL

Rohr Gedackt	8
Salicional	8
Voix Celeste	8
Spitz Principal	4
Nachthorn	4
Octavin	2
Scharff	III rks
Trompette	8
Tremulant	

GREAT

Quintaton	16
Principal	8
Bourdon	8
Octave	4
Rohr Flute	4
Super Octave	2
Mixture	IV rks

CHOIR

Gedackt	8
Erzahler	8
Gemshorn	4
Nazard	2 2/3
Block Flöte	2
Tierce	1 3/5
Quinte Flöte	1 1/3
Zimbel	II rks
Krummhorn	8
Tremuland	

ACCESSORIES

Swell Shutter Pedal
Choir Shutter Pedal
Crescendo Pedal

PEDAL

Principal	16
Bourdon	16
Octave	8
Gedackt	8
Choral Bass	4
Mixture	III rks
Posaune	16

COUPLERS

Swell to Great
Choir to Great
Swell to Choir
Swell to Pedal
Great to Pedal
Choir to Pedal

Killarney Park Lutheran Church, Vancouver, B.C. (30 stops, 4 ranks)

In 1968 the present church building was completed and it was believed that the current organ was also installed shortly afterwards. The instrument was designed and built by Waterloo, Ontario organ builder J.C. Hallman and was based on their stock designed mass produced unit organ line. The organ contains pipework from the Dutch builder Stinkens and is set up on a 4 extended rank pipe chest. The instrument was installed in the back east corner of the rear gallery by area representative John Darbyshire. It is in a dark stained plain wood paneled cabinet without pipe facade or screen front. The organ is entirely under expression and voiced in neo-classical style. The detached standard AGO compass and configuration two manual tab stop console is located at the front of the gallery and faces east. There are no pre-set pistons or couplers accept for the Automatic Pedal that couples to the Great manual. The console is connected to the pipe chest by direct electric action. The room has favourable acoustics and the instrument speaks quite well into the space.

Specifications:

SWELL

Bass Flute	16
Rohrflöte	8
Salicional	8
Flute	4
Violina	4
Nazard	2 2/3
Piccolo	2
Cor Oboe	8
Oboe Clarion	4
Tremulant	

GREAT

Principal	8
Rohrflöte	8
Salicional	8
Octave	4
Violina	4
Twelfth	2 2/3
Fifteenth	2
Dulcet	2
Nasat	1 1/3
Sifflöte	1
Cor Oboe	8
Oboe Clarion	4
Automatic Pedal	

PEDAL

Bourdon	16
Gedeckt	16
Flute	8
Quint	5 1/3
Choral Bass	4
Flute	4
Flautino	2
Cor Oboe	8
Oboe Clarion	4

ACCESSORIES

Expression Shutter Pedal
Crescendo Pedal

Knox United Church, Vancouver, B.C. (18 stops, 20 ranks)

The organ at Knox United was originally built by Casavant Frères Ltée. in 1950 as Opus 2037 and had 10 stops and ranks. In 1956, Andrew Chapman of Vancouver installed seven additional Casavant ranks. Adrian Koppejan, organ builder from Chilliwack, was contracted to rebuild and enlarge the instrument in 1989. He brightened the organ's sound somewhat and made the Pedal division more useful. The electro-pneumatic action organ is located behind a screen at the chancel right side with the detached two-manual full-compass tab stop console at the left facing it.

Specifications:

SWELL

Stopped Diapason *	8
Quintadena	8
Viola de Gamba *	8
Voix Celeste (1st G) *	8
Octave	4
Lieblich Flöte *	4
Piccolo *	2
Sesquialtera	II rks
Cornopean *	8
Oboe *	8
Tremulant	
Swell Sub	
Swell Super	

GREAT

Principal	8
Rohr Flöte	8
Gemshorn *	4
Mixture	III rks
Clarinet *	8
Great Super	

COUPLERS

Swell Sub to Great
Swell to Great
Swell Super to Great
Swell to Pedal
Swell Super to Pedal
Great to Pedal
Great Super to Pedal

PEDAL

Bourdon *	16
Octave Bass	8
Choral Bass (ext.)	4

ACCESSORIES

Finger Pistons:
- Manual I –
  - 3 Great & Pedal Pre-select
  - 3 Pedal Pre-select
- Manual II –
  - 3 Swell Pre-select

Great to Pedal Toe Stud
Swell Shutter Pedal
Crescendo Pedal

* = Casavant ranks

Ladner Christian Reformed Church, Delta, B.C. (17 stops)

In 1978, after the completion of the new church building, Hugo Spilker was contracted to install one of his largest lower mainland organ designs. The instrument was built using many pipes from the 1933 Woodstock Organ Co. organ that was at Vancouver's First Baptist Church. The pipework is displayed rather boldly in a cedar framed case that projects from the sanctuary's back wall. The two-manual tab stop console is detached and located in the front right of the room. There is very little borrowing in the stoplist.

Specifications:

SWELL

Stopped Diapason	8
Gamba	8
Celeste	8
Principal	4
Piccolo	2
Sesquialtra	II rks
Tremulant	
Swell Sub	
Swell Super	

GREAT

Principal	8
Flute	8
Dulciana	8
Open Flute	4
Super Octave	2
Mixture	II rks
Trumpet	8
Great Super	

ACCESSORIES

Swell Shutter Pedal
Crescendo Pedal

PEDAL

Bourdon	16
Octave	8
Bass Flute	8
Choral Bass	4

COUPLERS

Swell to Great Sub
Swell to Great
Swell to Great Super
Swell to Pedal
Great to Pedal

Lakeside Presbyterian Church, Summerland, B.C. (13 stops & ranks)

This building was originally constructed in 1911 as a Baptist Church and changed hands several times becoming a Methodist Church then United, a Masonic Temple in 1956, and finally a Presbyterian Church 1991 which it has been up until now. The organ was built in about 1900 by Edward Lye of Toronto, Ontario for Trinity (United) Church, Port Arthur, Ontario. In 1929 the organ was purchased and re-installed in this building while it was being used as a United Church and it has remained here ever since virtually unchanged. In 1997, it was cleaned and repaired under Chilliwack organ builder Adrian Koppejan's supervision. The organ stands front and centre in a large tiled floor room with good acoustics. Its tall majestic case of oak wood and gold painted speaking facade pipes has an attached drawstop keydesk of two 58-note manuals and 30-note concave straight pedal board. The Swell box stands above the Great division and the action is mechanical throughout. The organ easy fills this room with a clear forthright sound.

Lakeside Presbyterian Church, Summerland, B.C. Continued

Specifications:

SWELL

Open Diapason	8
Stopped Diapason	8
Aeoline	8
Dolce Flute	4
Piccolo	2
Oboe Gamba	8
Tremulant	

GREAT

Open Diapason	8
Melodia	8
Dulciana	8
Principal	4
Harmonic Flute	4
Fifteenth	2

ACCESSORIES

2 Swell Pre-set Hitchdowns
2 Great Pre-set Hitchdowns
Swell Shutter Pedal

PEDAL

Bourdon	16

COUPLERS

Swell to Great
Swell Super to Great
Swell to Pedal
Great to Pedal

Langley Canadian Reformed Church, Langley, B.C. (22 stops, 22 ranks)

The 1982 installed Hugo Spilker organ was proving to be inadequate for this church's needs in recent years and a search was started for a new instrument. Eventually they settled on a proposed instrument design offered in 2006 by Casavant Frères Ltée. This organ, Opus 3872, was installed in the church during May of 2008 and cost $370,000. This is the first all new original location design Casavant organ to be installed in this province in over 20 years and reflects the latest evolution in their designs. The instrument is located on a platform over the lecturn at the front of the church. The contemporary design facade with an angel-like appearance to the outline is made of oak wood, polished metal speaking pipes and side panels. Its 1,250 pipes on slider chests are controlled by electric action connected to a detached two manual and pedal board tab stop console located on the right side towards the front. There is an extensive combination action layout with eight levels of memory.

Langley Canadian Reformed Church, Langley, B.C. Continued

Specifications:

SWELL

Stopped Diapason	8
Gamba	8
Voix Celeste tc	8
Principal	4
Spindle Flute	4
Fifteenth	2
Nineteenth	1 3/5
Douçaine	16
Oboe	8
Tremulant	
Swell 16	
Swell Unison Off	
Swell 4	

GREAT

Prestant	8
Chimney Flute	8
Octave	4
Quinte	2 2/3
Flute	2
Seventeenth	1 1/3
Mixture	II - IV rks
Trumpet	8

PEDAL

Subbass	16
Octavebass	8
Octave (ext.)	4
Douçaine (Sw.)	16
Trumpet (Gr)	8

COUPLERS

Swell / Great 16
Swell / Great 8
Swell / Great 4
Swell / Pedal 8
Swell / Pedal 4
Great / Pedal 8

ACCESSORIES

Thumb Pistons:
- Manual I – Great to Pedal
  - 5 Great Pre-select
  - 4 General Pre-select
  - Full Organ
- Manual II – Swell to Great
  - Swell to Pedal
  - 5 Swell Pre-select
  - 4 General Pre-select

Swell / Pedal Toe Stud
Great / Pedal Toe Stud
3 Pedal Pre-select Toe Studs
8 General Pre-select Toe Studs
Full Organ Toe Stud
Swell Shutter Pedal
Crescendo Pedal

Living Hope Christian Reformed Church, Abbotsford, B.C. (8 stops & ranks)

This organ is the smallest but oldest organ in Abbotsford. It was built in 1910 by the Karn-Warren Organ Co. and spent many years in the old Masonic Temple in Vancouver. In 1940 it was changed from tubular to electro-pneumatic action. In 1967 the organ was dismantled and placed in storage while the old building was torn down. In 1972, Bert Blok of Abbotsford bought the organ and installed it on a platform in the front of Second Christian Reformed Church. The detached two-manual drawstop 30-note pedal board console is on the right facing inward.

Specifications:

SWELL	
Stopped Diapason	8
Viol di Gamba	8
Voix Celeste	8
Flauto Traverso	4
Swell Super	

GREAT	
Open Diapason	8
Dulciana	8
Principal	4
Great Super	

PEDAL	
Bourdon	16

COUPLERS

Swell Sub to Great
Swell to Great
Swell Super to Great
Swell to Pedal
Great to Pedal

ACCESSORIES

Swell Shutter Pedal
Crescendo Pedal

Lutheran Church of the Cross, Victoria, B.C. (17 stops, 10 ranks)

For many years this congregation worshiped in their church hall and used a three rank Hugo Spilker built unit organ. A new sanctuary was constructed with greater seating capacity, larger room volume, and good acoustic properties. In 2007, Grant Smalley completed his contract of removing and enlarging the existing organ, providing a new console, and installing it all in its new location. The organ chamber has a simple contemporary design of twin pipe facades in symmetrical order. The detached two-manual and Pedal tab stop console is moveable. An interesting feature of this organ are two 8 ft. Gemshorn pipe ranks for each manual division.

Specifications:

POSITIVE		GREAT		PEDAL	
Gedeckt	8	Principal	8	Bourdon	16
Gemshorn	8	Rohrflute	8	Octavebass	8
Principal	4	Gemshorn	8	Bourdon (Pos)	8
Flute (ext)	4	Octave (ext)	4	Choral Bass (ext)	4
Piccolo (ext)	2	Rohrflute (ext)	4	Flute (Pos)	4
		Superoctave (ext)	2	Positiv to Pedal	
		Mixture 1 1/3	III rks	Great to Pedal	
		Positive to Great			

Maranatha Canadian Reformed Church, Surrey, B.C. (41 stops, 44 ranks)

In 1975, through area representative John Darbyshire, Casavant Frères was contracted to build an organ for this new church building. The design incorporated Stinkens pipework from the 1960's organ at their former building as well as 13 ranks from Casavant's 1912 Opus 501 from the former building of Central Presbyterian Church in Vancouver. A new reverse key colour three manual and pedal board drawstop console was also provided. Minor changes were made to the organ over the years and the most recent has been the 2006 installation of a replacement pipechest and one-rank addition for the Positive division which are mid 1950s Hill, Norman & Beard of England components from the former Christ Church Cathedral organ in Victoria. This work was undertaken by Grant Smalley of Victoria. The organ is of electro-pneumatic action and is located on a platform in the front of the church. The speaking facade pipes are 1912 Casavant ones and the detached console is to the left facing inward. This is the largest pipe organ in Surrey and it speaks effectively in a room with good acoustics.

Maranatha Canadian Reformed Church, Surrey, B.C. Continued

Specifications:

SWELL

Bourdon *	16
Principal	8
Gedeckt	8
Aeoline	8
Voix Celeste *	8
Wald Flüte *	4
Nazard	2 2/3
Piccolo *	2
Mixture	III rks
Fagot	16
Trumpet	8
Oboe *	8
Tremulant	

COUPLERS

Swell to Great
Swell to Positive
Positive to Great
Swell to Pedal
Great to Pedal
Positive to Pedal

GREAT

Principal *	16
Principal	8
Geigen Principal	8
Doppel Flöte *	8
Rohr Flöte	8
Octave *	4
Quintade	4
Octave Quint	2 2/3
Super Octave *	2
Block Flöte	2
Mixture	IV rks
Trompette *	8

ACCESSORIES

Thumb Pistons:
- Manual I –
  - Positive to Pedal
  - 4 Positive Pre-select
  - 4 Pedal Pre-select
- Manual II –
  - Positive to Great
  - Great to Pedal
  - 4 Great Pre-select
- Manual III –
  - Swell to Pedal
  - 4 Swell Pre-select

Swell to Pedal Toe Stud
Great to Pedal Toe Stud
Positive to Pedal Toe Stud
4 General Pre-select Toe Pistons
Full Organ Toe Piston
Swell Shutter Pedal
Crescendo Pedal

POSITIVE

Holpijp	8
Gemshorn	8
Octave +	4
Koppel Flöte	4
Italian Principal	2
Larigot	1 1/3
Sesquialtera	II rks
Krummhorn	8
Tremulant	

PEDAL

Principal *	16
Bourdon	16
Gedeckt (Sw)	16
Spitz Principal	8
Bourdon *	8
Koral Bass (ext)	4
Trombone *	16
Trompette (Gr)	8
Clarion	4

* = 1912 Casavant Frères
+ = 1950's Hill, Norman, & Beard

Marpole United Church, Vancouver, B.C. (18 stops, 4 ranks)

It is interesting to find that the two extant organs in the province built by the London, England firm of J.W. Walker & Sons Ltd. represent one of their earliest and latest examples of organ building here. The early example is the 1859 one-manual ten-stop tracker at St. John's Anglican Church in Duncan and the recent example is the organ at Marpole United, built in 1962, an 18 stop unified instrument of four ranks which are extended. The action is electro-pneumatic and the voicing is neo-classical. The organ replaces a 1907 Spurdon Rutt organ from England. The Marpole organ is situated in a screened chamber at the front of the church and the detached two-manual 30-note Pedal tab stop console faces the case.

Specifications:

SWELL		GREAT		PEDAL	
Open Diapason	8	Open Diapason	8	Bourdon	16
Lieblich Gedeckt	8	Lieblich Gedeckt	8	Bass Flute	8
Dulciana	8	Dulciana	8	Fifteenth	4
Lieblich Flute	4	Principal	4	Octave Flute	4
Dulcet	4	Twelfth	2 2/3		
Nazard	2 2/3	Fifteenth	2		
Flautino	2	Mixture	III rks		
Tremulant					

COUPLER

Great to Pedal

ACCESSORIES

Expression Pedal
Crescendo Pedal

Nelson United Church, Nelson, B.C. (30 stops, 27 ranks)

In 1967, the 1910 two-manual Casavant tubular-penumatic organ in this church was destroyed by arson. The organist, in an effort to get the old organ rebuilt, was believed by some to have started the fire, however he was acquitted by the court. In 1969, the Keates Organ Co. of Acton, Ontario built a new instrument fully exposed across the front of the church and voiced it in neo-classical style. The organ had wind regulator problems in its design that eventually were corrected by Casavant's Jean Girouard of Vancouver. The organ is quite well developed in sound ideas with a fully developed Pedal and little borrowing of ranks. It is perhaps a bit too large for the room it is in, however it is the largest organ in the B.C. interior. The facade has Principal pipes with high mouth cutups and short feet. The two-manual and Pedal tab stop console is detached and faces the front.

Specifications:

SWELL		GREAT		PEDAL	
Rohr Flöte	8	Spitz Gedeckt	16	Resultant	32
Salicional	8	Principal	8	Contrabass	16
Celeste	8	Spitz Flöte	8	Bourdon	16
Principal	4	Salicional (Swell)	8	Spitz Gedeckt (Gr.)	16
Block Flöte	4	Octave	4	Octave Bass	8
Italian Principal	2	Gedeckt	4	Bass Flute	8
Scharff	IV rks	Flach Flöte	2	Choral Bass	4
Sesquialtera	II rks	Mixture	IV rks	Gedeckt (Great)	4
Contra Oboe	16	Trumpet	8	Super Octave	2
Trompette	8	Chimes		Posaune	16
Tremulant		Great Super		Fagotto (Swell)	16
Swell Sub					
Swell Super					
Swell Unison Off					

Nelson United Church, Nelson, B.C. Continued

COUPLERS

Swell Sub to Great
Swell to Great
Swell Super to Great
Swell to Pedal
Swell Super to Pedal
Great to Pedal
Great Super to Pedal

ACCESSORIES

Finger Pistons:
  Manual I – Swell to Great
    Great to Pedal
    4 Great Pre-select
    4 Pedal Pre-select
  Manual II – Swell to Pedal
    4 Swell Pre-select
Great to Pedal Toe Stud
4 General Pre-select Toe Pistons
Full Organ Toe Stud
Swell Shutter Pedal
Crescendo Pedal

New Westminster Christian Reformed Church, Burnaby, B.C. (31 stops, 32 ranks)

The Casavant Frères Ltée. organ, Opus 2950, was installed here by B.C. rep. J. Jean Girouard in 1967. Additions were made to it in 1970 and 1975. At that time, it was an unencased two manual electro-pneumatic action organ with 20 stops and 27 ranks of pipes on a platform above the pulpit area at the front. In 1990, Adrian Koppejan of Chilliwack, B.C. was contracted to enlarge and encase the organ. He re-arranged the original Positiv division by breaking down the two-rank Sesquialter into separate Quint and Tertz stops, transferring .the Viool Fluit, Spits Fluit and Praestant from it to a new Swell division, removing a three-rank Mixture from the Pedal, and adding seven new ranks of pipes throughout. The detached two-manual drawstop console at the front left side was given an additional Swell manual. The pleasing proportions of the simplified 17th century style oak case, built by congregation member Bert Breedveld, has helped to mellow the former brash sounding organ and the additional ranks of pipes have expanded its colour and dynamics.

New Westminster Christian Reformed Church, Burnaby, B.C. Continued

Specifications:

POSITIVE		GREAT		SWELL	
Gedekt	8	Quintadena	16	Vioolfluit	8
Prestant +	4	Prestant	8	Gamba +	8
Roerfluit +	4	Roerfluit	8	Celeste +	8
Quint	2 2/3	Oktaaf	4	Spitsfluit	4
Geemshoorn +	2	Blokfluit	2	Oktaaf	2
Tertz	1 3/5	Mixtuur	IV rks	Quint	1 1/3
Cymbel	III rks	Trompet	8	Oboe (ext)	16
Kromhoorn	8			Oboe +	8
Tremulant +				Oboe (ext)	4
				Tremuland	

\+ = Adrian Koppejan, 1990

COUPLERS	PEDAL	
Swell to Great	Subbas	16
Positive to Great	Quintadena (Gr)	16
Positive to Swell	Prestant	8
Swell to Pedal	Open Flute +	8
Great to Pedal	Oktaaf	4
Positive to Pedal	Oktaaf (ext)	2
	Fagot	16

North Lonsdale United Church, North Vancouver, B.C. (53 stops, 8 ranks)

In 1968, G. Herald Keefer installed a custom designed instrument behind the screen at the front of the church. It is believed that much of the 1930 Morton two-manual four-rank instrument that was in a Powell River theatre and moved to radio station CJOR by Stan Haddon in 1958 is in the present organ. The organ is extensively unified throughout and entirely under expression. It has electric action and a two-manual tab stop console built by Bill Hale. It is believed that this organ also has some reed pipes from the 1933 Woodstock organ that was at Vancouver's First Baptist Church.

Specifications:

SWELL

Major Bass	16
Stopped Flute	16
Contra Gamba	16
Diapason	8
Major Bass	8
Stopped Flute	8
Gamba	8
Quint	5 1/3
Principal	4
Flute	4
Concert Flute	4
Gambette	4
Nazard	2 2/3
Piccolo	2
Fifteenth	2
Tierce	1 3/5
Sifflote	1
Tuba	16
Tuba	8
Solo Reed	8
Oboe Horn	8
Vox Humana	8
Tuba	4
Oboe	4
Vox	4
Tremolo (entire organ)	
Swell Sub	
Swell Super	

GREAT

Contra Gamba	16
Diapason	8
Major Flute	8
Stopped Flute	8
Gamba	8
Principal	4
Flute	4
Concert Flute	4
Gambette	4
Nazard	2 2/3
Piccolo	2
Fifteenth	2
Tuba	8
Solo Reed	8
Oboe Horn	8
Vox Humana	8
Oboe	4
Vox	4
Great Super	

COUPLERS

Swell to Great
Swell Super to Great
Swell to Pedal
Swell Super to Pedal
Great to Pedal
Great Super to Pedal

PEDAL

Resultant Bass	32
Sub Bass	16
Gedackt	16
Diapason	8
Major Flute	8
Stopped Flute	8
Gamba	8
Tuba	8
Oboe Horn	8
Tuba	4

ACCESSORIES

Finger Pistons:
- Manual I –
  - 6 Great Pre-select
- Manual II –
  - 6 Swell Pre-select

Swell to Pedal Toe Stud
Great to Pedal Toe Stud
Expression Pedal
Crescendo Pedal

Olivet Baptist Church, New Westminster, B.C. (13 stops, 15 ranks)

One of Andrew Chapman's last organ installations in his long career in B.C. is the 1958 Opus 2458 instrument of Casavant Frères Limitee, St. Hyacinthe Quebec, found in this church. It had 12 stops in a chamber located above the baptismal tank in the front of the church. The front is screen covered. The detached electro-pneumatic action console has tab stops. In 1979, Ken Hodgson, a local organ technician, added a three-rank Mixture to brighten the organ up. Other than this, the organ hasn't been changed and remains as one of the province's most recent Casavant built romantically voiced instruments.

Specifications:

SWELL

Principal	8
Bourdon	8
Aeoline	8
Voix Celeste	8
Flute Traverso	4
Oboe	8
Tremulant	
Swell Sub	
Swell Super	

GREAT

Open Diapason	8
Melodia	8
Dulciana	8
Principal	4
Flute	4
Mixture +	III rks
Great Super	

ACCESSORIES

Finger Pistons:
- Manual I –
  - 3 Great & Pedal Pre-select
- Manual II –
  - 3 Swell Pre-select

Great to Pedal Toe Piston
3 General Pre-select Toe Pistons
Swell Shutter Pedal
Crescendo Pedal

PEDAL

Bourdon	16

COUPLERS

Swell Sub to Great
Swell to Great
Swell Super to Great
Swell to Pedal
Swell Super to Pedal
Great to Pedal
Great Super to Pedal

+ = Added by Ken Hodgson in 1979

Orpheum Theatre, Vancouver, B.C. (70 stops, 13 ranks)

The organ, located behind grilled screens in chambers at both sides of the stage was built in 1927 as Model 235 Opus 1746 by Rudolph WurliTzer Co., North Tonawanda, N.Y. It is the only extant original location theatre organ in Canada. It is unified with extended ranks, two divisions of which are under expression and has 12 different percussive effects. In 1978, Ken Hodgson of White Rock cleaned and rebuilt the organ. The three manual radiating tab stop-type console is mounted on a lift that elevates to stage level.

Specifications:

SOLO

Diphonic Diapason	8
Tibia Clausa	8
Piccolo	4
Tuba	16
Tuba	8
Trumpet	8
Oboe	8
Clarinet	8
Kinura	8
Clarinet	4
Bells	
Xylophone	
Glockenspiel	
Chimes	

PEDAL

Diaphone	16
Bourdon	16
Diaphonic Diapason	8
Tibia Clausa	8
Flute	8
Cello	8
Octave	4
Tuba	16
Tuba	8
Clarinet	8
Bass Drum	
Kettle Drum	
Crash Cymbal	

GREAT

Diapason	16
Bourdon	16
Viol	16
Diaphone Open	8
Horn Diapason	8
Tibia	8
Flute	8
Viol	8
Salicional	8
Celeste	8
Octave	4
Piccolo	4
Flute	4
Viol	4
Salicional	4
Celeste	4
Twelfth	2 2/3
Piccolo	2
Tierce	1 3/5
Fifteenth	2
Tuba	16
Tuba	8
Trumpet	8
Oboe	8
Clarinet	8
Kinura	8
Vox	8
Clarinet	4
Bells	
Sleigh Bells	

ACCOMPANIMENT

Bourdon	16
Viol	16
Open	8
Open II	8
Tibia	8
Flute	8
Viol	8
Salicional	8
Celeste	8
Piccolo	4
Flute	4
Viol	4
Salicional	4
Celeste	4
Twelfth	2 2/3
Piccolo	2
Tuba	8
Oboe	8
Clarinet	8
Kinura	8
Vox	8
Vox	4

COUPLERS

Solo to Great
Solo to Accompaniment

Orpheum Theatre, Vancouver, B.C. Continued

PEDAL	GREAT	ACCESSORIES
Cymbal	Xylophone	Finger Pistons:
	Glockenspiel	Manual I –
	Chimes	6 Pre-select
	Harp	Manual II –
		10 Pre-select
		Manual III –
		10 Pre-select
		Tremulants –
		Main
		Solo
		Tibia
		Tuba
		Vox Humana
		Accompaniment Shutter Pedal
		Solo Shutter Pedal

Our Lady of Sorrows Catholic Church, Vancouver, B.C. (36 stops, 8 ranks)

In 1960, Stan Haddon of Vancouver was contracted to build this organ for the rear gallery of the church. The pipes are situated in two expressive chambers with grills of ornamental concrete blocks at both corners of the gallery. The detached tab stop console of two manuals and Pedal was made by Laukhuff of West Germany and cost $1300. It is connected by electro-pneumatic action to the pipes. Of the eight ranks of pipes, two ranks were made by Stinkens of Holland. The organ is unified throughout and the pipes and action cost $6300. Stops marked "°" are connected to pipes in one chamber.

Specifications:

SWELL

Cello °	16
Conic Flute °	8
Rohr Flute °	8
Lieblich Gedeckt	8
Salicional °	8
Celest °	8
Principal	4
Salicet °	4
Gemshorn °	4
Nazard	2 2/3
Nachthorn °	2
Larigot	1 1/3
Horn	8
Tremulant °	

GREAT

Lieblich Gedeckt	16
Diapason	8
Chimney Flute °	8
Bourdon	8
Dulciana	8
Octave	4
Spitzflute °	4
Quint	2 2/3
Fifteenth	2
Quartane	II rks
Cornopean	8
Clairion	4

PEDAL

Bourdon	16
Quint Bass	10 2/3
Octave Bass	8
Bass Flute °	8
Cello	8
Quint Bass °	5 1/3
Choral Bass	4
Nineteenth	2 2/3
Fifteenth	2
Cornopean	8
Clairion	4

ACCESSORIES

2 Expression Pedals
Crescendo Pedal

Paroisse Notre Dame de Lourdes, Maillardville, B.C. (7 stops & ranks)

This church, a wooden building dating from about 1910, houses the largest French speaking congregation in the province. In about 1971, its first pipe organ was installed by local technician, Hector Viens, an apprentice of Stan Haddon. The pipework and chests behind a screen with dummy pipes are located at the front of the church and the two manual and Pedals tab stop console is to the left facing inward. The organ comes from various unknown origins, however the pipes and chests are mainly the work of Karn-Warren in 1907 and the console has the WurliTzer insignia on it. The action is slider chest with electro-pneumatic connections to the console, an offshoot of the Austin-Universal type. The Swell division is enclosed in its own expression box. There aren't any pre-set pistons at the console.

Specifications:

SWELL

Stopped Diapason	8
Viola	8
Flute	4
Swell Sub	
Swell Super	
Swell Unison On/Off	

GREAT

Open Diapason (tc)	8
Flute	8
Violina	4
Great Super	
Great Unison On/Off	

COUPLERS

Swell Sub to Great
Swell to Great
Swell Super to Great
Swell to Pedal
Great to Pedal

PEDAL

Bourdon	16

ACCESSORY

Swell Shutter Pedal

Pemberton Memorial Chapel, Royal Jubilee Hospital, Victoria, B.C. (29 stops, 6 ranks)

When Lawrence Phelps took over as tonal director of Casavant Frères, one of the first instruments he voiced was Opus 2469 built in 1958 for John Shaw who lived in Ontario at that time. He later moved to Victoria and had Hugo Spilker install it in his new home. The organ has since been relocated to the rear gallery of this chapel after it was donated by a School of Nursing alumnae member several years ago. A new facade was added in 2008 with gold painted dummy pipes. The organ is a neo-classically voiced unit style layout. The detached tab stop console with conventional two-manual and pedal board layout has its Great keyboard as the upper manual. The console is opposite to and faces the pipe chest at the other side of the gallery.

<u>**Specifications:**</u>

GREAT

Metal Gedeckt	16
Spitz Prinzipal	8
Rohr Flöte	8
Spitz Octav	4
Nacht Horn	4
Nasat Horn	4
Nasat	2 2/3
Block Flöte	2
Scharff	2/3

COUPLERS

Positiv to Great
Great to Pedal
Positive to Pedal

POSITIV

Nacht Horn	8
Block Flöte	4
Rohr Flöte	4
Nasat	2 2/3
Klein Prinzipal	2
Terz	1 3/5
Larigot	1 1/3
Sifflöte	1

ACCESSORIES

Finger Pistons:
- Manual I –
  - 3 Positiv Pre-select
  - 3 Pedal Pre-select
- Manual II –
  - 3 Great / Pedal Pre-select
  - 3 General Pre-select

3 General Pre-select Toe Pistons
No setter piston

PEDAL

Metal Gedeckt	16
Spitz Prinzipal	8
Nacht Horn	8
Rohr Quinte	5 1/3
Spitz Octave	4
Rohr Flöte	4
Terz	3 1/6
Nasat	2 2/3
Block Flöte	2
Nacht Horn	2
Terz	1 3/5
Scharff	1 1/3

6 RANKS

Bourdon/Rohr Flöte	16
Principal Conique	8
Gedeckt	8
Blockflöte	4
Tierce	3 1/5
Nasat	2 2/3

Penticton United Church, Penticton, B.C. (20 stops, 4 ranks)

This organ was built in 1928 by Franklin Legge of Toronto as Opus 57. It is a unified style instrument of two extended ranks in each of the two-manual divisions which are borrowed down to the Pedal division. The organ is located in a screen front divided case at the front of the church and the detached tab stop console faces the organ. The entire compliment of pipes are enclosed in two expression boxes.

Specifications:

SWELL		GREAT		PEDAL	
Lieblich Gedeckt	16	Open Diapason	8	Open Diapason	16
Open Diapason	8	Melodia	8	Echo Bourdon	16
Clarabella	8	Dulciana	8	Bass Flute	8
Salicional	8	Principal	4	Violincello	8
Flute	4	Fifteenth	2		
Violina	4	Cornopean	8		
Twelfth	2 2/3				
Nazard	2 2/3				
Piccolo	2				
Oboe	8				
Tremulant					
Swell Sub					
Swell Super					

ACCESSORIES

Finger Pistons:
- Manual I – 3 Great and Pedal Pre-select
- Manual II – 3 Swell Pre-select

Swell Shutter Pedal
Great Shutter Pedal

COUPLERS

Swell Sub to Great
Swell to Great
Swell Super to Great
Swell to Pedal
Great to Pedal

Philadelphia Church of Vancouver, Vancouver, B.C. (18 stops, 14 ranks)

The organ in the rear gallery of this church was built for the building's former owners, Surrey Christian Reformed Church, by the Praestant Organ Co. in 1977. The firm was a local one partnered by Adrian Koppejan of Chilliwack and Adrian de Jong of Abbotsford. This is the only organ they built. Adrian Koppejan continued to build organs under his own name, This organ is self-contained with a simple single flat of pipes at the front. The detached two-manual tab stop console is also in the gallery and is connected by electro-pneumatic action. Most of the organ has new components and pipes, however four ranks of pipes came from the 1925 Casavant Opus 1104, a 42-stop instrument from the University of Alberta in Edmonton, purchased by Adrian de Jong in 1976 for $10,500. Adrian Koppejan was the senior partner in the project and did the tonal finishing.

Specifications:

POSITIV

Höhl Flute *	8
Röhr Flute	4
Nazard	2 2/3
Prestant	2
Oboe *	8
Tremolo	

* = Used Casavant pipes 1909

GREAT

Open Diapason *	8
Gedeckt *	8
Octave	4
Fifteenth	2
Mixture	III rks
Trumpet	8
Clarion (ext.)	4
Great Super	

ACCESSORIES

Full Organ Toe Stud
Crescendo Pedal

PEDAL

Subbass	16
Bourdon (ext.)	8
Choral Bass (ext.)	4
Octave (ext.)	2
Trumpet (Gr)	8
Clarion (Gr)	4

COUPLERS

Positiv to Great
Positive Super to Great
Positive to Pedal
Great to Pedal

Queen Margaret's Private School Chapel, Duncan, B.C. (16 stops, 2 ranks)

In 1967-68, Hugo Spilker of Victoria built a two manual organ for this rustic log building. Replacing a previous organ of tracker action, this instrucment was made in the unified style with combined electric and electro-pneumatic action and placed upon a platform. The two extended ranks are comprised of Rohrflute which is in a swell box with Bourdon 16 extensions on both sides of it and a high tin content Principal placed in front of the swell box. The tab stop console was made by Hammond and converted for use in this organ.

Specifications:

SWELL		GREAT		PEDAL	
Soft Flute	8	Diapason	8	Bourdon	16
Viola	8	Flute (Swell)	8	Flute (Swell)	8
Principal	4	Principal	4	Choral Bass	4
Orchestral Flute	4	Flute	4	Flute	4
Quint	2 2/3	Fifteenth	2	Principal	2
Piccolo	2				

Queens Avenue United Church, New Westminster, B.C. (47 stops, 45 ranks)

This organ is the largest in New Westminster. It was built for this building in 1959 as Opus 2552 by Casavant Frères Ltée. and later revoiced in 1965 to neo-classical by Casavant's Lawrence Phelps. In 1981, Alex Bernhardt, the company's B.C. and Alberta rep, added a Resultant Bass 32 to the Pedal. The instrument is located behind a screen at the front of this lofty contemporary design building with very good acoustics. The detached full compass three-manual and AGO Pedal board drawstop console is at the front right side facing inward and connected by electro-pneumatic action.

Specifications:

SWELL		GREAT		CHOIR	
Geigen Principal	8	Quintaton	16	Cor de Nuit	8
Lieblich Gedeckt	8	Principal	8	Erzahler	8
Salicional	8	Bourdon	8	Unda Maris	8
Voix Celeste	8	Gemshorn	8	Prestant	4
Geigen Octave	4	Octave	4	Koppelflöte	4
Rohrflöte	4	Spitzflöte	4	Rohr Nazard	2 2/3
Octavin	2	Superoctave	2	Blockflöte	2
Cymbal	IV rks	Fourniture	IV rks	Tierce	1 3/5
Contrafagot (ext.)	16	Trompette Harmonique	8	Trompette Harm. (Gr)	8
Trompette	8	Chimes		Krummhorn	8
Fagot	8	Great 4		Rohr Schalmei	4
Clairon	4	Great Unison Off		Chimes	
Tremulant				Tremulant	
Swell 16				Choir 16	
Swell 4				Choir 4	
Swell Unison Off				Choir Unison Off	

Queens Avenue United Church, New Westminster, B.C. Continued

PEDAL

Resultant Bass	32
Contrabasse	16
Bourdon	16
Quintaton (Gr)	16
Erzahler (Ch)	16
Principal	8
Stopped Diapason (Ext)	8
Erzahler (Ch)	8
Nachthorn	4
Blockflöte	2
Mixture	III rks
Bombarde	16
Fagot (Sw)	16
Fagot (Sw)	8
Rohr Schalmei (Ch)	4

COUPLERS

Swell to Great 16
Swell to Great 8
Swell to Great 4
Swell to Choir 16
Swell to Choir 8
Swell to Choir 4
Choir to Great 16
Choir to Great 8
Choir to Great 4
Swell to Pedal 8
Swell to Pedal 4
Great to Pedal 8
Great to Pedal 4
Choir to Pedal 8
Choir to Pedal 4

ACCESSORIES

Finger Pistons:
- Manual I – Swell to Choir
  - Choir to Pedal
  - 5 Choir Pre-select
- Manual II – Swell to Great
  - Choir to Great
  - Great to Pedal
  - 5 Great Pre-select
  - 5 Pedal Pre-select
- Manual III – Swell to Pedal
  - 5 Swell Pre-select
  - 6 General Pre-select

Great to Pedal Toe Stud
5 Pedal Pre-select Toe Stud
6 General Pre-select Toe Studs
Full Organ Toe Stud
Swell Shutter Pedal
Choir Shutter Pedal
Crescendo Pedal

Residence of Mrs. D. Barrs, Victoria, B.C. (41 stops, 37 ranks)

In 1967, while living in this home, A.K. Smalley built this organ in a screen front chamber in his music room. He designed the organ to perform both theatre and classical music. Much of the pipework comes from the old organ at St. John's Shaughnessay Anglican Church in Vancouver, a combination of Casavant and Estey of the United States. The four-manual drawstop console was made by Casavant in 1933 and was bought from St. Andrew's-Wesley United Church in Vancouver for $800. The Swell and Great Diapson as well as Choir Geigen contain a Haskell designed 8′ Bass. The Solo Tuba was made by Gottfried. The Pedal Trombone is an S.R. Warren Diaphone from Victoria Capital Theatre's former organ. The action is electro-pneumatic.

Specifications:

SWELL

Diapason	8
Gedeckt	8
Gamba	8
Aeoline	8
Celeste	8
Flute	4
Flauto	4
Flautino	2
Cornopean	8
Vox Humana	8
Oboe	4
Chimes	
Tremolo	
Swell Sub	
Swell Super	

GREAT

Diapason	8
Gedeckt	8
Dolce	8
Octave	4
Flute	4
Quint	2 2/3
Fifteenth	2
Tierce	1 3/5
Trumpet	8
Clarion	4
Chimes	
Great Super	

SOLO

Diapason	8
Flute	8
Violin	8
Gamba	8
Tuba	8
Oboe	8
Clarinet	8
Vox Humana	8
Chimes	
Tremolo	
Solo Sub	
Solo Super	

PERCUSSION

Chimes
Snare Drum
Tambourine
Castenets
Tom-Tom
Block
Xylophone
Glockenspiel
Harp
Sleigh Bells
Bass Drum
Chinese Gong
Cymbal

CHOIR ECHO

Geigen	8
Dolce	8
Celeste	8
Flute	4
Clarinet	8
Choir Sub & Super	

PEDAL

Sub-Bass	16
Bourdon	16
Lieblich Gedeckt	16
Octave	8
Bass Flute	8
Bourdon	8
Trombone	16

Residence of Mrs. D. Barrs, Victoria, B.C. Continued

COUPLERS

Swell to Great
Swell Super to Great
Solo Sub to Great
Solo to Great
Solo Super to Great
Choir Sub to Great
Choir to Great
Choir Super to Great
Echo Sub to Great
Echo to Great
Echo Super to Great
Swell Sub to Choir
Swell to Choir
Swell Super to Choir
Echo Sub to Choir
Echo to Choir
Echo Super to Choir
Solo Sub to Choir
Solo to Choir
Solo Super to Choir
Solo to Swell
Echo on Great off
Echo on Choir off
Great to Solo
All Swells to Swell
Great to Pedal
Great Super to Pedal
Swell to Pedal
Swell Super to Pedal
Solo to Pedal
Solo Super to Pedal
Choir to Pedal
Choir Super to Pedal
Echo to Pedal

ACCESSORIES

Finger Pistons:
  Manual I –
    Swell to Choir
    Choir to Pedal
    5 Choir Pre-select
    3 Echo Pre-select
  Manual II –
    Swell to Great
    Choir to Great
    Solo to Great
    Great to Pedal
    6 Great Pre-select
    5 Pedal Pre-select
  Manual III –
    Swell to Great
    6 Swell Pre-select
  Manual IV –
    Solo to Pedal
    3 Solo to Pre-select
Great to Pedal Toe Stud
4 General Pre-select Toe Pistons
Full Organ Toe Stud
3 Expressive Pedals for Entire Organ
Crescendo Pedal

Residence of Albert Brennink, Duncan District, B.C. (6 stops, 8 ranks)

In 1972, the Uetikon, Switzerland organ building firm of Rudolf Ziegler-Heberlein built this organ as a demonstration example for an international congress of organ builders. Rudolf Ziegler owned it until he sold it in 1976 to Brennink, who was actively practicing architecture in Europe at this time. Upon his retirement, Brennink moved to Duncan and in 1981 set up his instrument in a music room in the house. The organ is this province's only example from a Swiss builder and is a masterpiece in workmanship and sound. The organ has neo-baroque voicing and mechanical key and stop action throughout. There are two reverse colour 56-note keyboards, and a 30-note pedal board. The stops controlling the ranks are set up in a unique way, being activated by vertically mounted rocker levers situated at both sides of the keydesk. The case is made of walnut with a facade of high tin content speaking Principal pipes. With a Subbass 16 in the Pedal, the overall prospect of this organ seems too small, however the bottom notes of this rank have been ingeniously mounted horizontally under the platform supporting the case and pedal board. The pipes' mouths speak upward into the back of the case.

Specifications:

POSITIV		GREAT		PEDAL	
Quintatön	8	Gedeck	8	Subbass	16
Mixtur 1′	III rks	Suavial	4		
		Principal	2		

COUPLERS

Great to Positive
Positiv to Pedal
Great to Pedal

Residence of Mike & Norma Kobald, Langley, B.C. (9 stops, 5 ranks)

Very little is known about this organ. The builder's name has not been found on it but its pipes were made in 1878 by Samuel L. Pierce of the Samuel Pierce Organ Pipe Co. of Reading, Mass. Judging from the stoplist and case design, an educated guess is that it was built by the large American firm Jardine but because of the French nomenclature on the stop labels it also quite possibly a rare surviving work of the Québec builder Napoléon Déry who also used pipes from Pierce. The organ was in Rupert Foursquare Church in Vancouver for a number of years, owned by one of its members. It then fell into disrepair and was subsequently put up for sale in 1977. Its case was in rough shape and the 17-note pedal board was disconnected. In 1979, it was sold to Adrian Koppejan of Chilliwack for $1,800. He rebuilt the organ, restoring it to its original appearance & sound and increased the pedal board to 24 notes. In late 1979, the organ was sold to Pieter Vanderpol for $6,500 and installed at his residence. Before selling his property and moving on, his daughter, Norma, obtained the organ and had it installed in her home where it is presently located. The organ stands in an integral dark wood case with a screen and simple facade of one flat of wood dummy pipes painted dark metallic with gold coloured mouths. It measures 8′ tall about 6 1/2′ wide & 5 1/2′ deep. The keydesk has a single 58-note manual with all stops but the Quint divided into bass and treble at middle C. The pedal board is straight and flat. The Pedal Sub Bass and Tremolo are marked but they haven't been installed yet. The organ still has mechanical action throughout and it is the oldest tracker action instrument in mainland B.C.

<u>**Specifications:**</u>

MANUAL		PEDAL	COUPLER
Diapason (Bass)	8	Pedal Sub Bass *	Pedal Coupler
Diapason (Treble)	8		
Dulciane (Bass)	8		**ACCESSORY**
Dulciane (Treble)	8		
Quinte	5 1/3		Tremolo *
Principal (Bass)	4		
Principal (Treble)	4		
Doublette (Bass)	2		
Doublette (treble)	2		

* = Prepared for at the console

Residence of Leonard Noort, New Westminster, B.C. (10 stops, 10 ranks)

In 1991, the Chilliwack organ builder Adrian Koppejan completed a new tracker action organ for Leonard Noort to be used as a residence instrument. Built in an oak case with a facade of polished high tin content speaking pipes of the Great Octave 2, this organ has an attached key-desk of two 56-note manuals and a concave 30-note pedal board. There is a Swell division in an enclosed box under expression. The whole instrument weighs in at 800 lbs and is located in the residence music room. The voicing is in neo-classical style and is a good example of this builder's quality workmanship.

Specifications:

SWELL		GREAT		PEDAL	
Holzgedeckt	8	Rohrflöte	8	Bourdon	16
Koppelflöte	4	Salicet	4		
Gemshorn	2	Nasard	2 2/3		
Dulzian	8	Octave	2	**ACCESSORY**	
Tremulant		Tertz	1 3/5		
				Swell Shutter Pedal	

COUPLERS

II - I
II – Pedal
I - Pedal

Residence of James Tarling, Burnaby, B.C. (77 stops, 15 ranks)

In 1927, Rudolph WurliTzer of North Tonawanda, N.Y. built Opus 1657 Model 260 theatre organ for Vancouver's Capitol Theatre. Sound was just starting to come into the films and the theatre wanted to cancel the order but the organ arrived anyway, was installed, but put to little use. Other theatres that acquired organs in this period were faced with the same dilema, however many were modified and moved to churches and funeral homes, one remains intact at the Orpheum Theatre, and a few were moved to private residences. The Capitol's organ was sold to, dismantled by, and reassembled in Jim Tarling's basement in 1972 where it shares company with an impressive collection of various mechanical instruments including an old Wurlitzer barrel organ, three one-manual reed organs, and a two manual and Pedal Karn reed organ. The theatre organ is the largest intact Wurlitzer in active use in the province with electro-pneumatic action controlling the pipes, 20 different percussive effects and the largest three-manual tab stop console in use in the province.

Specifications:

SOLO		GREAT			
Diaphonic Diapason	8	Diaphone	16	Ophicleide	16
Tibia Clausa	8	Tibia	16	Clarinet	16
String	8	Viol	16	Saxophone	16
Quintadena	8	Bourdon	16	Tuba	8
Piccolo	4	Diaphonic Diapason	8	Trumpet	8
Ophicleide	16	Tibia Clausa	8	Oboe	8
Tuba	8	Viol	8	Clarinet	8
Trumpet	8	String	8	Saxophone	8
Oboe	8	Flute	8	Kinura	8
Clarinet	8	Celeste	8	Vox	8
Saxophone	8	Piccolo	4	Clarinet	4
Kinura	8	Flute	4	Cathedral Chimes	
Clarinet	4	Viol	4	Bells	
Oboe	4	Celeste	4	Xylophone	
Xylophone		Twelfth	2 2/3	Glockenspiel	
Glockenspiel		Fifteenth	2	Chrysoglott	
Bells		Piccolo	2	Marimba	
Chimes		Tierce	1 3/5	Harp	
				Sleigh Bells	
				Great Sub	
				Great Super	

Residence of James Tarling, Burnaby, B.C. Continued

ACCOMPANIMENT

Viol	16
Bourdon	16
Diaphonic Diapason	8
Tibia Clausa	8
Flute	8
String	8
Viol d'Orchestre	8
Quintadena	8
Voix Celeste	8
Flute	4
Viol	4
Celeste	4
Twelfth	2 2/3
Piccolo	2
Vox	16
Tuba	8
Oboe	8
Clarinet	8
Saxophone	8
Vox	8
Vox	4
Marimba	
Harp	
Chrysoglott	
Snare Drum	
Tambourine	
Castanets	
Chinese Block	
Tom Tom	
Sand Block	
Accompaniment Super	

PEDAL

Diaphone	16
Tibia Clausa	16
Bourdon	16
Octave	8
Tibia	8
Flute	8
String	8
Cello	8
Flute	4
Ophicleide	16
Tuba	8
Clarinet	8
Saxophone	8
Bass Drum	
Kettle Drum	
Snare Drum	
Crash Cymbal	
Cymbals	

ACCESSORIES

Finger Pistons:
- Manual I –
  - 10 Solo Pre-select (5 adjustable)
- Manual II –
  - 10 Great Pre-select (5 adjustable)
- Manual III –
  - 10 Accompaniment Pre-select (5 adjustable)

Surf Button
Door Bell Button
Steamboat Whistle Button
Siren Toe Stud
Car Horn Toe Stud
Thunder Toe Stud
8 Various Toe Studs
2 Expression Pedals
Crescendo Pedal

COUPLERS

Solo to Great
Solo to Accompaniment
Solo to Pedal
Great to Pedal

STOP JAM ACCESSORIES

4 Great Second Touches
7 Accompaniment Second Touches
5 Various Tremulants
Pedal Ophicleide 16 on/off

Richmond Presbyterian Church, Richmond, B.C. (18 stops, 3 ranks)

The organ here was originally built by the Dutch firm of A. de Graaf of Ede, Holland in 1970 and sold by Hugo Spilker of Victoria to the Catholic Church in Penticton for $4,500 including installation. It stayed there only for a short period of time before being sold to Richmond Presbyterian Church and again installed by Hugo Spilker, this time upon a platform at the front of the sanctuary. The organ lost $5,000 for this installation. The instrument is de Graaf's only example in the province and is extensively unified with the three pipe ranks being Principal, Stopped Flute, and Salicional. The case is unenclosed and the polished tin pipes are completely visible from the front. The detached two 56-note manual 32-note Pedal tab stop console is at the right side facing inward and connected by electric action. There aren't any couplers or pre-set pistons.

Specifications:

SWELL		GREAT		PEDAL	
Gedeckt	8	Diapason	8	Bourdon	16
Salicional	8	Stopped Diapason	8	Bass Flute	8
Octave	4	Octave	4	Choral Bass	4
Lieblich Flöte	4	Viola	4	Cello	4
Nasard	2 2/3	Quint	2 2/3	Fifteenth	2
Nachthorn	2	Prestant	2		
Quint Flute	1 1/3				

Ruth Morton Baptist Church, Vancouver, B.C. (19 stops and 17 ranks)

In about 1919, the Ontario organ builder Karn-Warren built an instrument for the Dominion Theatre in Victoria. In 1943, it was sold to this church and re-installed in a chamber at the left side near the sanctuary front. In 1968, Casavant Frères' B.C. rep. J. Jean Girouard repaired the organ and replaced the original console with a rebuilt 1921 Casavant two-manual, 30-note pedal board drawstop one that was from Opus 920 in Edmonton, Alta. The organ's plain facade has a single flat of dummy pipes. There are 994 pipes which are controlled by electro-pneumatic action. The Swell Oboe stop is a reedless labial design voiced to sound like one.

Specifications:

SWELL

Bourdon	16
Stopped Diapason	8
Viola da Gamba	8
Quintadena	8
Aeoline	8
Voix Celeste (tc)	8
Flauto Traverso	4
Piccolo	2
Oboe	8
Vox Humana	8
Chimes	
Swell Super	

GREAT

Contra Viole	16
Open Diapason	8
Doppel Flute	8
Dulciana	8
Principal	4
Clarinet	8
Great Super	

COUPLERS

Swell to Great
Swell Super to Great
Swell to Pedal
Great to Pedal

PEDAL

Bourdon	16
Lieblich Gedeckt (Sw)	16
Violone (Gr)	16

ACCESSORIES

Great to Pedal Hitchdown
7 General Pre-select Hitchdowns
Swell Shutter Pedal
Crescendo Pedal

Ryerson United Church, Vancouver, B.C. (74 stops, 78 ranks)

In 1964, Casavant Frères Ltée. was contracted to build a 65-stop organ to a specification drawn up by Dr. Hugh McLean the church's organist. Opus 2795 was installed by J. Jean Girouard, Casavant's area representative. Due to a lack of funds, both Choir and Gallery divisions weren't installed so it had 46 stops. In fall of 2001, the church had the funds to complete the organ. Casavant was again asked to finish it but without the Gallery division. They also replaced the existing reed work's tongues and shallots, altered some other ranks, revoiced the rest of the organ for better sound balance, and refurbished and updated the console. A solid state combination system to improve stop pre-sets selection was added. The Pedal division's 32′ stops were made with electronic sampled sound. Completed in 2005 at a cost of just under $500,000, this organ is now the most versatile and one of the largest in B.C. It is located at the front of the sanctuary on a platform above and behind the choir stalls. In front of the open prospect pipework there is a detached and moveable full compass, four-manual drawstop console. The organ's voicing is German influence neo-classical.

Ryerson United Church, Vancouver, B.C. Continued

Specifications:

CHOIR

Gemshorn	16
Principal	8
Rohrflöte	8
Erzähler	8
Erzähler Celeste	8
Fugara	4
Nachthorn	4
Nasat	2 2/3
Blockflöte	2
Terz	1 3/5
Plein Jeu	III rks
Bombarde (ext)	16
English Horn (ext)	16
Trompette (Gr)	8
English Horn	8
Clairon (ext)	4
Tremulant	

SWELL

Gemshorn (Ch)	16
Principal (Ch)	8
Hohlflöte	8
Quintadena	8
Salicional	8
Voix Celeste	8
Principal	4
Koppelflöte	4
Flauto Veneziano	2
Cornet	V rks
Fourniture	IV rks
Cymbale	IV rks
Contre Trompette	16
Trompette	8
Hautbois	8
Tremulant	

GREAT

Bourdon	16
Principal	8
Bourdon	8
Octave	4
Spitzflöte	4
Waldflöte	2
Mixture	IV rks
Sesquialtera	II rks
Rauschquinte	II rks
Trompette	8
Carillon	
Zimbelstern	

POSITIVE

Violflöte	8
Holzegedeckt	8
Principal	4
Rohrflöte	4
Octave	2
Quinte	1 1/3
Sifflöte	1
Cornet (Sw)	V rks
Scharff	III rks
Krummhorn	8
English Horn (Ch)	8
Tremulant	

PEDAL

Soubasse	32
Principal	16
Subbass	16
Bourdon (Gr)	16
Gemshorn (Ch)	16
Quint (ext)	10 2/3
Octave	8
Principal (Ch)	8
Rohrgedeckt	8
Erzähler (Ch)	8
Nasat	5 1/3
Choralbass	4
Blockflöte	4
Nachthorn	2

COUPLERS

Choir to Great 16
Choir to Great 8
Choir to Great 4
Choir to Positive 16
Choir to Positive 8
Choir to Positive 4
Choir to Pedal 8
Choir to Pedal 4
Swell to Choir 16
Swell to Choir 8
Swell to Choir 4
Swell to Great 16
Swell to Great 8
Swell to Great 4

Ryerson United Church, Vancouver, B.C. Continued

PEDAL

Mixture	IV rks
Contre Posaune	32
Posaune	16
Contre Trompette (Sw)	16
English Horn (Ch)	16
Trompette	8
Trompette (Gr)	8
English Horn (Ch)	8
Schalmey	4
Clairon (Ch)	4

COUPLERS

Swell to Positive 16
Swell to Positive 8
Swell to Positive 4
Swell to Pedal 8
Swell to Pedal 4
Great to Positive 8
Great to Pedal 8
Positive to Great 16
Positive to Great 8
Positive to Great 4
Positive to Pedal 8
Positive to Pedal 4
Pedal to Great 8

ACCESSORIES

Finger Pistons:
- Manual I –
  - Choir to Pedal
  - Swell to Choir
  - 6 Choir Pre-select
  - Full Organ
- Manual II –
  - Choir to Great
  - Swell to Great
  - Positive to Great
  - Great to Pedal
  - 6 Great Pre-select
  - 6 Pedal Pre-select
- Manual III –
  - Swell to Pedal
  - 6 Swell Pre-select
  - 8 General Pre-select
- Manual IV –
  - Choir to Positive
  - Swell to Positive
  - Positive to Pedal
  - 6 Positive Pre-select

Toe Pistons:
- Great to Pedal
- 8 General Pre-select
- Full Organ

Carillon Expression Pedal
Choir Shutter Pedal
Swell Shutter Pedal
Crescendo Pedal

St. Aidan's United Church, Victoria, B.C. (21 stops, 8 ranks approx.)

This church's organ was built in 1970-71 by Hugo Spilker. It is extensively unified with electric action at the manuals and electro-pneumatic action in the Pedal. The pipes are divided into two free-standing sections at the front of the sanctuary. The acoustics are quite good thanks to the well known architect Dicastri. The detached tab stop 2-manual console is situated at the front left side and faces the cases. Two notable features: the Swell Oboe is unenclosed and the Pedal division is entirely borrowed from unenclosed manual pipes except fo the 12 bottom notes of the Bourdon.

Specifications:

SWELL		GREAT		PEDAL	
Rohr Flute	8	Diapason	8	Bourdon	16
Gemshorn	8	Bourdon	8	Octave Bass	8
Fugara	4	Octave	4	Bass Flute	8
Rohr Gedackt	4	Flute D'Amour	4	Choral Bass	4
Rohr Quint	2 2/3	Super Octave	2	Twenty-Second	2
Gemshorn	2	Mixture	III rks	Mixture	III rks
Tierce	1 3/5		.	Oboe	4
Oboe	8				

COUPLERS

Swell to Great
Swell to Pedal

ACCESSORIES

Finger Pistons:
Manual I – 5 Great & Pedal Pre-select
Manual II – 5 Swell Pre-select
2 General Pre-select Toe Pistons
Swell Shutter Pedal
Crescendo Pedal

St. Andrew's Anglican Church, Kelowna, B.C. (8 stops, 6 ranks)

Inside this church is an instrument built in Germany in 1992 and regarded by its builder / owner and those who are fond of it as "Leonhard Zack's Masterpiece". Leonhard Zack is an organ technician builder by trade and he lived in Egglham Bavaria at the time of this organ's construction. He studied organ building by apprenticing at a local Bavarian firm. Eventually he set up shop and serviced and rebuilt organs over there. Eventually he emigrated to Canada and this organ was transported by ship via the Panama Canal to Vancouver, where it was shipped inland and put on display at the 1998 Calgary International Organ Festival. Shortly afterwards, the organ was moved and installed at Christ Lutheran Church in Kelowna. On October 25th 1998 it was dedicated with a recital by Lorne Manweiler, former organist at St. John's Lutheran Church, Vernon. In early 2000, it was made available for relocation and installed at its present home at St. Andrew's Church. In the summer of 2003 a severe forest fire destroyed many buildings in the outskirts of Kelowna and this church building was threatened with destruction. The parishioners rushed in to remove and save what they could and this included the organ which made a television debut showing people taking pieces of it out of the building. The church was spared and the instrument re-installed. The organ here is a portative instrument standing about eight feet tall in an integral case of light coloured carved wood and with a facade of polished metal speaking pipes. There is a single 51-note keyboard without pedal board and the manual is divided at middle B into bass and treble stops. The Coppel 8 (stopped flute) and stopped bass part of the Flöte 4 which are comprised of wood were made by Leonhard Zacher. The rest of the pipework was provided by Karl Meisinger Orgelpfeifen Spezialwerkstätten, Simbach, Germany. The organ has mechanical key and stop action.

Specifications:

MANUAL

Bass		Diskant	
Coppel	8	Coppel	8
Flöte	4	Flöte	4
Prinzipal	2	Prinzipal	2
Mixtur	II-III rks	Mixtur	II-III rks

St. Andrew's Anglican Church, Trail, B.C. (12 stops and ranks)

The organ in this church is the building's original instrument built by Casavant Frères in 1955 and installed by Andrew Chapman of Vancouver. The Opus 2305 instrument has romantic voicing and is located in a screen covered chamber at the right side of the chancel. The detached two-manual and Pedal tab stop console is at the same side facing away from the case and connected by electro-pneumatic action. The instrument has good voicing which carries well in this brick interior with reasonably good acoustics.

Specifications:

SWELL

Principal	8
Stopped Diapason	8
Viola di Gamba	8
Vox Celeste	8
Harmonic Flute	4
Oboe	8
Tremulant	
Swell Sub	
Swell Super	

GREAT

Open Diapason	8
Melodia	8
Dulciana	8
Principal	4
Great Super	

COUPLERS

Swell Sub to Great
Swell to Great
Swell Super to Great
Swell to Pedal
Swell Super to Pedal
Great to Pedal
Great Super to Pedal

PEDAL

Bourdon	16
Stopped Flute	8

ACCESSORIES

Finger Pistons:
Manual I –
3 Great & Pedal Pre-select
Manual II –
3 Swell Pre-select
Great to Pedal Toe Stud
3 General Pre-select Toe Pistons
Swell Shutter Pedal
Crescendo Pedal

St. Andrew's Cathedral (Anglican), Prince Rupert, B.C. (8 stops & ranks)

Built by Casavant Frères Ltée., Ste. Hyacinthe, Québec, in 1926, this organ is the oldest one in Prince Rupert and the only one there not entirely enclosed in a swell box. It is located in the right corner of the chancel. The Opus 1161 instrument originally had tubular-penumatic action but has since been changed to electro-pneumatic. The oak case has a facade on two sides of gold painted speaking Diapason pipes. The two manual and Pedal keydesk, has tab stops and is all attached to the case. In the 1960s, Jean Girouard of Vancouver, replaced the Swell reed stop with a Quint.

Specifications:

SWELL

Violin Diapason	8
Stopped Diapason	8
Quint +	5 1/3
Principal	4
Oboe *	8
Swell Sub	
Swell Super	

GREAT

Open Diapason	8
Melodia	8
Dulciana	8
Great Super	

PEDAL

Bourdon	16

ACCESSORIES

Swell Shutter Pedal
Crescendo Pedal

COUPLERS

Swell Sub to Great
Swell to Great
Swell Super to Great
Swell to Pedal
Swell Super to Pedal
Great to Pedal
Great Super to Pedal

+ = Added by Jean Girouard in the 1960s.
* = Removed by Jean Girouard in the 1960s.

St. Andrew's Catholic Cathedral, Victoria, B.C. (26 stops & ranks)

In 1907, Casavant Frères was contracted to build their Opus 293 here which was one of their first organs on Vancouver Island. It had 23 stops controlling 27 ranks of pipes with a two-manual and pedal board console and tubular-pneumatic action. In the late 1940s, Chandos Dix of New Westminster unsuccessfully attempted to convert the action to electro-pneumatic which was to use electrical power from a car battery. Stan Haddon of Vancouver was then hired to restore it back to original. In 1966-68, Hugo Spilker electrified the action, provided a rebuilt three-manual console with prepared Positive division, removed some pipes, re-arranged some others, and added three new ranks. Grant Smalley installed a new three-manual drawstop console in 1989, did some restorative work, and re-leathered the manual chests in 2008. The console has been set up to include a future Positive division with proposed stoplist included in the specifications listed below. The organ, located in the upper of two rear galleries, has two cases with dark wood and a facade of speaking gold painted pipes with silver coloured mouths that are basses from the Great Open Diapason, Dulciana, and Pedal Open Diapason 8's. About 21 of the original Casavant organ ranks are still in use in the present instrument which speaks well into a room with good acoustics.

St. Andrew's Catholic Cathedral, Victoria, B.C. Continued

Specifications:

SWELL

Open Diapason	8
Stopped Diapason	8
Gamba	8
Gamba Celeste	8
Spitz Principal +	4
Harmonic Flute	4
Piccolo	2
Sesquialtera 2 2/3	II rks
Trumpet	8
Oboe	8
Tremulant	
Swell Sub	
Swell Super	

PEDAL

Open Diapason	16
Bourdon	16
Octave Bass (ext)	8
Stopped Flute	8
Choral Bass (ext)	4
Trombone	16
Trumpet (ext)	8
Clairon (prep)	4

+ = Added or altered by
Hugo Spilker in 1966-68

GREAT

Open Diapason	8
Flute	8
Dulciana	8
Octave	4
Open Flute +	4
Fifteenth	2
Nineteenth +	1 1/3
Mixture	III rks
Trumpet	8
Great Super	

COUPLERS

Great to Pedal 8
Great to Pedal 4
Swell to Pedal 8
Swell to Pedal 4
Positive to Pedal 8
Postive to Pedal 4
Swell to Great 16
Swell to Great 8
Swell to Great 4
Swell to Positive 8
Positive to Great 8

POSITIVE (proposed)

Gedeckt	8
Quintadena	8
Principal	4
Gemshorn	4
Nasard	2 2/3
Principal	2
Tierce	1 3/5
Cymbel 1	III rks
Cremona	8
Tremulant	

ACCESSORIES

Thumb Pistons:
- Manual I –
  - 6 Positive Pre-select
  - Swell to Pedal
  - Positive to Pedal
- Manual II –
  - Swell to Great
  - Positive to Great
  - Great to Pedal
  - 6 Great Pre-select
  - 4 General Pre-select
  - Full Organ
- Manual III –
  - 6 Swell Pre-select
  - 4 General Pre-select
  - Swell to Great

6 Pedal Pre-select Toe Pistons
8 General Pre-sel. Toe Pistons
Great to Pedal Toe Stud
Full Organ Toe Stud
Swell Shutter Pedal
Crescendo Pedal

St. Andrew's Presbyterian Church, Victoria, B.C. (35 stops, 39 ranks)

The history of the present instrument at St. Andrew's Church began in 1880 when the Toronto, Ontario organ builder S.R. Warren & Son completed construction of a new mechanical action instrument and sent it out to Victoria where it was installed early in 1881 at the previous location of this church. The organ had two manuals, approximately 20 stops, and cost about $3,100 including shipping via Cape Horn. In 1889, the organ was relocated to this newly constructed building. Unfortunately the organ proved to be inadequate partly because it was too small going from a sanctuary that seated 250 to one that held 650. The newer sanctuary also lacked the acoustic life the older location had. The organ was also beset with wind supply and mechanical problems. Over the years modifications were made. The detached console was reattached to the case in 1896 and in 1913 two new stops were installed. An electric blower replacing the water powered engine system was installed in 1920. In 1922, Karn-Warren, the merged successor to S.R. Warren & Son was contracted to convert the action to tubular-penumatic, add some new pipework, and move the console again. Two ranks of Casavant-made pipes from the 1930s were later added. By 1950, because of the failing state of the organ, it became necessary to rebuild the organ. In 1951, the T. Eaton Co., an offshoot of Toronto organ builder Franklin Legge, was hired to do the work. They electrified the action, provided a new three-manual drawstop console, and added more pipework. Costing just over $21,000, Opus 110 also involved moving the organ case forward 18 inches and relocating the speaking facade pipes to new pipe chests within the case. New pipework included a Clarinet in the Swell, a Laukhuff made Trumpet in the Great, and additional pipes in the Pedal to expand the compass from 30 to 32 notes. The front was left open and eventually copper netting was installed to cover it. In 1955, dummy pipes were installed to fill the empty part of the facade. In 1956, Hugo Spilker initiated a series of changes to the organ. In 1968, he rebuilt the organ to restore the pipe chests back up 4 to 5 feet to the original level and relocated and painted the speaking Diapason facade pipes to their rightful place in front. 1974 saw Hugo Spilker undertaking a major tonal revision of the organ by removing or re-voicing several ranks of pipes and adding about 400 new neo-classically voiced Stinkens-made pipes. A two-rank Positiv division was added in front of the facade bringing the total compliment to 34 ranks of pipes. Victoria's first Cymbelstern made its debut on this organ at that time.

St. Andrew's Presbyterian Church, Victoria, B.C. Continued

In 1996, Grant Smalley took over maintenance of the organ. He made modifications to improve sound and reliability which included re-leathering most of the chests and providing the bottom octave of pipes for the Clarinet now in the Choir at 16 foot pitch. The organ console was showing signs of failure around this period and other concerns motivated another change for the organ. A $190,000 donation was given to the church to undertake this project which started in 2001 and included strengthening the organ loft and choir platform as well as new lighting in the front. Michael Perkins was hired to install a new Rodgers model T967 three-manual reverse colour keys drawstop console, rewire the organ and add digital sampled pipe voices and other sounds with the real pipes to create a hybrid pipe and digital sound system with 2,190 pipes and the equivalent of 124 ranks on 72 stops. Eighteen ranks of pipes were purchased from Victoria's Christ Church Cathedral to be latter installed. Between 2002 and 2005, Grant Smalley voiced and installed the majority of these pipes into the organ. They were mostly made in 1957 by Hill, Norman, & Beard with the exception of the Swell Trumpet 8 which was made in 1872 by J.W. Walker of London England.The Spilker installed Cymbelstern is now gone and the organ only has seven ranks of the original 1881 S.R. Warren & Son organ still working but the impressive dark wood gothic style case is still standing across the front. The console contains a full complement of couplers and registration aids including 12 general pistons and six thumb or toe pistons for each division. This instrument now has the reputation of being the loudest organ on Vancouver Island. The following specifications are of the instrument's pipe ranks' stops only.

Specifications:

SWELL

Geigen Open Diapason *	8
Stopped Diapason *	8
Viola de Gamba +	8
Voix Celeste + (1st G)	8
Principal #	4
Flute #	4
Octavin #	2
Mixture ++# 1 1/3	III-V rks
Contra Fagotto #	16
Trumpet #	8
Oboe # (tc)	8
Clarion #	4
Tremulant	

* = S.R. Warren & Son 1881
\+ = Casavant Frères 1930's

GREAT

Open Diapason #	8
Doppel Flute *	8
Octave #	4
Lieblich Flöte *	4
Fifteenth #	2
Larigot ++	1 1/3
Mixture ++ # 2	IV rks
Trumpet+++	8
Great 4	

PEDAL

Open Diapason *	16
Bourdon *	16
Octave Bass *	8
Stopped Flute (ext)	8

CHOIR

Flute #	8
Rohr Gedeckt ++	4
Nazard ++	2 2/3
Block Flute ++	2
Tierce ++	1 3/5
Clarinet	16
Tremulant	
Octave Coupler	

SOLO

Gedeckt ++	8
Principal ++	4

St. Andrew's Presbyterian Church, Victoria, B.C. Continued

PEDAL

Choral Bass #	4
Posaune (Gr. ext) ++	16
Contra Fagotto (Sw.)	16

++ = Hugo Spilker 1974
\# = Grant Smalley 2002-05
+++ Grant Smalley from Casavant 1988, added 2009

St. Andrew's United Church, Nanaimo, B.C. (14 stops, 13 ranks)

The organ at this church was built by the Karn Organ Company in 1893 and had an Austin-Universal style of action. In 1955 it was rebuilt by Hugo Spilker of Victoria who changed the action to electro-pneumatic, provided a new two-manual tab stop console, and brightened up the sound by adding a rank of pipes to make a Mixture in the Great and borrowing into and extending the Pedal to develop it beyond the existing Bourdon 16 stop. The organ chest and pipes are located in a screened chamber at the front of the sanctuary and the console is detached and facing the case.

Specifications:

SWELL

Open Diapason	8
Salicional	8
Open Flute	4
Quint	2 2/3
Oboe	8
Tremolo	
Swell Sub	
Swell Super	
Swell Unison Off	

GREAT

Open Diapason	8
Gedackt	8
Principal	4
Fifteenth	2
Mixture +	III rks
Great Sub	
Great Super	
Great Unison Off	

COUPLERS

Swell Sub to Great
Swell to Great
Swell Super to Great
Swell to Pedal
Great to Pedal

PEDAL

Bourdon	16
Octave Bass #	8
Bass Flute #	8
Octave Bass #	4

ACCESSORIES

Finger Pistons:
Manual I –
4 Great & Pedal Pre-select
4 General Pre-select
Manual II –
4 Swell & Pedal Pre-select
4 General Pre-select Toe Pistons
Sforzando Toe Stud
Swell Shutter Pedal
Crescendo Pedal

= borrowed ranks into Pedal by Hugo Spilker in 1955
+ = added by Hugo Spilker in 1955

St. Andrew's United Church, North Vancouver, B.C. (47 stops, 34 ranks)

The organ in this church for the most part is derived from the organ that was built in 1934 by Henry Pitcher & Sons of Louisville, Kentucky for White Plains Presbyterian Church, White Plains, New York. It was bought for about $10,000 dismantled, crated, and loaded onto a truck and sent to St. Andrew's in 1963. Volunteer workers under the supervision of C.J. Williams refinished, repaired, and installed the organ. G. Herald Keefer was also involved in redesigning the organ by incorporating some pipes from the previous instrument and using some new ones. The organ steadily deteriorated to an almost unplayable condition until the late 1970s, when John Darbyshire was hired to repair the action step by step as funds were made available. At one time there were 55 stops and 40 ranks on the organ but changes by Keefer and the removal of the rear gallery five-rank Echo division reduced its size. The action is electro-pneumatic with a detached three-manual tab stop console facing the curtained facade at the front.

Specifications:

SWELL		GREAT		CHOIR	
Principal	8	Principal	8	Stopped Flute	8
Rohr Flute	8	Geigen Principal	8	Unda Maris	8
Gamba	8	Bourdon	8	Vox Angelica	8
Gamba Celeste	8	Octave	4	Flute Celeste	8
Harmonic Flute	4	Traverse Flute	4	Principal	4
Nazard	2 2/3	Twelfth	2 2/3	Gedeckt	4
Piccolo	2	Fifteenth	2	Nasat	2 2/3
Tierce	1 3/5	Mixture	III rks	Blockflöte	2
Sesquialtera	II rks	Trumpet	8	Terz	1 3/5
Fagotta	16	Great Sub		Sifflöte	1
Cornopean	8	Great Super		Cornet	V rks
French Horn	8	Great Unison Off		Cor Anglais	8
Fagotto	8			Choir Sub	
Clarion	4			Choir Super	
Swell Sub				Choir Unison Off	
Swell Super					
Swell Unison Off					

St. Andrew's United Church, North Vancouver, B.C. Continued

PEDAL

Resultant	32
Open Diapason	16
Sub Bass	16
Dulciana	16
Octave	8
Gedeckt	8
Dolce	8
Bombarde	16
Fagotto	16
Bombarde	8
Fagotto	8
Regal	4

COUPLERS

Swell Sub to Great
Swell to Great
Swell Super to Great
Swell Sub to Choir
Swell to Choir
Swell Super to Choir
Choir Sub to Great
Choir to Great
Choir Super to Great
Swell to Pedal
Swell Super to Pedal
Great to Pedal
Great Super to Pedal
Choir to Pedal
Choir Super to Pedal

ACCESSORIES

An abundance of pre-select Pistons on manuals and Pedal
Swell Shutter Pedal
Choir Shutter Pedal
Crescendo Pedal

St. Andrew's-Wesley United Church, Vancouver, B.C. (59 stops, 66 ranks)

The organ in this church has evolved, expanded, and reverted basically back, in this third rebuild, to romantic voicing and Casavant based design including the original bellows and 17 ranks from their Opus 390 of 1909. That organ was designed for and installed in St. Andrew's Presbyterian Church, Vancouver. After the United Church was born in 1925, St. Andrew's merged with Wesley Methodist, built the present structure, and hired Casavant Frères Ltée. to rebuild and enlarge St. Andrew's organ as Opus 1475 in 1932. In 1966, G. Herald Keefer & Associates were contracted to rebuild the organ, add classically voiced pipes from Stinkens of Holland, and provide a new console. The completed work, Keefer's largest job, turned out to be a less than satisfactory clash of voicing styles and other problems including uneven response times from one division to another. In 1994, Huestis Pipe Organ Associates of Ladner, were hired to rebuild the organ and restore the original pipework, incorporating other used pipes and new ranks to complete the ensemble, preserving the original English romantic sound and also making it flexible enough to accomplish a wider range of organ works. Reverting back to Casavant's electro-pneumatic action entailed the incorporation of pipechests and console shell of Casavant's Opus 2477 of 1955, installed originally in an Arizona church and obtained from the Texas organ builder Robert Sipe. The console was rebuilt by Huestis and new expressive division boxes were built by Helmuth Wolff Associates of Laval, Québec. The Casavant pipework was augmented with ranks as old as 100 years from the 1909 installation to those made by Austin, Midmer, Möller, Stinkens (1966 rebuild) among others, and new pipes made by Martin Pasi from Kent, Washington. The pipechests have been mounted higher up and closer to the chamber fronts than previously, with the Swell and Great in the south side and Choir and Pedal in the north side of the chancel. The result is a most satisfactory and balanced blend of romantic foundation tone with classically voiced upper and solo ranks added. By 1997, the main body of work was completed and the organ fully operational. The new Pasi pipes completed the specification in 2001 and they are yet to have the facades re-built. Total cost of the project was about 3/4 million dollars.

St. Andrew's-Wesley United Church, Vancouver, B.C. Continued

__Specifications:__

SWELL

Bourdon☞	16
Open Diapason*	8
Stopped Diapason*	8
Salicional	8
Vox Coelestis*	8
Principal+	4
Open Flute	4
Quint	2 2/3
Fifteenth	2
Mixture ☼	III
Trumpet ◈	16
Trumpet +	8
Oboe*	8
Clarion+	4
Chimes ☞	
Tremolo	

COUPLERS

Swell Sub to Great
Swell to Great
Swell Super to Great
Choir Sub to Great
Choir to Great
Choir Super to Great
Swell Sub to Choir
Swell to Choir
Swell Super to Choir
Swell to Pedal
Swell Super to Pedal
Great to Pedal
Great Super to Pedal
Choir to Pedal
Choir Super to Pedal

GREAT

Flute	16
Open Diapason	8
Doppel Flute*	8
Viola*	8
Octave*	4
Flute*	4
Quint+	2 2/3
Super Octave*	2
Mixture	IV rks
Cornet	III rks
Trumpet ✧(ext)	16
Trumpet ✧	8

PEDAL

Resultant	32
Double Diapason*	16
Contrabass	16
Subbass	16
Bourdon (Sw)	16
Octave (ext)	8
Open Wood	8
Flute*	8
Bourdon (Sw)	8
Quint	5 1/3
Octave	4
Mixture	III rks
Trombone ▪	16
Contra Trumpet	16
Cornopean (ext)	8
Clarion (ext)	4

CHOIR

Violin Diapason	8
Stopped Flute*	8
Viole*	8
Vox Angelica	8
Fugara+	4
Spire Flute	4
Nazard+	2 2/3
Piccolo*	2
Tierce+	1 3/5
Mixture+	III rks
Clarinet ⅄	8
Musette+	8
(Unenclosed)	
Solo Flute*	8
Solo Octaves	4
Cornet*	IV-V rks
Solo Trombone (Ped)	16
Solo Trumpet*	8
Tremolo	

ACCESSORIES

Thumb Pistons:
- Manual I –
  - Swell to Choir
  - Choir to Pedal
  - 5 Choir Pre-select
- Manual II –
  - Swell to Great
  - Choir to Great
  - Great to Pedal
  - 5 Great Pre-select
  - 5 Pedal Pre-select
  - Full Organ

St. Andrew's-Wesley United Church, Vancouver, B.C. Continued

⅄ = 1890s S.R. Warren
* = 1909 Casavant Opus 390
▪ = 1925 Midmer Organ Co.
☞ = Möller Organ Co.
✧ = Austin Organ Co.
+ = 1966 Stinkens
* = Martin Pasi 1997- 2001

ACCESSORIES

Manual III –
Swell to Pedal
5 Swell Pre-select
6 General Pre-select
Great to Pedal Toe Stud
6 General Pre-select Toe Studs
Full Organ Toe Stud
Schulmerich Bells expression
Swell Shutter Pedal
Choir Shutter Pedal
Crescendo Pedal

St. Andrew's-Wesley United Church Chapel, Vancouver, B.C. (13 stops, 11 rks.)

The G. Herald Keefer organ in the chapel was proving to be unreliable and was replaced by a tracker action organ in the front built by the English firm of Martin Goetze & Dominic Gwynn, Welbeck Abbey Estate, near Worksop. The 1986 work is made in the manner of the 18th century English builder, Richard Bridge. The heavily mitred top case is made of English oak and measures 13'9" x 7' x 3'. The facade has five flats of 25% tin pipes. The single manual has 54 keys and the pedal board, a copy of a 1740 Dutch design, has 24 notes. The wind is supplied through a double fold wedge reservoir and the pitch is A440.

<u>**Specifications:**</u>

MANUAL		PEDAL		COUPLER
Open Diapason	8	Bourdon	16	Manual to Pedal
Stopped Diapason	8			
Principal	4			
Flute	4			
Twelfth	2 2/3			
Fifteenth	2			
Tierce (bass & treb)	1 3/5			
Sesquialtera (bass & treb)	II rks			
Trumpet (bass & treb)	8			

St. Ann's Chapel Museum, Victoria, B.C. (10 stops, 9 rks.)

The ornately decorated chapel housing the organ listed below is a heritage site that was originally a Roman Catholic Convent. Provincial government departments now use most of the space and some parts, like the chapel, are open to the public as museum space. The organ in the chapel's rear gallery was built for it in 1913 by Casavant Frères Ltée. Opus 516 is a tubular-penumatic organ of two 61-note manuals and a 30-note concave radiating pedal board. The voicing and stop nomenclature are French romantic. The case is made of ashwood. The draw-stop knobs are solid ebony, the ivory surfaces still have their original finish, and the organ is in pristine condition. The Bourdon 16 in the Pédale is on a split wind system to give a softer volume when the same rank is drawn as a Gedeckt. The Souffleur is a stop which, when pulled, rings a bell to tell the bellows pumper to commence. There is also a gauge at the side next to the pump level to indicate air volume in the reservoir. At some point along the way, an electric blower was installed but the organ can still be hand pumped.

Specifications:

RECIT		GRAND-ORGUE		PÉDALE	
Bourdon	8	Montre	8	Bourdon	16
Salicional	8	Mélodie	8	Gedeckt	16
Voix Celeste (tc)	8	Dulciane (tc)	8		
Flute Harmonique	4	(Bass from Mélodie)			
Hautbois (tc)	8				
Tremolo					

ACCESSORIES

Récit Shutter Pedal
Crescendo Pedal
Souffleur

COUPLERS

Récit Grave au Grand-Orgue
Récit au Grand-Orgue
Récit Aigue au Grand-Orgue
Grand-Orgue Aigue
Récit à la Pédale
Grand-Orgue à la Pédale

St. Augustine's Roman Catholic Parish, Vancouver, B.C. (41 stops, 31 ranks)

In 1980, a fire which heavily damaged the church, devastated the three-manual 34-stop organ. The Keates Organ Co. of Acton, Ontario was contracted to build a new instrument of three manuals and 1700 pipes into two cases at the rear gallery. The instrument, with drawstops at the console and electric action, has oak panelled cases with plain facades of metal and wood speaking pipes all of which complements the new back window they frame. The organ was installed in March of 1982 with the assistance of John Darbyshire of Abbotsford, the B.C. representative. The voicing was done by the company's tonal director Dietrich Geissler.

Specifications:

SWELL

Stopped Flute	8
Salicional	8
Celeste	8
Octave Geigen	4
Cor de Nuit	4
Gemshorn	2
Mixture	III rks
Double Trumpet	16
Trompette	8
Clarion (extended)	4
Swell Sub	
Swell Super	
Tremulant	

COUPLERS

Swell Sub to Great
Swell to Great
Swell Super to Great
Swell Sub to Choir
Swell to Choir
Swell Super to Choir
Choir Sub to Great
Choir to Great
Choir Super to Great
Swell to Pedal
Swell Super to Pedal
Great to Pedal
Great Super to Pedal
Choir to Pedal

GREAT

Pommer Gedeckt	16
Open Diapason	8
Pommer (extended)	8
Gemshorn	8
Octave	4
Rohr Pommer (ext.)	4
Fifteenth	2
Mixture	II-IV rks
Trumpet	8

PEDAL

Resultant	32
Violone	16
Subbass	16
Gedeckt (Great)	16
Octavbass	8
Bassflöte (extended)	8
Choralbass (ext.)	4
Pommer (Great)	4
Posaune	16
Trumpet (Swell)	16
Tromba (extended)	8
Clarion (extended)	4
Cromorne (extended)	4

CHOIR

Rohrflöte	8
Erzähler	8
Prestant	4
Koppelflöte	4
Nazard	2 2/3
Sifflöte	2
Tierce	1 3/5
Trumpet (Great)	8
Cromorne	8
Choir Sub	
Choir Super	
Tremulant	

ACCESSORIES

Finger Pistons:
- Manual I – Swell to Choir
  - Choir to Pedal
  - 5 Choir Pre-select
- Manual II – Swell to Great
  - Choir to Great
  - Great to Pedal
  - 5 Great Pre-select
  - 5 Pedal Pre-select
- Manual III – Swell to Pedal
  - 5 Swell Pre-select
  - 6 General Pre-select

Great to Pedal Toe Stud
6 General Pre-select Toe Studs
5 Pedal Pre-select Toe Studs

St. Augustine's Roman Catholic Parish, Vancouver, B.C. Continued

ACCESSORIES

Choir Super to Pedal
Full Organ Toe Stud
Swell & Choir Pedals
Crescendo Pedal

St. Catherine's Anglican Church, North Vancouver, B.C. (13 stops, 17 ranks)

This organ was built as Opus 3240 in 1974 by Casavant Frères of Ste-Hyacinthe, Québec. It was a stock design of their modular style line of instruments and has French classical voicing with electro-pneumatic action. The organ is situated at the back of the church on a platform over the rear gallery and has its own mahogany panelled case with a plain facade of silver painted speaking Montre pipes. The two-manual tab stop console is detached and located at the left side of the gallery. There is also a second one-manual keydesk with four stops in the middle front of the gallery used as a supplementary console to direct the choir from. The main console's manuals are 56 notes each.

Specifications:

RECIT		GRAND ORGUE		PEDALE		
Bourdon	8	Montre	8	Soubasse		16
Flute	4	Flute à Cheminée	8	Octave Bass		8
Doublette	2	Prestant	4	Flute à Cheminée	(Grand Orgue)	8
Trompette	8	Fourniture	IV rks	Octave		4
Tremblant		Cornet	III rks			

COUPLERS	ACCESSORIES
Récit à Grand Orgue	Swell Shutter Pedal
Récit à Pédale	Crescendo Pedal
Grand Orgue à Pédale	

St. Christopher's Anglican Church, West Vancouver, B.C. (14 stops, 10 ranks)

This organ was built by Hill, Norman & Beard of London, England in 1963 and cost $16,000 including installation by Stan Haddon of Vancouver. It is the only intact newly built example from this company in the province. The pipes are located on a platform at the front of the church behind a screen. The detached two-sliding manual and Pedal tab stop console is at the right side facing the front. The action is electro-pneumatic and the Pedal division is completely borrowed and extended from the manual divisions. The Great Stopped Flute and Gemshorn are extensions of the Stopped Diapason and Spitz Principal ranks respectively, and the Swell Mixture has one break in it. The organ is in good running and sounding condition and fills the room quite adequately.

Specifications:

SWELL		GREAT		PEDAL	
Spitz Flute	8	Open Diapason	8	Bourdon	16
Salicional	8	Stopped Diapason	8	Principal	8
Octave	4	Spitz Principal	4	Gedeckt	4
Mixture	III rks	Stopped Flute	4	Fagotto	16
Fagotto	8	Gemshorn	2		
Octave 4 Coupler					

COUPLERS

Swell to Great
Swell to Great 4
Swell to Pedal
Swell to Pedal 4
Great to Pedal

ACCESSORIES

Finger Pistons :
Manual I –
3 Great & Pedal Pre-select
Manual II –
3 Swell Pre-select
Great to Pedal Toe Stud
Swell Shutter Pedal
Crescendo Pedal

St. David's Anglican Church, Vancouver, B.C. (11 stops and ranks)

This organ was built in 1913 by Casavant Frères and is # 521. It is a romantically voiced organ with two manuals and Pedals with tubular-penumatic action connecting an oak, drawstop console with the case situated behind the right corner of the choir. The organ has remained unchanged from its time of building except for the painted guild work done on the gold coloured face pipes in 1972 by Jack Archbald.

Specifications:

SWELL

Open Diapason	8
Stopped Diapason	8
Aeoline	8
Voix Celeste	8
Harmonic Flute	4
Oboe	8
Tremulant	

GREAT

Open Diapason	8
Melodia	8
Dulciana	8
Principal	4
Great Super Octaves	

ACCESSORIES

3 Reversible Swell Toe Iron Pre-select Pistons
2 Reversible Great & Pedal Toe Iron Pre-select Pistons
Bellows Signal
Swell Shutter Pedal
Crescendo Pedal

PEDAL

Bourdon	16

COUPLERS

Swell Sub to Great
Swell to Great
Swell Super to Great
Swell to Pedal
Great to Pedal

St. David's United Church, West Vancouver, B.C. (27 stops, 22 ranks)

This organ was built by Vancouver organ technician Stan Haddon of Haddon Custom Pipe Organs. The work was completed in 1961 and cost $11,000. The instrument is located in a paneled case with screen front at the centre front of the room. The detached three-manual drawstop console in the left front side near the case is a Casavant one from the Opus 1269 1928 organ at Canadian Memorial United Church, Vancouver which just purchased a new Hill, Norman & Beard one. The pipework at St. David's contains 11 ranks from Stinkens of Holland and ten ranks from Laukhuff of Germany.

Specifications:

SWELL

Violin Diapason	8
Gamba	8
Quintadena	8
Voix Celeste	8
Flute Ouverte	4
Piccolo	2
Contra Fagotto (ext.)	16
Oboe	8
Schalmei (ext.)	4
Chimes	
Swell 16 to Swell	
Swell 4 to Swell	

COUPLERS

Swell 16 to Great
Swell 8 to Great
Swell 4 to Great
Swell 16 to Choir
Swell 8 to Choir
Swell 4 to Choir
Choir 16 to Great

GREAT

Open Diapason	8
Concert Flute	8
Octave	4
Flute D'Amour	4
Twelfth	2 2/3
Fifteenth	2
Great 16 to Great	
Great 4 to Great	

PEDAL

Sub Bass	16
Bourdon	16
Octave Bass (Gr.)	8
Bass Flute (Gr.)	8
Choral Bass (ext.)	4
Contra Fagotto (Sw.)	16

CHOIR

Gedackt	8
Gemshorn	8
Rohr Gedackt	4
Principal	2
Sesquialtera	II rks
Krummhorn	8
Chimes	
Tremolo	
Choir 16 to Choir	
Choir 4 to Choir	

ACCESSORIES

Thumb Pistons:
- Manual I –
  - Swell to Choir
  - Choir to Pedal
  - 3 Choir Pre-select
- Manual II –
  - Swell to Great
  - Choir to Great
  - Great to Pedal

St. David's United Church, West Vancouver, B.C. Continued

COUPLERS

Choir 8 to Great
Choir 4 to Great
Chimes to Great
Swell 8 to Pedal
Swell 4 to Pedal
Great 8 to Pedal
Choir 8 to Pedal
Chimes to Pedal

ACCESSORIES

3 Great Pre-select
3 Pedal Pre-select
Manual III –
Swell to Pedal
4 Swell Pre-select
Great to Pedal Toe Stud
3 General Pre-select Toe Pistons
Swell Shutter Pedal
Choir Shutter Pedal
Crescendo Pedal

St. Helen's Anglican Church, Surrey, B.C. (21 stops, 6 ranks)

In 1970, Surrey resident Norman Starr, decided to design and build his own house organ. With Jean Girouard of Vancouver as consultant, he succeeded in building this two 61-note manuals 30-note pedal board unified type organ. The pipework is comprised of two ranks of wood pipes that he made himself, metal pipes from Stinkens of Holland, and 13 facade pipes from the 1912 Casavant Frères Opus 501 from Central Presbyterian Church's former organ in Vancouver. Mr. Starr also built the walnut panelled console which also has an unusual arrangement of two rows of drawstops over the keyboards. The instrument is partially enclosed and runs on a wind pressure of 2 1/2 inches. In 1982, the organ was moved and installed in the rear gallery of this church, one of Surrey's oldest and most elegant. The console was placed in the front right side of the nave. This room also has rather nice acoustics.

Specifications:

SWELL		GREAT		PEDAL	
Principal	8	Principal	8	Bourdon	16
Rohrflöte	8	Bourdon	8	Principal	8
Flute d'Amour	4	Geigen Principal	4	Bass Flute	8
Nazard (tc)	2 2/3	Rohrflöte	4	Choral Bass	4
Spitz Flute	2	Nazard (tc)	2 2/3	Rohrflöte	4
Tierce (tc)	1 3/5	Super Octave	2	Twenty-second	2
Sifflote	1	Larigot	1 1/3	Nazard (tc)	1 1/3

ACCESSORIES

Finger Pistons:
- Manual I –
  - 4 Great Pre-select
- Manual II –
  - 4 Swell Pre-select

3 Pedal Pre-select Toe Pistons
Swell Shutter Pedal
Crescendo Pedal

St. Helen's Anglican Church, Vancouver, B.C. (33 stops, 10 ranks)

The organ in this building originally was a 1951 Möller instrument unified with five ranks of pipes. In 1977, G. Herald Keefer & Associates of Vancouver were contracted to rebuild and enlarge the organ. They did this in stages starting with overhauling the action and putting in a solid-state keying system, revoicing the original pipework, adding pipes and electronic sounds to the specifications, and finally adding a second case of exposed pipework comprising the Great division over the console at the front lefthand side. The original case is at the front right. This project under the guidance of Fred Geoghegan resulted in an instrument unified with electric action and a large stoplist for a two-manual console in a rather small building. This instrument, Keefer's Opus 21, is set up for possible additions in the future.

Specifications:

SWELL

Contra Gamba	16
Principal	8
Gedeckt	8
Salicional	8
Salicional Celeste	8
Octave	4
Rohr Flute	4
Salicet	4
Flautina	2
Contra Fagotto	16
Trompette	8
Hautbois	8
Clairon	4
Chimes	
Tremolo	
Swell Super	

COUPLERS

Swell Super to Great
Swell to Great
Swell Sub to Great
Swell to Pedal
Swell Super to Pedal
Great to Pedal

GREAT

Principal	8
Metallgedackt	8
Erzähler	8
Prinzipal	4
Spillflöte	4
Nasat	2 2/3
Octav	2
Blokflöte	2
Terz	1 3/5
Scharff	III rks
Dulzian	8
Tremolo	

ACCESSORIES

Great Reeds Expressive
Couplers Normal
Swell Strings II
Erzähler Celeste
Finger Pistons:
  Manual I –
    Great to Pedal
    4 Great Pre-select
    4 Pedal Pre-select
  Manual II –
    4 Swell Pre-select
    4 Genral Pre-select
Great to Pedal Toe Stud

PEDAL

Untersatz	32
Principal	16
Bourdon	16
Gamba	16
Octave	8
Choral Bass	4
Contra Posaune	32
Posaune	16
Fagotto	16
Trompette	8
Dulzian	4

St. Helen's Anglican Church, Vancouver, B.C. Continued

ACCESSORIES

4 General Pre-select Toe Studs
Trumpet Reverse Toe Stud
Sforzando Toe Stud
Swell Shutter Pedal
Crescendo Pedal

St. James Anglican Church, Vancouver, B.C. (35 stops, 35 ranks)

This organ was originally built for this church by Casavant Frères as Opus 1605 in 1938. It had three manuals and 31 stops controlling 1760 pipes and cost $10,000. In 1948, the organ's console along with the choir were relocated from a gallery under the organ chamber to a gallery on the west side. In an adjacent enclosure a new pipe chest was added to the Choir division with three ranks of pipes discarded from Vancouver's Christ Church Cathedral Casavant organ being rebuilt at the time. In the 1960s, G. Herald Keefer unsuccessfully attempted to brighten up the sound but in 1971, Casavant rep. J. Jean Girouard restored the organ back to its original English romantic voicing style. In 1973, another attempt to modify the organ to more current voicing trends fell through after Casavant placed a bid. Water damage in the 1980s necessitated repairs and renovations to modify the organ were undertaken by Casavant's area rep. Herb Huestis in 1984-85 and new pipework was provided by the firm. In 2003 Casavant was contracted to rebuild the original drawstop console whereupon they converted it to solid state circuitry, added a few more coupler switches, computerized the combination action to offer eight levels of memory, and prepared drawstops for future additions. The organ is located in a chamber in the north gallery behind a screen and pipe facade designed by the church's architect, Adrian Gilbert Scott. Due to lack of space there is much borrowing in the Pedal, however this organ speaks quite effectively in its grand style in a room with very good acoustics.

Specifications:

SWELL		GREAT		CHOIR	
Open Diapason	8	Bourdon	16	Violin Diapason +	8
Stopped Diapason	8	Open Diapason	8	Geigen Principal *	8
Viola da Gamba	8	Hohl Flute	8	Melodia	8
Voix Celeste	8	Gemshorn *	8	Rohr Flöte +	8
Flauto Traverso	4	Principal	4	Viola ++	8
Violina	4	Open Flute	4	Dulciana *	8

St. James Anglican Church, Vancouver, B.C. Continued

Grave Mixture	II rks
Contra Fagotto (ext)	16
Cornopean	8
Oboe	8
Tremulant	
Swell Sub	
Swell Super	

ACCESSORIES

Thumb Pistons:
- Manual I –
  - 4 Choir Pre-select
- Manual II –
  - 4 Great Pre-select
  - 4 Pedal Pre-select
- Manual III –
  - 4 Swell Pre-select

8 General Pre-select Toe Pistons
Great to Pedal Toe Stud
Full Organ Toe Stud
Swell Shutter Pedal
Choir Shutter Pedal
Crescendo Pedal

Flute	2
Mixture ++	IV rks
Cornet ++	II rks
Trumpet	8
Great Super	

PEDAL

Open Diapason	16
Sub Bass	16
Bourdon (Gr.)	16
Octave (Gr.)	8
Bourdon (Gr.)	8
Trombone	16
Fagotto (Sw.)	16

Principal ++	4
Gedeckt Flute *	4
Dulcet +	4
Nazard ++	2 2/3
Fifteenth	2
Clarinet	8
Tremulant	
Choir Sub	
Choir Super	

COUPLERS

Swell Sub to Great
Swell to Great
Swell Super to Great
Swell Sub to Choir
Swell to Choir
Swell Super to Choir
Great to Choir
Choir Sub to Great
Choir to Great
Choir Super to Great
Swell to Pedal
Great to Pedal
Choir to Pedal

* = Removed from original specification
\+ = Pipes from Christ Church Cathedral added in 1948
++ = New Casavant pipes added 1984-85

St. John The Divine Anglican Church, Burnaby, B.C. (29 stops, 4 ranks).

The organ here was built as Opus 402 in 1944 by the Ontario piano and organ building firm Quido. It once was in St. Anthony's Catholic Church, Trail, B.C. until 1952, when it was sold to this church for $2,700. While it was in the Kingsway location the organ underwent modifications by Ken Hodgson starting with the 1961 relocation to the back of the nave and electrification of the action. The console was also replaced by a new two-manual 30-note pedal board tab stop one. In 1978, he removed the Vox Humana rank and replaced it with an Oboe one. In 1998, the congregation merged with St. Stephens Anglican Church on Smith Ave. In the newer A-frame building the two things that prevailed from the former location was the church name and the pipe organ which was re-installed in a screen and wood frame faced chamber on the front left side. The console was placed on the same side but at the back of the nave and facing to the right. Because the organ is extensively unified the console does not have couplers or pre-set pistons.

Specifications:

SWELL		GREAT		PEDAL	
Gedeckt	16	Bourdon	16	Bourdon	16
Gamba	16	Geigen	8	Geigen	8
Geigen	8	Clarabella	8	Gedeckt	8
Bourdon	8	Viola d'Gamba	8	Cello	8
Viola d'Gamba	8	Prestant	4	Octave	4
Octave	4	Flute	4	Flute	4
Flute d'Amour	4	Gemshorn	4	Oboe +	8
Violin	4	Twelfth	2 2/3		
Piccolo	2	Fifteenth	2		
Oboe +	16	Oboe +	8		
Oboe +	8	Oboe +	4		
Tremolo					

ACCESSORIES

Full Organ Toe Stud
Expression Pedal
Crescendo Pedal

+ = Added by Ken Hodgson in 1978

St. John's Anglican Church, Duncan, B.C. (10 stops, 12 ranks)

In 1859, J.W. Walker and Sons of London, England was contracted to build an organ for the British Consulate in Nice, France. By some obscure deal, the completed organ was purchased instead by Lady Burdett-Coutts and sent to the Old Iron Church of St. John's (Anglican) in Victoria. That church was demolished in about 1911 when the organ was transferred to neighbouring St. Barnabas Anglican where it resided for only two years. It was then finally sold to St. John's Anglican Church and later moved to the present church where it now stands at the left side of the chancel. In 1960, the organ's action and windchest were repaired and the pipes tonally refinished for the new location. In that decade Hugo Spilker installed a three-rank Mixture. In 1980-81, Grant Smalley did more repairs replacing worn out wood parts and gaskets, and rebuilding the main chest at a cost of $4,600. The instrument has been carefully maintained with much of its pipework being original and tracker action throughout. The drawstop keydesk has one 56-note manual with a 27-note straight flat pedal board. The dark stained pine wood case has a single flat facade of speaking Diapason pipes with painted spotted metal to 8 ft. C. Containing 619 pipes, this organ is one of the oldest, most historically significant and important design examples in the province.

St. John's Anglican Church, Duncan, B.C. Continued

Specifications:

MANUAL

Double Diapason (tc)	16
Open Diapason	8
Stopped Diapason	8
Dulciana (tc)	8
Principal	4
Rohr Flute	4
Twelfth	2 2/3
Fifteenth	2
Mixture +	III rks

PEDAL

Subbass	16

ACCESSORY

Hitchdown Swell Pedal

COUPLER

Manual to Pedal

+ = added by Hugo Spilker in the 1960s

St. John's Lutheran Church, Vernon, B.C. (20 stops, 20 ranks)

After a nine year period without new organ contracts in this province, Casavant Frères Ltée. of Ste. Hyacinthe, Québec, was contracted in 1984 to build an electro-pneumatic action neo-classically voiced instrument. Opus 3672 cost $135,000 and assisted by the Alberta rep. Steven Millct, was the first job as Casavant's B.C. organ sales rep. for local technician Herb Huestis. The organ is located at the front centre of the sanctuary, with a left side detached tab stop console with two 56-note manuals and a 32-note Pedal board.

Specifications:

SWELL		GREAT		PEDAL	
Major Flute	8	Bourdon	16	Violin Bass	16
Gemshorn	8	Principal	8	Bourdon (Sw.)	16
Conical Flute	4	Bourdon	8	Octave	8
Principal	2	Octave	4	Bourdon (Gr.)	8
Quint	1 1/3	Flute	2	Fifteenth	4
Trumpet	8	Mixture	IV rks	Trombone (ext.)	16
		Cornet	II rks	Trumpet (Gr.)	8
		Chimes			

ACCESSORIES	COUPLERS
Finger Pistons :	Swell 16 to Great
Manual I –	Swell to Great
5 General Pre-select	Swell 4 to Great
Toe Pistons –	Swell to Pedal
6 General	Swell 4 to Pedal
Great to Pedal	Great to Pedal
Swell Shutter Pedal	Sub off Crescendo
Crescendo Pedal	

St. John's Shaughnessy Anglican Church, Vancouver, B.C. (71 stops, 69 rks.)

After this building was completed, bids were submitted by two organ companies. Casavant Frères' proposal was to build the entire organ in the rear gallery only with the detached console and choir lofts up front. J.C. Hallman Organ Company's proposal was to build the organ in two sections with the main organ in a chamber by the chancel. The Waterloo, Ontario company's proposal was accepted and in 1968 they undertook the project for $86,000 and it was the largest organ they built. Fred Carter was the consultant in the project and the organ has neo-classical voicing with an electric action direct chest design. It has three cases: the main is in a chamber at the left transcept and has a wood screen front with an unenclosed projecting Positiv division mounted on a platform. The two other cases are unenclosed and situated in the back two corners of the rear gallery along with the copper State Trumpet 8, projecting from the gallery rail. Another interesting feature is that this is the largest multiple console organ in the province, with the main four-manual drawstop console, controlling all six divisions, located at the front right in the chancel and a second smaller console, for the gallery pipes, located at the edge of the rear gallery. Another unusual feature, besides the builder providing drawstops, is that there is little borrowing among the ranks of pipes, however due to the poor designing of the building and the organ layout in a deep narrow chamber and gallery, this interior is a difficult one for effective sound projection.

St. John's Shaughnessay Anglican Church, Vancouver, B.C. Continued

Specifications:

GALLERY

Spitz Flöte	8
Rohr Bourdon	8
Flute Celeste	8
Principal	4
Singen Gedeckt	4
Sifflöte	2
Kleine Mixture	II rk
State Trumpet	8
Tremulant	

PEDAL

Bourdon	16
Spitz Flöte	8
Principal	4

SWELL I

Violone	16
Viola	8
Viole Celeste	8
Geigen Octave	4
Doublette	2
Plein Jeu	IV rks
Rauschquinte	II rks
Fagot	16
Trompette	8
State Trumpet (Gal.)	8
Clarion	4
Tremulant	
Swell Division I Sub	
Swell Division I Super	
Swell Division I Off	

SWELL II

Holz Gedeckt	8
Erzähler	8
Erzähler Celeste	8
Nachthorn	4
Gemshorn	4
Nazard	2 2/3
Wald Flöte	2
Tierce	1 3/5
Rohr Schalmei	8
Tremulant	
Swell Division II On	

GREAT

Quintaden	16
Principal	8
Bourdon	8
Quintadena	8
Octave	4
Koppel Flöte	4
Super Octave	2
Fourniture	IV rks
Scharf	III rks
Trompette Harmonique	8
State Trumpet (Gal.)	8
Trompette Harmonique	4

POSITIV

Gedeckt	8
Prestant	4
Spillflöte	4
Block Flöte	2
Nasat	1 1/3
Sifflöte	1
Cymbel	III rks
State Trumpet (Gal.)	8
Krummhorn	8
Tremulant	

PEDAL

Untersatz	32
Contrabass	16
Violone	16
Subbass	16
Gedeckt	16
Quintaten	16
Principal	8
Violone	8
Stopped Flute	8
Octave	4
Block Flöte	4
Gemshorn	4
Block Flöte	2
Mixture	III rks
Bombarde	16
Fagot	16
Trompette	8
Rohr Schalmei	4

St. John's Shaughnessay Anglican Church, Vancouver, B.C. Continued

COUPLERS

Gallery to Great
Gallery to Positiv
Swell I Sub to Great
Swell I to Great
Swell I Super to Great
Swell I Sub to Positiv
Swell I to Positiv
Swell I Super to Positiv
Swell II to Great
Swell II to Positiv
Positiv to Great
Gallery to Pedal
Swell I to Pedal
Swell I Super to Pedal
Swell II to Pedal
Swell II Super to Pedal
Great to Pedal
Positiv to Pedal

ACCESSORIES

Great & Pedal Pistons Coupled
Finger Pistons:
- Manual I –
  - Positive to Pedal
  - 4 Positive Pre-select
- Manual II –
  - Great to Pedal
  - 7 Great Pre-select
  - 7 Pedal Pre-select
- Manual III –
  - Swell I to Pedal
  - Swell II to Pedal
  - 6 Swell I Pre-select
  - 4 Swell II Pre-select
  - 7 General Pre-select
- Manual IV –
  - Gallery to Pedal
  - 3 Gallery Pre-select
  - Reeds Off
  - Full Organ
- Toe Pistons –
  - Great to Pedal
  - 7 Pedal Pre-select
  - 7 General Pre-select
  - Full Organ
- Swell I Shutter Pedal
- Swell II Shutter Pedal
- Crescendo Pedal

St. Luke's Anglican Church, Victoria, B.C. (22 stops, 23 ranks)

In 1925, Casavant Frères built their Opus 1103 as a theatre organ for Vancouver's Kerrisdale Theatre. The $8,500 cost included the traps which were Chimes, Marimba Harp, and Xylophone. In 1958, Vancouver organ technician Stan Haddon relocated the instrument which became the second organ to be installed in the present building of St. Luke's. Between 1995 and 2001, Victoria organ builder Grant Smalley altered and enlarged the organ somewhat. The Swell Violin Diapason was moved to the Great and the Great Open Diapason and Tuba moved to the Pedal. The new Pedal ranks were extended and additions included the Swell Mixture from the former 1932 Casavant organ at Victoria's First United Church. The Trumpet rank was made by Laukhuff of Germany and a new Swell Principal 4 was made by Richmond, B.C. pipemaker Jack Pearson. The organ is located in a chamber which projects out of the conventional roof line of the building at the front left side. Behind a screen facade, all pipes but one Great rank are in two expressive boxes. The detached theatre-style tab stop console of two manuals and 30-note pedal board is at the right side in front and controls the pipes by electro-pneumatic action.

<u>**Specifications:**</u>

SWELL

Stopped Diapason	8
Viola d'Gamba	8
Voix Celeste	8
Principal +	4
Flauto Traverso	4
Nazard	2 2/3
Piccolo	2
Mixture + 2	III rks
Sesquialtera +	II rks
Oboe	8
Chimes	
Zimbelstern +	
Tremulant	
Swell Sub	
Swell Super	

+ = Added by Grant Smalley 1995 - 2001

GREAT

Diapason	8
Bourdon	8
Dulciana	8
Octave	4
Octave	2
Trumpet +	8
Great Super	

COUPLERS

Swell Sub to Great
Swell to Great
Swell Super to Great
Swell to Pedal
Great to Pedal
Great Super to Pedal

PEDAL

Bourdon	16
Octave Bass	8
Bass Flute	8
Octave (ext)	4
Tuba + (ext)	16
Tuba	8

ACCESSORIES

Thumb Pistons:
- Manual I –
  - Great to Pedal
  - 4 Great Pre-select
- Manual II –
  - Swell to Pedal
  - 4 Swell Pre-select

Full Organ Toe Stud
Swell Shutter Pedal
Great/Pedal Shutter Pedal
Crescendo Pedal

St. Mark's Anglican Church, Qualicum Beach, B.C. (18 stops, 3 1/2 ranks)

The organ at this church was built and installed here by Hugo Spilker of Victoria during 1976. It is a unified instrument of two manuals and Pedal with a detached WurliTzer drawknob console at the right front side of the chancel. There are no couplers but there is a setterboard type piston system. The vibrato has a fan type design. The case is at the opposite side at the front with un-enclosed pipe facade.

Specifications:

SWELL		GREAT		PEDAL	
Gedeckt	8	Dulciana (tc)	16	Bourdon	16
Salicional	8	Principal	8	Bass Flute	8
Salicet	4	Bourdon	8	Cello	8
Quint Flute	2 2/3	Octave	4	Choral Bass	4
Piccolo	2	Flute d"Amour	4	Choral Flute	4
Clarinet (synth)	8	Super Octave	2		
Vibrato		Sesquialtera	II rks		

St. Mark's Evangelical Lutheran Church, Vancouver, B.C. (21 stops, 7 ranks)

In 1972, Hugo Spilker of Victoria was contracted to build a unified style organ of two manuals for this church. The pipework was divided into two walnut cabinets at both sides of the altar, with some pipes of the Bourdon 16 behind a screen and the blower and reservoirs installed in the existing organ chamber. The following is a typical example of pipe set up in a unified organ of this size by this builder:

a) Bourdon	16′-8′ 1-24 wood, 25-73′:33% tin	73 pipes
b) Principal	8′-4′ 1-20 zinc, 21-73 75% tin	73 pipes
c) Chimney Flute	4′-2′ (Rohr Flöte) 1-73 50% tin	73 pipes
d) Mixture 2 ranks	1′ 75% tin	122 pipes
e) Tierce	1 3/5′ from tenor C (49 notes) 50% tin	37 pipes
f) Oboe	4′ from tenor C 50% tin	49 pipes
Total		427 pipes

The action as a rule is electric with electro-pneumatic Pedal and there usually aren't any couplers or pre-set pistons at the console. When new pipes are called for, Jacques Stinkens of Holland is a favourite supplier but more recently, pipes have been obtained from Ireland and England. Hugo usually made his own wood pipes and did the tonal finishing and voicing himself. Much of the action work came from England.

Specifications:

MANUAL I		MANUAL II		PEDAL	
Principal	8	Rohr Flöte	8	Bourdon	16
Bourdon	8	Gedackt	4	Octave Bass	8
Octave	4	Quint Flöte	2 2/3	Bass Flute	8
Rohr Gedackt	4	Principal	2	Choral Bass	4
Super Octave	2	Spitz Flöte	2	Choral Flute	2
Scharff	II rks	Tierce	1 3/5	Mixture	II rks
Oboe-Schalmai (tc)	8	Sifflöte (Tenor C)	1	Oboe-Schalmei	4

St. Martin's Anglican Church, North Vancouver, B.C. (25 stops, 7 ranks)

This organ was originally built for St. Margaret's Anglican Church, Vancouver by Casavant Frères in 1938 and is Opus 1590. In 1969, it was moved to St. Martin's Anglican and installed in a screen front expressive chamber at the front left side of the interior. The detached two-manual and Pedal tab stop console was placed at the right side of the front and connected by electro-pneumatic action. The organ is extensively unified throughout and there aren't any couplers or pre-set pistons at the console.

Specifications:

SWELL		GREAT		PEDAL	
Geigen Principal	8	Bourdon	16	Bourdon	16
Lieblich Gedeckt	8	Geigen Principal	8	Geigen	8
Dulciana	8	Lieblich Gedeckt	8	Gedeckt	8
Quintadena	8	Dulciana	8	Dulciana	8
Lieblich Flute	4	Lieblich Flute	4	Violina	4
Violina	4	Violina	4	Dolce	4
Dulcet	4	Nazard	2 2/3	Trompette	8
Trompette	8	Super Octave	2		
Oboe	8	Clarion	4		
Tremulant					

ACCESSORIES

Expression Pedal
Crescendo Pedal

St. Mary's Anglican Church, Vancouver, B.C. (41 stops, 47 ranks)

In 1955, Casavant Frères built Opus 2296 for this church. In 1964, Jean Girouard with Casavant rebuilt and revoiced the organ to neo-classical calling it Opus 2786. In 1995 and 1997, Huestis Pipe Organ Associates of Ladner re-leathered the chests, revoiced sections particularly the manual reeds and mixtures, added 12 pipes to the Swell Hautbois changing it to 8′ from 4′, and replaced the Pedal Rohr Schalmei with a new Clarion rank. The organ is situated in the chancel with the main case on the left side and the unenclosed Choir division with an open single flat facade of speaking polished scaled metal Erzähler pipes along with the 1955 full scale three-manual drawstop console on the right side.

Specifications:

SWELL		GREAT		CHOIR	
Nachthorn	8	Quintaton	16	Gedackt	8
Salicional	8	Principal	8	Erzähler	8
Quintadena	8	Rohr Flöte	8	Prestant	4
Voix Celeste	8	Gemshorn	8	Koppel Flöte	4
Geigen Principal	4	Octave	4	Bach Flöte	2
Rohr Flöte	4	Spitz Flöte	4	Quint Flöte	1 1/3
Gemshorn	2	Quinte	2 2/3	Cymbal	III rks
Plein Jeu	II-III rks	Wald Flöte	2	Solo Trumpet (Gr)	8
Basson	16	Mixture	III-IV rks	Cromorne	8
Trompette	8	Sesquialtera	II rks	Tremulant	
Hautbois	8	Solo Trumpet	8		
Tremulant					
Swell Sub					
Swell Super					

St. Mary's Anglican Church, Vancouver, B.C. Continued

COUPLERS

Swell Sub to Great
Swell to Great
Swell Super to Great
Swell Sub to Choir
Swell to Choir
Swell Super to Choir
Choir Sub to Great
Choir to Great
Choir Super to Great
Swell to Pedal
Swell Super to Pedal
Great to Pedal
Great Super to Pedal
Choir to Pedal
Choir Super to Pedal

PEDAL

Contrebass	16
Subbass	16
Quintaton (Gr)	16
Principal	8
Pommer Gedact	8
Choral Bass	4
Mixtur	IV rks
Bombarde	16
Solo Trumpet (Gr)	8
Clarion	4

ACCESSORIES

Finger Pistons:
- Manual I –
  - Swell to Choir
  - Choir to Pedal
  - 4 Choir Pre-select
- Manual II –
  - Swell to Great
  - Choir to Great
  - Great to Pedal
  - 5 Great / Pedal Pre-select
  - 4 Pedal Pre-select
- Manual III –
  - Swell to Pedal
  - 5 Swell Pre-select

Great to Pedal Toe Stud
5 General Pre-select Toe Pistons
Full Organ Toe Stud
Swell Shutter Pedal
Crescendo Pedal

St. Mary's Anglican Church, Victoria, B.C. (20 stops, 25 ranks)

In 1921 Casavant Frères completed their Opus 890, a 14-stop twin case, electro-pneumatic action instrument with a two-manual full compass drawstop console. In 1986, Herb Huestis, from the lower mainland, rebuilt the organ retaining nine original ranks and adding 16 new ones. The console was replaced with a 1971 Casavant tab stop type bought from a Florida location. The facade is comprised of polished high tin content speaking pipes from the Great Montre 8 and Pedal Montre 8 and Octave 4. The organ is voiced French neo-classical and is a good example for its size.

Specifications:

SWELL

Bourdon à Cheminée *	8
Viole de Gambe *	8
Voix Celeste *	8
Flute Ouverte *	4
Doublette *(old Prin 4)	2
Quinte	1 1/3
Cymbale	III rks
Clarinette	16
Trompette *	8
Tremulant	

* = Casavant pipes 1921

GREAT

Montre	8
Bourdon (* 1 - 12)	8
Prestant	4
Flute	2
Fourniture 1 1/3	IV rks
Cornet	II rks

PEDAL

Soubasse *	16
Montre	8
Bourbon *	8
Octave (ext)	4
Bombarde	16
Trompette (prep)	8

COUPLERS

Swell to Great
Swell to Pedal
Great to Pedal

ACCESSORIES

Thumb Pistons:
- Manual I –
  - Swell to Great
  - Great to Pedal
  - 4 Great Pre-select
  - 4 Pedal Pre-select
- Manual II –
  - Swell to Pedal
  - 4 Swell Pre-select

Swell to Pedal Toe Stud
Great to Pedal Toe Stud
4 General Pre-select Toe Studs
Full Organ Toe Stud
Swell Shutter Pedal
Crescendo Pedal

St. Mary's Roman Catholic Church, Ladysmith, B.C. (16 stops, 2 ranks)

The organ in the rear left-hand gallery of this contemporary design building is Opus 1797 built by Casavant Frères Ltée. in 1945. It is believed that this organ was originally made for the residence of Dr. Hermann Robertson in Victoria. At one point in time, St. John The Divine Anglican Church in the same city owned it, and finally it was acquired by St. Mary's and moved to its present location in 1968. This is one of Casavant's smallest unit organ designs with a self contained oak paneled case and attached full compass two manual and AGO pedal board keydesk. There are no pre-set pistons or couplers and tab stops are used. All pipes are under expression and the two voices are stopped flute and salicional. The Oboe is a derived stop. The facade contains one simple flat of crudely made dummy pipes which are not from the original design. The case, without keydesk, measures 7 1/2' wide x 5' deep x 10' tall.

Specifications:

SWELL		GREAT		PEDAL	
Rohr Flôte	8	Rohr Flôte	8	Bourdon	16
Salicional	8	Salicional	8	Stopped Flute	8
Lieblich Flôte	4	Lieblich Flôte	4	Cello	8
Violina	4	Violina	4	Principal	4
Oboe	8	Nazard	2 2/3	Flute	4
Tremulant		Piccolo	2		

ACCESSORIES

Expression Shutter Pedal
Crescendo Pedal

St. Matthia's Anglican Church, Victoria, B.C. (20 stops, 16 ranks)

In 1957, Wm. Hill & Son and Norman & Beard Ltd. of London, England built this neo-classically voiced electro-pneumatic action organ and installed it at the left choir side of this then new building. Hugo Spilker of Victoria did later modifications by adding ranks to the Great. In 1987, Herb Huestis of Ladner, transferred the Swell Trumpet to the Great and added ranks to the Swell. More recently, Grant Smalley of Victoria, added ranks to the Swell and Pedal as well as wind system improvements. The detached tab stop two-manual console faces the organ case from the right choir side. The case has a facade of polished high tin content speaking pipes derived from the Great Principal 4 and Octave 2 ranks.

Specifications:

SWELL

Stopped Diapason +++ rblt	8
Aeoline	8
Geigen Octave ++	4
Stopped Flute (ext)	4
Fifteenth ++	2
Quint ++	1 1/3
Oboe +++ (Casavant)	8
Tremulant	
Swell Sub	
Swell Super	

+ = added by Hugo Spilker
++ = added by Herb Huestis in 1987
+++ = rebuilt or added by Grant Smalley

GREAT

Open Diapason	8
Lieblich Gedeckt	8
Principal +	4
Flute (ext) +	4
Super Octave +	2
Mixture 1 1/3 +&+++	III rks
Trumpet	8
Chimes	
Great Super	

COUPLERS

Swell Sub to Great
Swell to Great
Swell Super to Great
Swell to Pedal
Swell Super to Pedal
Great to Pedal

PEDAL

Sub Bass	16
Lieblich Gedeckt (1/2wp)	16
Open Bass +++	8
Bass Flute (ext)	8
Open Bass (ext) +++	4
Trumpet (Gr) ++	8

ACCESSORIES

Thumb Pistons:
- Manual I –
  - Great to Pedal
  - 4 Great Pre-select
- Manual II –
  - Swell to Great
  - 4 Swell Pre-select
  - Full Organ

Swell to Great Toe Stud
Great to Pedal Toe Stud
4 General Pre-select Toe Studs
Swell Shutter Pedal
Crescendo Pedal

St. Michael & All Angels Anglican Church, Kelowna, B.C. (23 stops & ranks)

The organ here was originally an English tracker action one built in about 1876 by Bevington, Abbot & Smith, or Walker. In 1901, it was moved to the first church of Wesley Methodist, Vancouver, and converted to tubular-penumatic action. The action was later electrified by Chandos Dix in 1921. In 1935, it was sold to the present church congregation, who in 1950 had Casavant install their Opus 2004 three-manual drawstop console and do repairs to the organ. Stan Haddon of Vancouver rebuilt the chests in 1965 and the latest overhaul was done by John Darbyshire of Abbotsford, who also moved the console and added a Bass Flute 8 to the Pedal in 1971. The case is located at the left side of the chancel and is made of oak with a two-turreted facade of speaking pipes made of stenciled cardboard with wood mouths.

Specifications:

SWELL		GREAT		CHOIR	
Lieblich Bourdon	16	Double Open Dia.	16	Melodia	8
Stopped Diapason	8	Open Diapason	8	Lieblich Gedeckt	8
Viola da Gamba	8	Doppelflöte	8	Gemshorn	8
Aeoline	8	Dulciana	8	Harmonic Flute	4
Voix Celeste	8	Principal	4	Clarinet	8
Flauto Traverso	4	Fifteenth	2	Tremulant	
Cornopean	8	Great Super		Choir Sub	
Oboe Bassoon	8			Choir Super	
Tremulant					
Swell Sub					
Swell Super					

St. Michael & All Angels Anglican Church, Kelowna, B.C. Continued

PEDAL

Open Diapason	16
Bourdon	16
Lieblich Bourdon	16
Bass Flute	8

ACCESSORIES

Finger Pistons:
- Manual I –
  - Swell to Choir
  - Choir to Pedal
  - 3 Choir Pre-select
- Manual II –
  - Swell to Great
  - Choir to Great
  - Great to Pedal
  - 3 Great Pre-select
- Manual III –
  - Swell to Pedal
  - 3 Swell Pre-select

Great to Pedal Toe Stud
3 General Pre-select Toe Pistons
Full Organ Toe Stud
Swell Shutter Pedal
Choir Shutter Pedal
Crescendo Pedal

COUPLERS

Swell Sub to Great
Swell to Great
Swell Super to Great
Swell Sub to Choir
Swell to Choir
Swell Super to Choir
Choir Sub to Great
Choir to Great
Choir Super to Great
Swell to Pedal
Swell Super to Pedal
Great to Pedal
Great Super to Pedal
Choir to Pedal
Choir Super to Pedal

St. Michael's Anglican Church, Vancouver, B.C. (15 stops & ranks)

The organ here was originally built by Casavant Frères in 1926 as Opus 1111, a theatre organ for Vancouver's Windsor Theatre. St. Michael's Church obtained it in 1940 for $2,500 and had it installed by Stan Haddon in a chamber to the left of the chancel. The facade is of oak wood and gold painted pipes with silver coloured mouths. The two-manual tab stop console is at the opposite side in the chancel and controls the organ by electro-pneumatic action. The Great and Pedal divisions are in a second expressive box. An unusual feature is the Swell to Great 2 2/3 coupler. There was a Pedal Resultant Bass 32 but has since been disconnected.

Specifications:

SWELL

Violin Diapason	8
Stopped Diapason	8
Viola da Gamba	8
Voix Celeste (tc)	8
Flauto Traverso	4
Oboe	8
Vox Humana	8
Chimes	
(Marimba) Harp	4
Tremulant	
Swell Sub	
Swell Super	
Swell Super 2 2/3	
Swell Unison Off	

GREAT

Open Diapason	8
Melodia	8
Dulciana	8
Octave	4
Harmonic Flute	4
Tuba	8
Chimes	
(Marimba) Harp	4
Tremulant	
Great Sub	
Great Super	
Great Unison Off	

COUPLERS

Swell Sub to Great
Swell to Great
Swell Super to Great
Swell to Great 2 2/3
Swell to Pedal
Great to Pedal

PEDAL

Bourdon	16
Flute	8
Pedal Chimes	

ACCESSORIES

Finger Pistons:
- Manual I –
  - Great to Pedal
  - 4 Great / Pedal Pre-select
- Manual II –
  - Swell to Pedal
  - 4 Swell Pre-select

Swell to Pedal Toe Stud
Great to Pedal Toe Stud
Swell Shutter Pedal
Great / Pedal Shutter Pedal
Crescendo Pedal

St. Paul's Anglican Church, Esquimalt, B.C. (24 stops, 27 ranks)

In 1890, Peter Conacher & Co., Huddersfield, England, was contracted to build an organ to be the second instrument for St. John The Divine Anglican Church (The Iron Church) in Victoria. Its cost including $800 duty but excluding the water motor for pumping the bellows was $4,000. The instrument was sent over seas to the east coast of the United States and transported by train across the country before being off loaded and shipped up to Victoria. In December 1912, the organ was sold to St. Paul's for $500 and installed by Adolf Fosness of Vancouver. The American firm of Hilborne L. Roosevelt did work on the organ at one time and in 1973, Hugo Spilker did pipework alterations to "brighten it up". Grant Smalley of Victoria recently restored pipework as best he could back to original. The organ is situated at the left side of the choir with a facade of carved fir and ornately painted speaking Diapason pipes. The divisions are mounted on one level with Great, Swell, and unenclosed Choir front to back and Pedal on the sides. The attached drawstop keydesk has three 56-note manuals and 30-note pedal board. It is a historically significant instrument being the oldest tracker organ of three manuals in the province.

Specifications:

SWELL		GREAT		CHOIR	
Violin Diapason *	8	Double Open Diapason	16	Lieblich Gedact	8
Hohl Flöte	8	Large Open Diapason	8	Dulciana *	8
Voix Celestes (tc)	8	Small Open Diapason	8	Clear Flute	4
Vox Angelica	8	Stopped Diapason	8	Nasat +	2 2/3
Octave	4	Octave	4	Principal +	2
Harmonic Piccolo	2	Harmonic Flute	4	Clarionet	8
Sesquialtera +	II rks	Octave Quint	2 2/3		
Cornopean	8	Super Octave	2		
Oboe	8	Scharff + 1 1/3	III rks		
Tremulant		Trumpet *	8		

St. Paul's Anglican Church, Esquimalt, B.C. Continued

COUPLERS

Swell to Great
Swell to Choir
Swell to Pedal
Great to Pedal
Choir to Pedal

PEDAL

Open Diapason	16
Bourdon	16

ACCESSORIES

3 Swell Select Non-adjust Toe Pistons
3 Great Select Non-adjust Toe Pistons
Swell Shutter Pedal

* = Removed from original specifications by Hugo Spilker in 1973
+ = Reworked or new pipes added by Hugo Spilker in 1973

St. Paul's Anglican Church, Nanaimo, B.C. (24 stops, 5 ranks)

In 1942, Casavant Frères Ltée. B.C. representative, Andrew Chapman, installed a new electro-pneumatic action romantically voiced unit organ in a screen fronted enclosure mounted over the right side of the chancel. Opposite to it is located the detached tab stop console with full keyboard and AGO pedal board compass. As with most Casavant unit organs, there are no pre-set pistons. Opus 1694 contains extended rank voices: 8′ based Open Diapason, Stopped Flute, Salicional, & Dulciana, and a 16′ based Pedal Bourdon. All ranks are under expression.

Specifications

SWELL

Contra Dulciana (tc)	16
Rohr Flöte	8
Salicional	8
Dulciana	8
Lieblich Flöte	4
Salicet	4
Dulcet	4
Nazard	2 2/3
Piccolo	2
Tierce	1 3/5
Tremulant	

GREAT

Lieblich Gedeckt	16
Open Diapason	8
Rohr Flöte	8
Salicional	8
Dulciana	8
Octave	4
Dulcet	4
Nazard	2 2/3
Fifteenth	2

ACCESSORIES

Expression Shutter Pedal
Crescendo Pedal

PEDAL

Bourdon	16
Octave	8
Stopped Flute	8
Cello	8
Dulcet	4

COUPLERS

Swell to Great
Swell to Pedal
Great to Pedal

St. Paul's Anglican Church, Vancouver, B.C. (21 stops, 20 ranks)

The organ here, Opus 264 of 1906, is the oldest extant Casavant Frères built original installation in the province. In 1952, Andrew Chapman changed the action from tubular to electro-pneumatic and installed a new Casavant two-manual drawstop console. At some point in time some of the pipe ranks were re-arranged but in the 1990s Herb Huestis re-configured the organ to original layout. Starting in 2001 with Casavant's area representative, Steven Miller supervising, the organ was shipped to the factory for cleaning, overhaul and some modification. This included new wind system reservoirs, electrifying some remaining old tubular action components and replacing or revoicing of four ranks of pipes. The locations of the Clarinet and Tuba ranks were also reversed. The organ's case is situated at the left front side of the chancel and is built out from the wall. It has a facade of ornately stencilled pipes on three sides of the case. The detached console is at the opposite side in front and faces the alter. The organ is a good example of English style romantic voicing and its sound fills the acoustically favourable room quite adequately.

St. Paul's Anglican Church, Vancouver, B.C. Continued

Specifications:

SWELL

Lieblich Bourdon	16
Open Diapason	8
Stopped Diapason	8
Viola di Gamba *	8
Voix Celeste *	8
Aeoline *	8
Traverse Flute	4
Piccolo	2
Tuba	8
Oboe	8
Tremulant	
Swell Sub	
Swell Super	

GREAT

Open Diapason	8
Melodia	8
Gamba *	8
Dulciana	8
Octave	4
Harmonic Flute	4
Fifteenth	2
Clarinet	8
Great Super	

COUPLERS

Swell Sub to Great
Swell to Great
Swell Super to Great
Swell to Pedal
Swell Super to Pedal
Great to Pedal
Great Super to Pedal

PEDAL

Double Open Diapason	16
Bourdon	16
Violoncello (Gr)	8

ACCESSORIES

Thumb Pistons:
- Manual I –
  - 4 Great Pre-select
- Manual II –
  - 4 Swell Pre-select
- Great to Pedal Toe Stud
- 4 General Pre-select Toe Pistons
- Full Organ Toe Stud
- Swell Shutter Pedal
- Crescendo Pedal

* = new pipes or revoiced ones by Casavant in 2001

St. Paul's Lutheran Church, Nanaimo, B.C. (11 stops, 12 ranks)

Picture: - Slide Tray #1 - Slide nos. 5 to 7.

This organ was built in the early 1900s by Edward Lye & Sons, Church Organ Builders, Toronto, Ontario. It was in Marpole Presbyterian Church, Vancouver, for many years. While there, its stop list read:

SWELL		GREAT		PEDAL	
Stopped Diapason Bass	8	Open Diapason (bass f)	8	Bourdon	16
Stopped Diapason (tc)	8	Stopped Diapason Bass	8		
Viola (tc)	8	Melodia	8		
Aeoline	8	Dulciana	8		
Dolce Flute	4	Principal	4		

Hugo Spilker then bought it from the church and had it in his shop for two years where he rebuilt the organ, removed the Aeoline and Dulciana and added six ranks of pipes which included a Principal 2 and Mixture III by Stinkens and a Casavant Rohr Flöte. He also changed the stopknob nomenclature on some of the original ranks but retained the organ's mechanical action. The organ was sold by him to this church and installed at the front right side of the sanctuary. The case, measuring 9′ wide x 12′ tall x 5′3" deep, is dark stained oak with gold painted speaking Diapason pipes. The Pedal Bourdon makes up the sides of the case. The keydesk, measuring 2′ more in depth, has two 61-note manuals and a 30-note concave radiating pedal board. The Tremolo effects the entire organ.

Specifications:

SWELL		GREAT		PEDAL	
Bass Flute (12n)	8	Principal (bass f)	8	Bourdon	16
Gedeckt (tc)	8	Rohr Flöte +	8	Krummhorn +	4
Salicional (tc)	8	Octave	4		
Hohl Flöte	4	Mixture + 1 1/3	III rks		
Principal +	2				

COUPLERS

Swell to Great
Swell to Pedal
Great to Pedal

ACCESSORIES

Tremolo
Swell Shutter Pedal

+ = ranks added by Hugo Spilker

St. Peter's Catholic Church, New Westminster, B.C. (9 stops & ranks)

This organ was built in 1923 by Casavant Frères and is number 967. It is located in the left side of the rear gallery of the church. The instrument's action was originally tubular-penumatic with the two manuals and Pedals integral with the case, but later it was converted by an unknown person to electro-pneumatic action with the original key desk and Pedals split from the case and added to a plain designed tab stop console, now located in the front middle of the gallery facing the choir. The case was built into the wall and choir stalls placed in front of it to help hide the gap left with the console conversion. The Swell is enclosed in a box behind the Great. The Tremulant is for the entire organ.

Specifications:

SWELL

Melodia	8
Salicional	8
Aeoline	8
Celeste	8
Oboe Gamba	8
Swell Sub	
Swell Super	

GREAT

Open Diapason	8
Dulciana	8
Wald Flute	4
Great Super	

ACCESSORIES .

Tremulant
Swell Shutter Pedal
Crescendo Pedal

PEDAL

Bourdon	16

COUPLERS

Swell Sub to Great
Swell to Great
Swell Super to Great
Swell to Pedal
Great to Pedal

St. Philip's Anglican Church, Vancouver, B.C. (33 stops, 41 ranks)

In 1961, Jean Girouard completed the installation of the new Casavant Frères Opus 2645, in an open chamber at the left side of this church's chancel. This is an early example of an all new installation neo-classical style voiced organ done under Lawrence Phelps' guidance. In 2007, Casavant provided a Harmonic Flute 4 and Hautbois 8 to the Swell which originally had that reed stop in 4' based pitch. The addition done under area rep. Steve Miller's supervision cost $45,000 and brought the total pipe complement to 2,192 pipes. The organ's pipework can be seen from two sides of its location. There is a simple single flat facade of grey metal speaking Principal 8 pipes along the opening into the nave and the chancel side has a projecting chest facade of Mixture and upperwork ranks from the Great as well. The Swell and Choir boxes can be seen behind and above the Great and Pedal divisions. The detached full compass three-manual and AGO pedal board drawstop console faces the front from the opposite side of the chancel from the case.

St. Philip's Anglican Church, Vancouver, B.C. Continued

Specifications:

SWELL

Gedeckt	8
Salicional	8
Voix Celeste	8
Geigen Principal	4
Harmonic Flute	4
Blockflöte	2
Plein Jeu	III rks
Fagot	16
Trompette	8
Hautbois	8
Tremulant	
Swell Sub	
Swell Super	
Swell Unison Off	

GREAT

Quintaton	16
Principal	8
Spitzflöte	8
Octave	4
Koppelflöte	4
Super Octave	2
Fourniture	IV rks

PEDAL

Contrabass	16
Subbass	16
Quintaton (Gr)	16
Principal	8
Stopped Flute	8
Choralbass	4
Mixture	IV rks
Bombarde	16

CHOIR

Rohrflöte	8
Erzähler	8
Unda Maris	8
Nachthorn	4
Klein Prinzipal	2
Quinte Flöte	1 1/3
Sesquialtera	II rks
Krummhorn	8
Tremulant	
Choir Sub	
Choir Super	
Choir Unison Off	

COUPLERS

Swell to Great
Swell to Choir
Choir to Great
Great to Choir
Swell to Pedal
Great to Pedal
Choir to Pedal
Choir Super to Pedal

ACCESSORIES

- Finger Pistons:
  - Manual I –
    - Choir to Pedal
    - 4 Choir Pre-select
  - Manual II –
    - Great to Pedal
    - 4 Great Pre-select
    - 4 Pedal Pre-select
    - Full Organ
  - Manual III –
    - Swell to Pedal
    - 4 Swell Pre-select
- Great to Pedal Toe Stud
- 4 General Pre-select Toe Pistons
- Full Organ Toe Stud
- Swell Shutter Pedal
- Choir Shutter Pedal
- Crescendo Pedal

St. Saviour's Anglican Church, Penticton, B.C. (29 stops, 5 ranks)

The organ in this church is a custom installation by Ken Hodgson of White Rock completed in 1961. The previous instrument, a Morton theatre organ from Kitsilano United Church in Vancouver, was badly damaged by fire and removed by Hodgson. Parts of the action and pipework were salvaged and used for the new organ but new chests and a two-manual tab stop console were provided by Balcom & Vaughan of Seattle. The organ is extensively unified and the pipes are entirely under expression in a chamber at the right side of the choir. There is a simple facade of dummy pipes on two sides of the chamber. The console does not have pre-set pistons or couplers.

Specifications:

SWELL		GREAT		PEDAL	
Bass Flute	16	Contra Bass	16	Bourdon	16
Violone	16	Contra Viol	16	Octave	8
Diapason	8	Diapason	8	Flute	8
Bourdon	8	Flute	8	Cello	8
Gedeckt	8	Gedeckt	8	Octave	4
Viola	8	Viola	8		
Dulciana	8	Dulciana	8	**ACCESSORIES**	
Principal	4	Octave	4		
Flute	4	Flute	4	Expression Pedal	
Viola	4	Voila	4	Crescendo Pedal	
Nazard	2 2/3	Quint	2 2/3		
Flautina	2	Octavin	2		

St. Saviour's Anglican Church, Victoria, B.C. (11 stops, 10 ranks)

This organ was built in 1870 by Albert E. Pease of Grayling Rd., Stoke, Newington, England. It was shipped around Cape Horn to Victoria on the sailing ship Red Rock, and installed here in 1901 for $1,500. In 1931 an electric Casavant blower was added. In the late 1960s, Hugo Spilker moved the Swell Violin Diapason 8 to a Quint 2 2/3. The organ is located at the left side of the choir and has a facade of ornately painted pipes. The attached two-manual keydesk has 56 notes each and the concave straight pedal board has 30 notes. The drawstops and key action are still of the original mechanical type. The enclosed Swell is controlled by a hitchdown pedal. The original hand pumping is to be restored.

Specifications:

SWELL

Lieblich Gedact	8
Flauto Traverso	4
Quint	2 2/3
Piccolo	2
Oboe	8
Tremolo	

GREAT

Open Diapason	8
Stopped Dia. Bass	8
Clarabella (Treble)	8
Viol d'Amour	8
Principal	4

ACCESSORIES

Swell Shutter Pedal

PEDAL

Bourdon	16

COUPLERS

Swell to Great
Swell to Pedal
Great to Pedal

St. Saviour's Pro-Cathedral (Anglican), Nelson, B.C. (11 stops, 10 ranks)

Inside this elegant stone building is an organ built for it in 1934 by Casavant Frères as Opus 1497 and installed by Andrew Chapman of Vancouver. The case, with facade pipes on two sides, is situated in a corner location at the right side of the choir. The detached electro-pneumatic action two-manual drawstop console faces the front of the church from the righthand side where the choir meets the nave.

Specifications:

SWELL

Violin Diapason	8
Stopped Diapason	8
Aeoline	8
Harmonic Flute	4
Oboe	8
Tremulant	
Swell Sub	
Swell Super	

GREAT

Open Diapason	8
Melodia	8
Dulciana	8
Principal	4
Great Sub	
Greater Super	

ACCESSORIES

Swell Sub to Great
Swell to Great
Swell Super to Great
Swell to Pedal
Swell Super to Pedal
Great to Pedal
Great Super to Pedal

PEDAL

Bourdon	16
Gedeckt (Swell ext.)	16

ACCESSORIES

Finger Pistons:
- Manual I –
  - Great to Pedal
  - 3 Great & Pedal Pre-select
- Manual II –
  - 3 Swell Pre-select

Great to Pedal Toe Stud
Swell Shutter Pedal
Crescendo Pedal

St. Thomas Anglican Church, Chilliwack, B.C. (32 stops, 4 ranks)

In 1968, the Hallman Organ Co. built this organ which was installed here by John Darbyshire of Abbotsford. The instrument is extensively unified with electric action controlling four ranks of pipes: Principal, Flute, Salicional, and Oboe. The voicing is a quite chiffy classical type. The pipes are in a chamber at the right side of the choir and are entirely under expression behind shutters visible from the outside. The detached two-manual tab stop console is at the opposite side of the choir facing the chamber. Apart from the Automatic Pedal, there aren't any couplers or pre-set pistons at the console.

Specifications:

SWELL		GREAT		PEDAL	
Bass Flute	16	Principal	8	Bourdon	16
Rohrflute	8	Rohrflute	8	Gedect	16
Salicional	8	Salicional	8	Octave	8
Flute	4	Octave	4	Flute	8
Violina	4	Violina	4	Salicional	8
Nazard	2 2/3	Twelfth	2 2/3	Quint	5 1/3
Piccolo	2	Fifteenth	2	Choral Bass	4
Cor Oboe	8	Dulcet	2	Flute	4
Oboe Clarion	4	Nasat	1 1/3	Flautino	2
		Sifflött	1	Cor Oboe	8
		Cor Oboe	8	Oboe Clarion	4
		Oboe Clarion	4		

ACCESSORIES

Tremulant
Automatic Pedal
Expression Pedal
Crescendo Pedal

Sands Memorial Chapel of Chimes, Victoria, B.C. (22 stops, 3 ranks)

In 1932, when the present chapel was completed, W.W. Kimball of Chicago, Illinois was contracted to build a three-rank unified electro-pneumatic action organ for a chamber provided in the front of the room. The organ's console of two manuals and Pedal is detached from the screen front pipe enclosure and has tab stops. The voicing is in the romantic style. This is the only pipe organ in a funeral home in Victoria.

Specifications:

SWELL		GREAT		PEDAL	
Contre Viola	16	Gedeckt	8	Bourdon	16
Gedeckt	8	Viola	8	Flute	8
Viola	8	Flute D'Amour	4	Viola	8
Flute D'Amour	4	Violina	4	Vox Humana	8
Violina	4	Nazard	2 2/3		
Nazard	2 2/3	Flautina	2	**ACCESSORIES**	
Flautina	2	Vox Humana	8		
Vox Humana	8	Vox Humana	4	Expression Pedal (entire organ)	
Orchestral Oboe (synthetic)	8			Crescendo Pedal	
Vox Humana	4				
Tremolo					

Second Church of Christ Scientist, Vancouver, B.C. (31 stops, 11 ranks)

For the sum of $5,100, Casavant Frères Ltée. was contracted to build in 1925, Opus 1109, an 11-rank tubular-penumatic action organ installed at this church within five months of the contract signing. The organ was set up in a screen front chamber at the front of the sanctuary. A detached two 61-note manual 30-note concave radiating pedal board tab stop console facing the organ was also provided. Over the years the organ's action was electrified. the Great division pipes removed (used on the present St. Mary's Anglican Church organ in Ganges), Swell Vox Humana removed, new ranks added including a Dutch made Stinkens Trumpet, and pipework reconfigured into a unified stop specification. G. herald Keefer was responsible for many of these changes. More recently, Herb Huestis rebuilt the original console by adding a solid state capture piston system. The organ is entirely under expression.

__Specifications:__

SWELL		GREAT		PEDAL	
Block Flute	16	Open Diapason	8	Resultant	32
Viole	8	Concert Flute	8	Bourdon	16
Bourdon	8	Rohr Flute	8	Open Diapason	8
Aeoline	8	Gamba	8	Stopped Flute	8
Voix Celeste tc	8	Principal	4	Principal	4
Flauto Traverso	4	Lieblich Flute	4	Trombone	16
Lieblich Flute	4	Nazard	2 2/3	Trumpet	8
Nazard	2 2/3	Fifteenth	2	Clarion	4
Piccolo	2	Trumpet	8		
Tierce	1 3/5	Trumpet Clarion	4	**ACCESSORIES**	
Trumpet	8	Great 16			
Oboe	8	Great 8		Expression Shutter Pedal	
Clarion	4	Great 4		Crescendo Pedal	
Tremulant		Swell 16 to Great			
Swell 16		Swell 8 to Great			
Swell 8		Swell 4 to Great			
Swell 4					

Shaughnessy Heights United Church, Vancouver, B.C. (35 stops, 33 ranks)

In November of 1956, Andrew Chapman installed Casavant Frères' last major example in late romantic style voicing in the province its Opus # 2355. The instrument has a detached three-manual and Pedal drawstop console and electro-pneumatic action. The pipes are situated in a chamber at the front lefthand side of the sanctuary but unfortunately have difficulty in speaking out into the room due to the heavy screen of concrete and wood which conceal them. In 1978, Alex Bernhardt, Casavant's B.C. representative, replaced the Swell Cornet III rks with a three-rank Mixture. Chimes were also installed then.

Specifications:

SWELL		GREAT		CHOIR	
Open Diapason	8	Bourdon	16	Geigen Principal	8
Stopped Diapason	8	Open Diapason	8	Melodia	8
Viola di Gamba	8	Hohlflöte	8	Dulciana	8
Voix Celeste	8	Gemshorn	8	Lieblich Flöte	4
Flauto Traverso	4	Principal	4	Nazard	2 2/3
Violina	4	Harmonic Flute	4	Flautino	2
Mixture	III rks	Fifteenth	2	Tromba	8
Contra Fagotto	16	Mixture	III rks	Clarinet	8
Cornopean	8	Tromba (Choir)	8	Tremulant	
Oboe	8	Chimes		Choir Sub	
Tremulant		Great Super		Choir Super	
Swell Sub					
Swell Super					

Shaughnessy Heights United Church, Vancouver, B.C. Continued

COUPLERS

Swell Sub to Great
Swell to Great
Swell Super to Great
Swell Sub to Choir
Swell to Choir
Swell Super to Choir
Choir Sub to Great
Choir to Great
Choir Super to Great
Swell to Pedal
Swell Super to Pedal
Great to Pedal
Great Super to Pedal
Choir to Pedal
Choir Super to Pedal

PEDAL

Contra Bass	16
Bourdon	16
Gedeckt (Great)	16
Stopped Flute (ext)	8
Cello (extended)	8
Choral Bass (ext.)	4
Trombone	16
Fagotto (Swell)	16

ACCESSORIES

Finger Pistons :
- Manual I –
  - Swell to Choir
  - Choir to Pedal
  - 4 Choir Pre-select
  - Full Organ
- Manual II –
  - Swell to Great
  - Choir to Great
  - 4 Great Pre-select
  - 4 Pedal Pre-select
- Manual III –
  - Swell to Pedal
  - 4 Swell Pre-select

Great to Pedal Toe Stud
4 General Pre-select Toe Pistons
Full Organ Toe Stud
Swell Shutter Pedal
Choir Shutter Pedal
Crescendo Pedal

Shawnigan Lake School, Shawnigan Lake, B.C. (29 stops, 25 ranks)

This organ was originally installed here in 1928 by Fosness & Dix from the Vancouver area and started with several pipe ranks from Laukhuff of Germany. The action was tubular-pneumatic but has since been changed to electro-pneumatic. The organ was located in a chamber in the left choir of the chapel. In 1965, Graham Anderson, assisted by Hugo Spilker, rebuilt, enlarged, and moved the organ to a platform at the back of the room. A new American built two-manual drawstop console was also installed. This was the first of several transformations of the organ with most of the original pipes being removed and replaced from no less than 11 different makers! These included Anderson, Bance, Hill, Norman & Beard, Karn-Warren, Laukhuff, Pearson, Smalley, Spilker, Stinkens, and Walker. The organ also grew in size and in 2003-04 the organ and console were re-installed in a new rear gallery. The case is quite imposing with speaking facade pipes.

Specifications:

SWELL

Gedeckt	8
Principal	4
Rohrflute	4
Nazard	2 2/3
Principal	2
Tierce	1 3/5
Sifflute	1
Scharff	II rks
Clarinet	8

COUPLERS

Swell to Great
Great to Great Super
Swell to Pedal
Great to Pedal

GREAT

Geigen Principal (prep)	16
Principal	8
Geigen Principal (Ped ext)	8
Gedeckt	8
Salicional	8
Octave	4
Flute	4
Gemshorn	2
Larigot	1 1/3
Mixture 1 1/3	III rks
Trumpet (Ped)	8

PISTONS

Manuals: 6 each
Pedal: 4
6 Generals: toe & thumb
2 reversibles: Gt/Ped, Sw/Gt
Full Organ

PEDAL

Geigen Principal	16
Subbass	16
Bourdon	16
Octavebass	8
Octave Geigen (ext)	8
Gedeckt (ext)	8
Super Octave (ext)	4
Posaune (ext)	16
Trumpet	8
Clarion (ext)	4

Tapestry Church (C.R.C.), Richmond, B.C. (23 stops, 16 ranks)

In 1967, Hugo Spilker of Victoria was contracted to build an instrument for the residence of the late Dr. D.B. Roxburgh also in Victoria. The organ was installed under grilled openings to the living room floor in an enclosure blasted out of rock. The organ was eventually sold and re-installed in this church by Hugo Spilker in May of 1987. The $40,000 cost included loft renovations, organ facade, and minor alterations. The instrument is situated on a platform at the front centre of the sanctuary and has a facade of speaking Principal pipes coloured satin light grey and framed by wood panels. The manuals are straight un-extended ranks except for the Gedeckt and reed and the Pedal is borrowed except for 12 notes of the Bourdon and 12 of the Fagott. There are about 1,000 pipes altogether. The action is electric in the manuals and electro-pneumatic in the Pedal. The detached tab stop console of standard key compass and AGO pedal board is situated off to the right of the case and faces inward. It was made by the W.H. Reisner Manufacturing Co. Inc. of Hagerstown, Maryland. This instrument is the largest pipe organ in Richmond.

Specifications:

SWELL		GREAT		PEDAL	
Gedeckt	8	Gedeckt (ext)	16	Bourdon (ext)	16
Erzähler	8	Principal	8	Octave Bass (Gr)	8
Erzähler Celeste	8	Bourdon	8	Bass Flute (ext)	8
Koppel Flute	4	Spitz Principal	4	Choral Flute (ext)	4
Rohr Quint	2 2/3	Chimney Flute	2	Contra Fagott (ext)	16
Principal	2	Mixture 1 1/3	III rks	Oboe (Gr)	8
Tierce	1 3/5	Oboe	8	Schalmei (Gr)	4
Nasard	1 1/3	Schalmei (ext)	4		
Tremolo		Great Super			
Swell Sub					
Swell Super					

COUPLERS

Swell to Great Super
Swell to Great
Swell to Pedal
Great to Pedal

ACCESSORIES

Great to Pedal Toe Stud
Swell Expression Pedal
Crescendo Pedal

Terrace Christian Reformed Church, Terrace, B.C. (20 stops, 3 ranks)

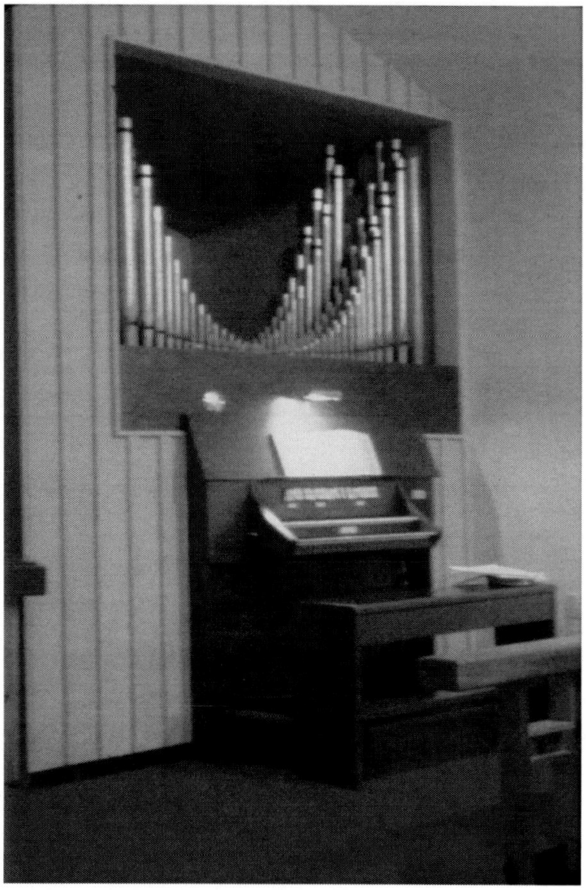

In 1937, the W.W. Kimball Co. of Chicago, Illinois built a small unified organ that was set up at radio station CJOR in Vancouver. It was later moved to First Christian Reformed Church in Vancouver by Stan Haddon. In 1973, the organ was sold and moved to Terrace and remains as the town's only church pipe organ. The instrument is situated in an open front chamber at the front right side of the interior.

Specifications:

SWELL

Bourdon	16
Diapason	8
Flute Ouverte	8
Viol d'Amour	8
Flute	4
Viole	4
Nazard	2 2/3
Flageolet	2
Orchestral Oboe	8
Tremolo	
Swell Unison 8	

GREAT

Diapason	8
Flute Ouverte	8
Viol d'Amour	8
Prestant	4
Flute	4
Viole	4
Doublette	2

PEDAL

Bourdon	16
Flute	8
Fifteenth	4
Flute	4

ACCESSORIES

Crescendo Pedal

Trinity Baptist Church, Vancouver, B.C. (16 stops, 15 ranks)

This organ was built in 1960 by Casavant Frères Ltée. as opus 2584 and has late-romantic period voicing and electro-pneumatic action. It was also the last organ that Andrew Chapman, the company's B.C. representative, installed in his long career before his retirement. Built for $18,000, the organ is located in the rear gallery of the church. Its screen fronted twin cases were built out from the corners of the back wall adjacent to the window. The detached two-manual tab stop console faces the choir loft from next to the gallery rail.

Specifications:

SWELL

Gedeckt	8
Salicional	8
Voix Celeste	8
Gemshorn	4
Nazard	2 2/3
Octavin	2
Oboe	8
Tremulant	
Swell Sub	
Swell Super	

GREAT

Principal	8
Bourdon	8
Dulciana	8
Octave	4
Rohr Flöte	4
Rausch Quint	II rks
Great Super	

COUPLERS

Swell Sub to Great
Swell to Great
Swell Super to Great
Swell to Pedal
Swell Super to Pedal
Great to Pedal
Great Super to Pedal

PEDAL

Subbass	16
Gedeckt	16
Bass Flute	8

ACCESSORIES

Finger Pistons:
Manual I –
3 Great Pre-select
Manual II –
3 Swell Pre-select
3 General Pre-select Toe Pistons
Great to Pedal Toe Stud
Swell Shutter Pedal
Crescendo Pedal

Trinity Christian Reformed Church, Abbotsford, B.C. (36 stops, 35 ranks)

The story of this organ begins with Casavant Frères Ltée completing their 1925 Opus 1104, an organ of three manuals and 30 stops, for the convocation hall in the University of Alberta in Edmonton. Casavant enlarged it in 1947 to 42 stops and 35 ranks of pipes. In 1975, it was put up for sale to make way for a new Casavant tracker organ. Adrian de Jong of Abbotsford purchased it for $10,500 and oversaw installation of its console and seven ranks of pipes in a temporary chapel in the new Christian Education building of Trinity Church in 1978. Four ranks of pipes were also sold and incorporated into the 1977 Praestant Organ Co. installation in the former Surrey Christian Reformed Church now Philadelphia Church. After Trinity Church was completed, de Jong, assisted by Adrian Koppejan and church members, re-installed the rebuilt and tonally modified organ which included the original console, pipe chests, 17 of the 1925, and ten of the 1947 Casavant ranks of pipes. Adrian Koppejan provided eight ranks of reworked or new pipes and did the tonal finishing. When the project was complete, they had an instrument with 2,098 pipes which cost the church $35,000. The organ is located against the chancel wall in front. The facade is not from Edmonton but was a Toledo Organ Co. one purchased from Kamloops United Church.

__Specifications__

SWELL		GREAT		POSITIVE	
Stopped Diapason	8	Gemshorn (ext)	16	Quintadena +	8
Viol D'Gamba	8	Open Diapason	8	Wald Flöte	4
Voix Celeste	8	Rohr Flute *	8	Principal +	2
Principal *	4	Gemshorn	8	Quint +	1 1/3
Flute Traverso	4	Octave	4	Cymbel +	II rks
Nazard *	2 2/3	Harmonic Flute	4	Clarinet	8
Piccolo *	2	Fifteenth *	2	Chimes	
Tierce +	1 3/5	Seventeenth *	1 3/5	Tremulant	
Cornet	III rks	Mixture *	II-IV rks	Positive 16	
Cornopean	8	Sesquialter +	II rks	Positive 4	
Chimes		Trumpet	8		
Tremulant		Clarion (ext)	4		
Swell 16		Chimes			
Swell 4		Great 16			
		Great 4			

Trinity Christian Reformed Church, Abbotsford, B.C. Continued

PEDAL

Open Diapason	16
Bourdon	16
Gemshorn (Gr)	16
Octave (ext)	8
Stopped Flute (ext)	8
Gemshorn (Gr)	8
Super Octave *	4
Trombone *	16

COUPLERS

Swell 16 to Great
Swell 8 to Great
Swell 4 to Great
Swell 16 to Positive
Swell 8 to Positive
Swell 4 to Positive
Positive 16 to Great
Positive 8 to Great
Positive 4 to Great
Swell 8 to Pedal
Swell 4 to Pedal
Great 8 to Pedal
Great 4 to Pedal
Positive 8 to Pedal
Positive 4 to Pedal

ACCESSORIES

Finger Pistons:
- Manual I –
  - Swell to positive
  - Positive to Pedal
  - 4 Positive Pre-select
- Manual II –
  - Swell to Great
  - Positive to Great
  - Great to Pedal
  - 4 General Pre-select
  - 4 Great Pre-select
  - Full Organ
- Manual III –
  - Swell to Pedal
  - 4 Swell Pre-select

4 Pedal Pre-select Toe Studs
Swell Shutter Pedal
Crescendo Pedal

* = Ranks added by Casavant in 1947
+ = Ranks reworked or new by Koppejan in 1978

Trinity Lutheran Church, Richmond, B.C. (21 stops, 10 ranks)

The organ for this church is the first completely new organ built by an American firm for a church in this province. It was built in June of 1975 by the Wicks Organ of Highland, Illinois with the installation done under the supervision of Mr. Charles Allen, their representative in Seattle, Washington. The organ is located in the rear gallery of this lofty A-frame building. The two-manual drawstop console is detached and placed in the gallery choir loft and the freestanding case is located above it supported by beams. The organ has 653 pipes with moderate unification and borrowing and the action is electric. The voicing is classical and there is an enclosed Swell division within the case. There is a Resultant in the Pedal which is an unusual stop for so small an instrument.

Specifications:

SWELL

Rohr Flöte	8
Salicional	8
Koppel Flöte	4
Nasat	2 2/3
Flageolet (ext.)	2
Sifflöte (ext.)	1
Fagot	8
Tremolo	
Swell Sub	
Swell Super	

GREAT

Principal (ext.)	8
Salicional (Swell)	8
Holz Gedeckt	8
Octave	4
Nachthorn	4
Flach Flöte	2
Mixture (ext.)	II rks
Fagot (Swell)	8

ACCESSORIES

Finger Pistons:
Manual I –
Great to Pedal
Manual II –
3 General Pre-select
3 General Pre-select Toe Pistons
Great to Pedal Toe Stud
Sforzando Toe Stud
Swell Shutter Pedal
Crescendo Pedal

PEDAL

Resultant (com.)	32
Sub Bass (ext.)	16
Principal Bass	8
Gedeckt (Great)	8
Choral Bass (ext.)	4
Fagot (Swell)	8

COUPLERS

Swell Sub to Great
Swell to Great
Swell Super to Great
Swell to Pedal
Great to Pedal

Trinity Western University, Langley (15 stops, 13 ranks)

In 1979, the Edmonton, Alberta music teacher Karl Rose contracted Casavant Frères Ltée. To build Opus 3429, a two-manual and Pedal 7-rank mechanical action instrument voiced by Albert Brunzema. Several years later Karl and the organ moved to a house in Surrey. The organ was enlarged to 12 stops in 2000-2001 by Adrian Koppejan. He heightened and extended the oak panelled case, added Pedal Bourdon pipes to the left side, and made some pipe chest enlargements. The Pedal's original Spitzgedeckt was extended and transferred into Manual I and the new pipes were made by Stinkens. In 2009, the organ was acquired by Trinity Western University and Adrian Koppejan was persuaded to come out of retirement to again modify, enlarge, and re-install the instrument in a music room on the campus. The project included relocating the Spitzgedeckt back to the Pedal, moving the Stinkens Dulzian from Manual II to the Pedal and extending both ranks by mechanical transmission, adding an Octave 4 to Manual II, and an Octave 2 to the Pedal. These alterations to the orginal Casavant design have complemented and added a rich smooth and clear plenum sound to this very fine instrument. The organ is not under expression and the facade has a simple flat of polished tin speaking Octave 2' pipes. The reverse colour keys of the manuals are comprised of 56 notes each and there is a 32-note concave radiating pedal board.

Specifications:

MANUAL I		MANUAL II		PEDAL	
Flute *	8	Quintade *	8	Subbass	16
Principal	4	Octave	4	Gedeckt (ext) *	8
Nasard	2 2/3	RohrFlute *	4	Spitzgedeckt *	4
Octave *	2	Quinte *	1 1/3	Octave	2
Terz	1 3/5	Tremulant		Dulzian	8
				Dulzian (ext)	4

COUPLERS

Manual II to Manual I
Manual I to Pedal

* = Original Casavant pipework, 1979.

University of British Columbia Music Building, Vancouver, B.C. (43 stops, 64 ranks)

In 1970, Casavant Frères was contracted to build their only original location tracker action organ in B.C., their Opus 3055, installed by Jean Girouard in the front gallery of the Music Building's Recital Hall. Dr. Hugh MacLean was the consultant and Lawrence Phelps voiced it in neo-baroque style. The organ has a shallow broad integral case with a facade in front. The Great and Pedal are divided at both sides of the glass shuttered Swell division in the middle. There is a three-manual 56-note reverse colour keyboard with 32 note Pedal and the drawstop action is electric. Apart from being the largest mechanical action three-manual organ in the province, it is also one of Casavant's largest installations and the first instrument to have a Ruckpositief in B.C.

In 1978 a new solid state pre-set piston system was installed to replace the old defective design one. Herb Huestis also did some revoicing work.

University of British Columbia Music Building, Vancouver, B.C. Continued

Specifications:

SWELL

Gedackt Flöte	8
Salizional	8
Vox Coelestis	8
Offen Flöte	4
Gemshorn	2
Klein Mixtur	III rks
Sesquialtera	III rks
Oboe	8
Vox Humana	8
Tremulant	

GREAT

Quintaton	16
Prinzipal	8
Rohrflöte	8
Oktav	4
Spitzflöte	4
Quinte	2 2/3
Oktav	2
Mixtur	V rks
Cornet	V rks
Dulzian	16
Trompete	8

POSITIEF

Metal Gedackt	8
Prinzipal	4
Koppel Flöte	4
Nasat	2 2/3
Oktav	2
Block Flöte	2
Terz	1 3/5
Quinte Flöte	1 1/3
Scharf	IV rks
Zimbel	III rks
Krummhorn	8
Tremulant	

PEDAL

Prinzipal	16
Subbass	16
Octav	8
Bordun	8
Choral Bass	4
Rohrpfeife	4
Nachthorn	2
Mixtur	V rks
Posaune	16
Fagott	16
Trompete	8
Schalmei	4

COUPLERS

Swell to Great
Positief to Great
Swell to Pedal
Great to Pedal
Positief to Pedal

ACCESSORIES

Finger Pistons:
- Manual I –
  - Positief to Pedal
  - 6 Positief Pre-select
- Manual II –
  - Swell to Great
  - Positief to Great
  - Great to Pedal
  - 6 Great Pre-select
  - 6 General Pre-select
- Manual III –
  - Swell to Pedal
  - 6 Swell Pre-select
  - 6 Pedal Pre-select

Positief to Great Toe Stud
Great to Pedal Toe Stud
Positief to Pedal Toe Stud
6 Pedal Pre-select Toe Pistons
Swell Shutter Pedal

University of Victoria, Auditorium, Victoria, B.C. (24 stops, 35 ranks)

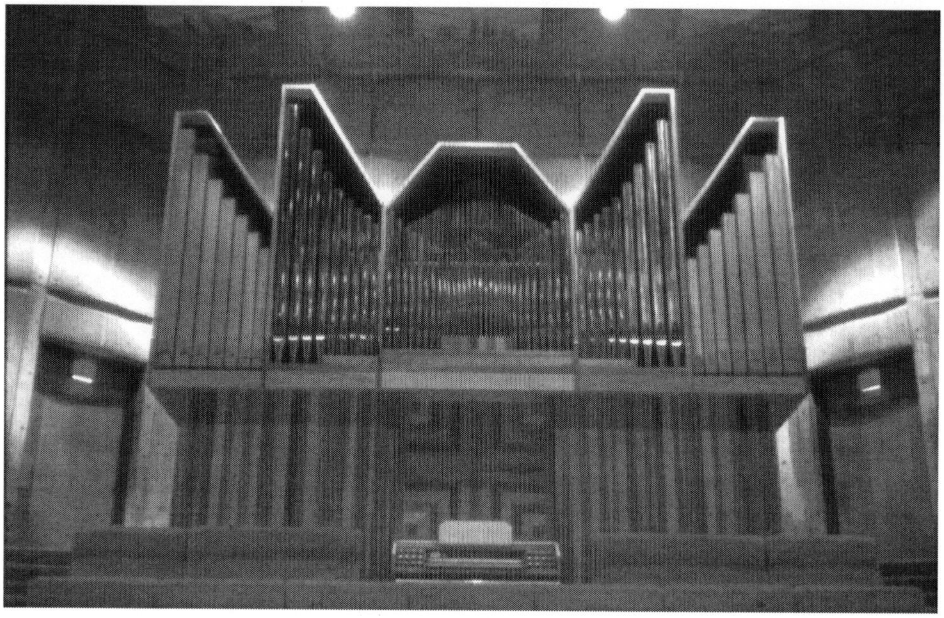

In 1966, the harpsichord maker Georges Mayer of Sarre-Union, Alsace, France built one of three tracker action organs with neo-classical voicing. It was sent to this country and installed in the 300-seat parish church of St. Mathias in Arvida, Québec. The change in climate from France to Québec caused a rapid deterioration in the organ and it was subsequently put up for sale. In 1978, by recommendation of the university harpsichord professor, Erich Schwardt, it was purchased with funds donated by Dr. Joyce Clearhue and installed in the 1,100 seat Auditorium. Victoria organ builder Hugo Spilker did the work which included a very complementary case design adapted to blend well with the room decor. The instrument was placed in the centre at one end of the Auditorium; it had cost $40,000. The organ's voicing proved quite unique for the province but the small scale pipework has made the organ inadequate to fill the room with sound despite efforts to increase its wind pressure. The instrument has two 56-note manuals and a 30-note pedal board in an attached tracker action keydesk. The mechanical action drawstops are without combination assists.

Specifications:

POSITIF

Bourdon à Cheminée	8
Montre	4
Flûte	4
Quint	2 2/3
Octave	2
Tierce	1 3/5
Larigot	1 1/3
Cymbale 1/2	III rks
Crommorne	8
Tremblant	

GRAND ORGUE

Quintaton	16
Montre	8
Bourdon	8
Prestant	4
Doublette	2
Principal	1
Cornet (mc)	V rks
Fourniture 1 1/2	IV rks
Cymbale 1	III rks
Trompette	8

PEDALE

Bourdon	16
Flûte	8
Principal	4
Dulciane	16
Clarine	4

COUPLERS

Positif au Grand Orgue
Positif au Pedale
Grand Orgue au Pedale

University of Victoria, Victoria, B.C. (3 stops and ranks)

There is a practice organ besides the larger auditorium organ. Hugo Spilker, in 1962, added new Stinkens pipework to an otherwise 1890s English-built pipe chest and reservoir of a single manual mechanical action intrument.

Specifications:

MANUAL

Gedeckt	8
Rohr Flöte	4
Principal	2

Vancouver School of Theology Chapel, Vancouver, B.C. (9 stops, 6 ranks)

The only example in the province of a modern tracker action design organ built by a Dutch company can be found here. It is also the first post 1950 modern mechanical action example to be found in B.C. The organ was built in 1963 by Verschueren of Heythuysen, The Netherlands and installed in St. David's Anglican Church, Westview by Stan Haddon of Vancouver. The stock design was known as the "Bach" model and had neo-classical voicing. In 1993, St. David's Church disbanded and the organ was eventually sold to V.S.T. where it was set up in the front of the sanctuary and replaced an electronic substitute. The self-contained organ is in a harp-shaped roof case with a simple flat of polished metal speaking pipes. The keydesk has a single 56-note manual split into bass and treble halves for the stop action. The 30-note concave straight pedal board doesn't have independent stops but is automatically coupled to the manual. The sound is quite bright and clear, a bit overpowering at the console but quite pleasant further out in the room.

Specifications:

MANUAL

Bass		Treble	
Hohlpfeife	8	Hohlpfeife	8
Principal	4	Gemshorn	8
Flöte	2	Principal	4
Mixture	II-III rks	Flöte	2
		Mixture	II-III rks

Victoria Conservatory of Music, Victoria, B.C. (56 stops, 54 ranks)

In the early 1900s, Casavant Frères Ltée. of St. Hyacinthe, Québec was contracted to build a medium size four-manual organ for a church in Boston, Mass. The instrument proved too costly for them and the deal fell through. It remained at the shop until 1910, when Metropolitan Church bought it. Opus 400 remained as original until 1966 when Casavant provided a new full compass four-manual and AGO pedal board drawstop console for $12,000. This electro-pneumatic instrument is the largest Casavant of English Romantic voicing in B.C. It is located across the front of the auditorium and has an open topped facade of gold-painted speaking 16′ Diapason pipes. Unfortunately the console was disconnected in about 1998 and the organ has been silent ever since. Replacement value on this organ is one of the highest in B.C.

<u>**Specifications:**</u>

SOLO

Gross Flöte	8
Gamba	8
Harmonic Flute	4
Harmonic Piccolo	2
Tuba	8
Cor Anglais	8
Tremulant	
Solo Sub	
Solo Super	

CHOIR

Open Diapason	8
Melodia	8

SWELL

Bourdon	16
Open Diapason	8
Stopped Diapason	8
Viola di Gamba	8
Clarabella	8
Aeoline	8
Voix Celeste (T.C.)	8
Principal	4
Flauto Traverso	4
Piccolo	2
Sesquialtera	III rks
Bassoon	16
Cornopean	8
Oboe	8

GREAT

Double Open	16
Open Diapason	8
Principal	8
Violin Diapason	8
Stopped Diapason	8
Doppel Flöte	8
Salicional	8
Octave	4
Wald Flöte	4
Twelfth	2 2/3
Fifteenth	2
Mixture (2′)	III rks
Trumpet	8
Posaune	8
Chimes	

Victoria Conservatory of Music, Victoria, B.C. Continued

CHOIR

Dulciana	8
Harmonic Flute	4
Violina	4
Flageolet	2
Clarinet	8
Tremulant	
Choir Sub	
Choir Super	

SWELL

Vox Humana	8
Harp	
Tremulant	
Swell Sub	
Swell Super	

PEDAL

Double Open (Ext.)	32
Open Diapason (Gr)	16
Open Wood	16
Violone	16
Bourdon	16
Gedeckt (Sw)	16
Octave	8
Bourdon (ext)	8
Violoncelle (ext)	8
Choral Bass	4
Mixture	2 2/3
Nachthorn	2
Trombone	16
Trumpet (ext)	8

COUPLERS

Solo to Swell
Solo to Great
Solo Super to Great
Solo to Choir
Swell Sub to Great
Swell to Great
Swell Super to Great
Swell to Choir
Swell Super to Choir
Choir to Great
Solo to Pedal
Solo Super to Pedal
Swell to Pedal
Swell Super to Pedal
Great to Pedal
Choir to Pedal

ACCESSORIES

Finger Pistons:
- Manual I –
  - Solo to Choir
  - Swell to Choir
  - Choir to Pedal
  - 4 Choir Pre-select
  - 6 Pedal Pre-select
- Manual II –
  - Solo to Great
  - Swell to Great
  - Choir to Great
  - Great to Pedal
  - 6 Great Pre-select
  - 6 General Pre-select
  - Full Organ
- Manual III –
  - Solo to Swell
  - Swell to Pedal
  - 6 Swell Pre-select
- Manual IV –
  - Solo to Pedal
  - 4 Solo Pre-select

Great to Pedal Toe Stud
6 General Pre-select Toe Studs
Full Organ Toe Stud
Swell Shutter Pedal
Solo Choir Shutter Pedal
Crescendo Pedal

West Point Grey United Church, Vancouver, B.C. (15 stops, 14 ranks)

In 1926, Casavant Frères Ltée. built Opus 1137, a theatre-style organ for the no longer extant Alma Theatre in Vancouver. With the arrival of sound to the motion picture film, the organ was no longer needed and eventually was sold to this church in 1941. Vancouver's Stan Haddon installed it minus the percussive traps: Marimba Harp and Xylophone. This is one of 14 theatre organs that Haddon was involved in re-locating to various churches and funeral homes in the lower mainland in his career. The organ is located in a chamber at the front left side choir. There is a screen and dummy pipes facade which for symmetry's sake is copied at the right choir side which is where the radiating tab stop two 61-note manuals 30-note pedal board console is located. The entire pipe work is enclosed in two expressive boxes and the action is electro-pneumatic.

Specifications:

SWELL

Violin Diapason	8
Stopped Diapason	8
Viola da Gamba	8
Voix Celeste	8
Flauto Traverso	4
Oboe	8
Vox Humana	8
Chimes	
Marimba Harp Sub *	
Marimba Harp *	
Tremulant	
Swell Sub	
Swell Super	
Swell Unison Off	

GREAT

Open Diapason	8
Melodia	8
Dulciana	8
Octave	4
Harmonic Flute	4
Tuba	8
Chimes	
Xylophone *	
Marimba Harp *	
Great Sub	
Great Super	
Great Unison Off	

PEDAL

Bourdon	16
Flute (Gr)	8
Chimes	

ACCESSORIES

Finger Pistons:
- Manual I –
  - Great to Pedal
  - 4 Great Pre-select
- Manual II –
  - Swell to Pedal
  - 4 Swell Pre-select

Swell Shutter Pedal
Great & Pedal Shutter Pedal
Crescendo Pedal

* = Removed by Haddon in 1941

COUPLERS

Swell Sub to Great
Swell to Great
Swell Super to Great
Swell to Pedal
Great to Pedal

West Vancouver United Church, West Vancouver, B.C. (31 stops, 36 ranks)

The original organ installed in this building in 1963 by Jean Girouard and Hugo Spilker were the chests, console, and 12 ranks of Vancouver's Ryerson United Church organ, Casavant's 1928 Opus 1249 plus 17 ranks of Stinkens pipes. The limitations and imbalances in this organ eventually made it unsuitable for the music needs of the congregation. It was decided to improve the sanctuary acoustics and have a new tracker organ designed with a fusion of historic Dutch, German, and modern ideas. The Roy, Washington firm of Pasi Organ Builders, Inc. was contracted and in 1998 at a cost of about $450,000 they installed a stunning mechanical action organ that weighed 8 tons was 28′ high with 31 stops and 36 ranks of pipes, and had two 58-note manuals and 30-note straight flat pedal board. Both the key and stop action are mechanical and there are no pre-set pistons. The 1851 pipes are tuned in the Kelner/Bach temperment. The walnut and cherry wood case has seven flats of polished metal speaking pipes. This organ is one of the finest in B.C.

West Vancouver United Church, West Vancouver, B.C. Continued

Specifications:

SWELL		GREAT		PEDAL	
Bourdon	8	Bourdon	16	Principal	16
Gamba	8	Principal	8	Subbass	16
Celeste	8	Suavial	8	Octave (ext)	8
Principal	4	Hohlflöte	8	Bourdon (ext)	8
Rohrflöte	4	Salicional	8	Choral Bass	4
Waldflöte	2	Octave	4	Nachthorn	2
Mixture	IV rks	Spitzflöte	4	Posaune	16
Dulcian	16	Nasat	2 2/3	Trumpet	8
Trumpet	8	Super Octave	2		
Oboe	8	Tierce	1 3/5		
Nachtigall		Mixture	V rks		
Zimbelstern		Trumpet	8		
Tremulant		Vox Humana	8		

ASSESSORY	COUPLERS
Swell Shutter Pedal	I / II
	I / Pedal
	II / Pedal

Westminster Abbey (Seminary of Christ the King), Mission, B.C. (41 stops, 39 ranks)

Inside the stunning 1982 built main chapel of the abbey is an instrument that culminates a dream of forty years for its resident organist, Fr. Basil Foote. In 1960, he supervised the installation of Casavant Frères Ltée. Opus 2572, a two-manual 15-stop rebuilt and enlarged organ, which was placed in a temporary chapel at the abbey. It was moved into a screened front chamber at the right side of the chancel in the new chapel, the same as the present organ. In 1995, the abbey acquired the Casavant three-manual 26-stop organ, Opus 397 of 1910, which was in Vancouver's Evangelistic Tabernacle formerly St. Giles Church. Then came a seven-year project of meticulously cleaning, appraising components, joining together, and adding some new pieces into what became virtually the complete restoration of Opus 397 with the console shell and a few ranks of pipes from Opus 2572 plus additional ranks in the Great; Octave 4 from Casavant Opus 1465 of 1932 out of First United Church, Victoria, as well as a new Cornet and Mixture. Brother Peter did most of the work assisted by others. Martin Pasi was also involved in the project. What they achieved was a beautifully restored romantically voiced organ enhanced by the wonderful acoustics of the chapel.

Specifications:

SWELL		GREAT		CHOIR	
Bourdon	16	Diapason	8	Gemshorn	16
Principal	8	Violin Diapason	8	Melodia	8
Stopped Flute	8	Doppel Floete	8	Flauto d'Amore	8
Viola	8	Octave	4	Dulciana	8
Aeoline	8	Harmonic Flute	4	Gemshorn (ext.)	8
Voix Celeste	8	Fifteenth	2	Wald Floete	4
Principal	4	Mixture	III-IV rks	Piccolo	2
Octave Horn	4	Cornet	II rks	Trumpet (Gr.)	8
Chimney Flute	4	Trumpet	8	Clarinet	8
Principal	2	Sub Octave		Tremolo	
Mixture	III rks	Super Octave		Sub Octave	
Fagotto (ext.)	16			Unison Off	
Cornopean	8				
Oboe	8				
Tremolo					
Sub Octave					
Super Octave					

Westminster Abbey, Mission, B.C. Continued

PEDAL

Open Flute	16
Subbass	16
Bourdon (Sw.)	16
Gemshorn (Ch.)	16
Violin Principal	8
Bass Flute	8
Gemshorn (Ch.)	8
Trombone	16
Fagotto (Sw.)	16

COUPLERS

Swell Sub to Great
Swell to Great
Swell Super to Great
Swell Sub to Choir
Swell to Choir
Swell Super to Choir
Choir Sub to Great
Choir to Great
Choir Super to Great
Swell to Pedal
Swell Super to Pedal
Great to Pedal
Great Super to Pedal
Choir to Pedal
Choir Super to Pedal

ACCESSORIES

Finger Pistons:
- Manual I –
  - Swell to Choir
  - Choir to Pedal
  - 5 Choir Pre-select
- Manual II –
  - Swell to Great
  - Choir to Great
  - Great to Pedal
  - 5 General Pre-select
  - 5 Great Pre-select
- Manual III –
  - Swell to Pedal
  - 6 Swell pre-select

9 Miscellaneous Toe Studs
Multi-switch computerized pre-set system
½ tone transposer switch
Swell Shutter Pedal
Choir Shutter Pedal
Crescendo Pedal

Westminster Abbey (Seminary of Christ The King), Mission, B.C. (23 stops, 5 ranks)

There are 3 chapels within Westminster Abbey and all have pipe organs. The two lessor known smaller chapels have two manual instruments. One has a 3-rank unit organ with a Kilgen console from Ralph Spitzer's Mt. Carmel, California home and was donated to them by him. The other, which is being described here, is a small Casavant Frères Ltée. unit organ, Opus 1584 built in 1938. It was originlly installed in the Centre & Hanna Funeral Home in Vancouver. At some time in the 1960s, J. Jean Girouard re-installed it in a new funeral home in Burnaby. Westminster Abbey purchased it for $5,000 in 1989 and had Brother Peter install it in his own design simple case of wood and cloth screen at the back of the chapel. The full compass two-manual and AGO pedal board tab stop console is beside the case facing forward and connected by electro-pneumatic action. There are no couplers or pre-set pistons and all pipes are under expression. The Oboe is a synthetic stop but the Vox Humana, however is genuine.

Specifications:

SWELL		GREAT		PEDAL	
Geigen Principal	8	Bourdon (tc)	16	Bourdon	16
Lieblich Gedeckt	8	Geigen Principal	8	Gedeckt	8
Dulciana	8	Lieblich Gedeckt	8	Geigen	4
Quintadena	8	Dulciana	8	Flute	4
Lieblich Flute	4	Lieblich Flute	4	Dolce	4
Violina	4	Violina	4		
Dulcet	4	Dulcet	4	**ACCESSORIES**	
Oboe	8	Nazard	2 2/3		
Vox Humana	8	Super Octave	2	Swell Shutter Pedal	
Tremulant		Chimes		Crescendo Pedal	

Willowby Christian Reformed Church, Langley, B.C. (11 stops, 12 ranks)

In 1975, Hugo Spilker was contracted to install an organ at this church. Much of the pipework in it dates from 1905, when W.W. Kimball & Co. of Chicago, built an instrument which spent several years in a Seattle, Washington, Methodist church. In 1968, it was bought and moved to the residence of Adrian de Jong in Abbotsford, and then sold to this church after some modification by Hugo Spilker. He rebuilt the windchests and provided a new blower, rectifier, and two-manual 30-note Pedal tab stop console. Pipework changes included the replacement of 12 Salicional pipes, two ranks added to an existing 2′ stop to make a Mixture, and some revoicing. The case panelling of mahogany and facade came fron the 1913 Canadian Pipe Organ Co. instrument that was at the old First Baptist Church in Victoria. The pipes are situated on a platform at the front of the sanctuary, with the detached console off to the left. This organ is the oldest one in Langley, and contains the oldest examples of Kimball's pipework in the province.

Specifications:

SWELL

Stopped Diapason	8
Salicional *	8
Principal	4
Piccolo	2
Oboe	8
Tremolo	

GREAT

Diapason	8
Melodia	8
Octave	4
Mixture +	III rks
Great Super	

ACCESSORIES

Swell Shutter Pedal

PEDAL

Bourdon	16
Bass Flute (ext.)	8

COUPLERS

Swell Sub to Great
Swell to Great
Swell Super to Great
Swell to Pedal
Great to Pedal

+ = 2 ranks added to original 2′ stop by Hugo Spilker in 1975
* = partially changed by Hugo Spilker in 1975

LIST III: DICTIONARY OF STOP NAMES

The following abbreviations after the stop names indicate the language origin of their spelling:

D	=	Dutch
E	=	English
F	=	French
G	=	German
I	=	Italian
L	=	Latin
S	=	Swiss origin

Acuta - A mixture with ranks of high pitch.

Aeoline - Gentle sounding stop usually in 8′ pitch.

Bach. Flöte (G) - See Gemshorm.

Baritone - A loud reed stop usually found in the Pedal.

Bass - Prefix to a stop to indicate that it sounds at one octave lower than its usual pitch.

Bassoon, Basson (F) - A relatively soft sounding capped reed stop often found in 16′ pitch and useful as a chorus stop.

Block Flute, Blockflöte (G), **Blok Fluit** (D) - Like a recorder or copy of a flute stop.

Bombarde (F) - A loud freely vibrating shallot or reed stop usually in the 16′ pitch.

Bourdon, Bordun (G) - A stopped flute usually found in 16′ or 8′ pitch.

Celeste, Celest - A soft sounding stop slightly tuned sharp to create an undulating effect when blended with another suitable rank of pipes.

Cello - A string stop considered as a fundamental.

Chimney Flute - A flute stop partially capped and usually containing a small-open tube extension to the top.

Choral Bass - The top end 4′ stop on a Pedal principal chorus.

Clarabella, Claribella, Claribel Flute - A bright sounding open wood flute stop often used as a solo.

Clarinet, Clarionet - A solo reed stop usually found at the 8′ pitch in the Choir division.

Clarion, Clairion - A 4′ open resonator strong reed stop usually found in a Pedal reed chorus.

Clear Flute - An open wood flute.

Concert Flute - An open flute like that found in an orchestra.

Conic Flute - A metal flute with an open top.

Contra - An adjective denoting one octave below the normal pitch of a stop.

Contrabasse - A full length principal stop in the Pedal.

Cor Anglais (F) - A solo reed with a bell on top imitating an orchestral english horn.

Cor de Nuit (F) - A quiet flue stop with a slight edge in tone. The pipes are usually uncapped.

Cor Oboe - See Oboe.

Cornopean - A chorus reed usually found in the Swell.

Cornet - A solo mixture stop that should contain at least 4 unbroken ranks which are usually flute pipes.

Cornet Regal - An open top solo reed stop of baroque voicing usually found in the Pedal.

Cromhorne, Cromorne (F) - A solo reed stop of baroque voicing usually found in the Choir division.

Cymbel, Cymbal, Cymbale - A mixture comprised of principal pipes with many breaks in it.

Diapason - An uncapped principal foundation stop of romantic voicing usually made of metal and often used in organ facades.

Diapason Phonon, Diaphone, Diaphonic Diapason - A principal stop of high wind pressure created by Robert Hope-Jones and mainly used in theatre organs.

Dolce - A romantically voiced soft flute stop.

Dolce Cornet - A soft Cornet. See Cornet.

Doppel Flute - An open flute with two mouths on opposite sides.

Double - An adjective before some stops indicating that it is an octave below its normal range.

Doublette (F) - A 2′ flute similar to the Fifteenth.

Dulciana, Dulcet, Dulcian, Dulciane (F) - A soft hybrid diapason of gentle string-like character.

Dulzian - A soft reed stop.

Echo - Prefix to indicate a quieter sound in a stop.

English Horn - See Cor Anglais.

Erzahler - A gentle sounding stop similar to a Gemshorn.

Erzahler Celeste - As above but tuned as a Celeste.

Fagot, Fagott (G), Fagotto - See Bassoon.

Fife - A high pitched open flute used mainly as a solo stop.

Fifteenth, Fifteen - A 2′ superoctave or principal stop.

Flach Flöte (G) - An uncapped flute of metal or wood.

Flageolet - A high pitched romantically voiced uncapped flute made of metal.

Flauto Traverso - An uncapped narrow scale stop imitating an orchestral flute.

Flauto Veneziano - A soft flute with chiffy sound voiced in the Italian style.

Flotgedeckt - A Gedeckt emphasizing the flute characteristics of it.

Flute, Flautino, Fluit (D), **Flautina** - General term indicating a stop of the flute family. The suffixes -ino and -ina indicate registration one octave higher than usual.

Flute à Chemineé (F) - See Chimney Flute.

Flute d'Amour (F) - A soft sounding flute made of wood.

Fourniture (F) - A principal mixture of 3 or 4 ranks of pipes.

French Horn - A muffled reed stop imitating the orchestral horn.

Fugara - An open hybrid flue stop giving a string-like tone.

Gamba, Gambette - A foundation string stop using small scale uncapped metal pipes.

Gamba Celeste - Gamba stop tuned sharp to make an undulating effect when combined with a suitable stop.

Gedackt (G), **Gedeckt, Gedact, Gedakt, Gedeck** (S) - A gentle sounding stopped flute usually made of wood.

Geigen - Indicating a stop with blending ability that is comprised of flue pipes voiced between principal and string sound. It is usually made of metal and uncapped.

Gemshorn - An uncapped flue stop with good blending ability made of metal and tapered towards the top.

Grand Bourdon Bass - A 32′ Pedal stop which is a 16′ Open Wood modified with stoppers.

Grand Chorus - A mixture of several ranks of pipes in the Bombarde division.

Grand Open Diapason - A large scale rank of open wood pipes in the Pedal.

Gross - Indicating a loud large scale stop.

Harmonique (F), **Harmonic** - Indicating high wind pressure solo stops built to twice the length of their register and containing drilled holes used for creating their desired effect.

Hautbois (F) - See Oboe.

Hohl Flöte (G), **Hohlpfeife**ı **Holpijp** (D) - An open wood chorus flute.

Holtz Gedackt (G) - A soft stopped wood flute.

Horn - An orchestral reed stop in romantic voicing.

Horn Diapason - A slotted principal designed to blend well with other stops.

Italian Principal - A gentle chiffy sounding principal stop.

Kinura - A moderately loud reed stop found in some theatre organs.

Klein (G) - A term used to describe a small scaled stop.

Koppel Flöte (G) - An uncapped metal flute with good blending abilities.

Koral Bass (G) - See Choral Bass.

Krummhorn (G), Kromhoorn (D) - See Cromhorne.

Kwint (D) - See Quint.

Larigot - A mutation stop of 2 2/3 or 1 1/3 pitch.

Lieblich - Used to indicate a narrow scaled stop of gentle tone.

Major Bass - A principal tone stop.

Melodia - A wide scaled, uncapped, solo flute of romantic voicing.

Mixture (F), **Mixtur** (G), **Mixtuur** (D) - A principal tone stop combining two or more pipes at each note, used to add brilliance and fullness to tone and give more effective stop blending ability.

Montre (F) - A foundation principal stop.

Musette (F) - A stop similar in tone to the orchestral oboe.

Nachthorn (G), Nacht Horn - See Cor de Nuit.

Nasard (F), **Nasat** (G), **Nazard** - A mutation flute stop of 2 2/3′ pitch.

Nineteenth - A 2′ flue chorus stop.

Oboe - A solo reed stop commonly found in the Swell.

Oboe Bassoon - A combination of the two stops with the Bassoon voiced into the bottom part of the rank.

Oboe Gamba - An imitation reed stop using string type pipes.

Octave (E), **Octav** (G), **Octaaf** (D) - An open metal principal chorus stop of 8′ or 4′ pitch.

Octave Bass - An 8′ principal in the manual.

Octave Wood - A wood stop, revoiced to imitate the Octave stop.

Octavin - A 2′ version of the Octave.

Offen Flöte (G) - An uncapped flute stop.

Open, Ouverte (F) - An uncapped rank of pipes.

Ophicleide - A loud high pressure reed stop usually found in the Pedal.

Orchestral Flute - An uncapped narrow scaled stop imitating the flute found in an orchestra.

Orchestral Oboe - A reed stop imitating its namesake.

Piccolo - A 2′ flute with uncapped pipes.

Plein Jeu (F) - A mixture with at least 3 pipes sounding at each note and having breaks in its ranks.

Pommer - See Gedackt.

Posaune (G) - A loud reed similar to a Trombone, usually found at 16′ pitch in the Pedal or 8′ pitch in the Great.

Praestant (D), **Prestant** (F) - An Octave or 4′ principal stop.

Principal (E), **Prinzipal** (G) - A foundation or Diapason stop.

Processional Trumpet - A solo trumpet stop.

Quartane - A small 2 rank mixture in the Great.

Quint, Quinte - A mutation stop at 5 1/3 in the manual and 10 2/3 in the Pedal.

Quintade - A capped metal flute with wide scaling.

Quintaden, Quintadena, Quintadeen (D) - Similar to Quintatön but a little louder in volume.

Quintatön - A capped flute with a prominent twelfth tone.

Rankett - A reed stop imitative of a baroque period instrument of the same name.

Rausch Zimbel - A high pitched 2 rank mixture with many breaks in it.

Rauschquinte, Rausquint - A 2 rank mixture usually containing 2 2/3′ and 2′ pitch ranks.

Regal - A reed stop with its name and sound derived from the baroque period.

Resultant, Resultant Bass - A rank or unification of pipes, usually stopped, added as a fifth to the Pedal 16′ foundation rank to give a 32′ effect sound.

Rohr (G), **Roer** (D), **Rhor** - Prefix to a stop indicating that it is partially capped or softer and chiffier than usual in sound.

Salicional, Salizional (G) - A narrow scaled uncapped metal string stop in 8 and sometimes 16 foot pitches.

Salicet - A 4′ pitch Salicional.

Salicional Celeste - A Salicional stop tuned sharp to create an undulating effect with properly blended stops.

Sanft Bass - A 16′ pitch gentle sounding stopped flute.

Saxophone - A reed stop imitating an orchestra saxophone.

Schalmei - A 4′ reed stop imitating a baroque instrument.

Scharff - A mixture with a high pitch.

Schwiegel (G) - A flute stop with shortened pipes.

Sesquialter, Sesquialtera - A 2 rank mixture with 2 2/3 and 1 3/5 foot ranks creating a noticeable sixth tone.

Sifflöte (G) - A 1′ flue stop with narrow open metal pipes.

Singend Gedackt - A capped wooden flue stop.

Spill Flöte (G), **Spillflute** (E), **Sillflöte** - A soft sounding metal flute capped by an inverted cone.

Spire Flute (E), **Spitz Flöte** (G), **Spits Fluit** (D) - A metal flue stop with the pipe shape tapered towards a point near its top. There is a notable seventeenth tone in its voicing.

State Trumpet - A horizontally mounted solo trumpet with fairly loud volume.

Still - Adjective to a stop name indicating that it is gentle in volume.

Stopped - A rank of pipes with caps or stoppers at the top.

Stopped Diapason - A principal flute usually made of wood with stoppers at the top.

String - A name indicating a narrow scaled open metal rank of pipes imitating orchestral strings.

Suavial (S) - A 4′ open wood flute stop.

Sub Bass, Subbass (G), **Sub-bass, Subbas** (D), **Soubasse** (F) - A 16′ Pedal Bourdon stop which is made of wood and capped with a stopper.

Sub Bourdon - A 32′ version of a Sub Bass.

Super - Adjective indicating a pitch one octave higher than normal.

Tibia, Tibia Clausa - Principal flute with broad tonal qualities mainly used in theatre style organs.

Tierce (F), **Terz** (G) - A 1 3/5′ pitch mutation in the seventeenth tone.

Trombone, Tromba - A 16 or 8 foot reed stop of loud and close toned character that has good blending ability.

Trompete, Trompette (F), **Trompet** (D), **Trumpet** (E) - A loud reed usually found in the Great, Swell, or Pedal division and used in a chorus or as a solo stop.

Trompette en Chamade (F) - A trumpet stop mounted horizontally.

Trumpet Magna - A form of trumpet stop.

Twelfth - A 2 2/3′ pitch mutation stop used for blending.

Twenty-second - A 2′ stop in the Pedal, usually a principal.

Tuba - A loud reed stop similar to the trumpet but with a somewhat tubby sound. In the manuals, it is usually at 8′ pitch and used as a solo stop. In the Pedal, it is usually at 16 feet.

Unda Maris - A single rank of pipes tuned flat or sharp to create a very gentle celeste-like effect when used with appropriate stops.

Untersatz (G) - A Sub Bass in the Pedal.

Viol, Viole, Viool (D) - A narrow scaled metal open flue stop.

Viol d'Orchestre (F) - A string stop of narrow open metal pipes imitating a viola.

Viola - A string stop like the Gamba that is good for blending.

Viola d'Amour - A soft sounding string stop.

Viola di Gamba (I), **Viole de Gambe** (F), **Viol d'Gamba** - A string stop with sound derived from an old Italian instrument.

Violes - A 2 rank stop of small narrow scaled open metal flue pipes.

Violin Celeste - An imitative open metal flue stop voiced slightly off pitch to create an undulating effect when blended with appropriate stops.

Violin Diapason - See Geigen.

Violina - An open metal flue stop imitating the violin.

Violincello (I), **Violoncelle** (F) - An open flue stop imitating the cello.

Violone (I) - An open flue stop of 16′ pitch that is a combination of a principal and a string in sound.

Vox Angelica - A celeste-like stop with a slower undulation.

Vox Celeste (F), **Vox Coelestis** (L) - A string-like stop tuned sharp to create an undulating effect.

Vox Humana - A partially capped short resonator reed stop of ancient origin used to imitate the human voice.

Wald Flute, Wald Flöte (G) - An uncapped flute, usually made of wood.

Zart Flute - A gentle flute-like stop with harmonics like that of a Ouintatön.

Zimbel (G) - See Cymbel.

Zingen Gedeck - A capped flute made of wood.

BIBLIOGRAPHY

Edge, Kathy - *History of Early Pipe Organs in Victoria* - Victoria, B.C., 1980.

Goode, Jack C. - *Pipe Organ Registration* - Nashville, Tennessee, U.S.A.: Abingdon Press, 1964.

Nye, Eugene M. - (A listing of pipe organ installations in B.C.) - Seattle, Washington, U.S.A., 1971 - partially revised in 1975; a copy received through the courtesy of D. Stuart Kennedy, Calgary, Alberta.

Owen, Barbara – An Early New England Organ on the West Coast (an article in the Journal of the Organ Historical Society) *The Tracker*, Volume 27, No. 4, Richmond, Virginia, U.S.A., 1983.